T0283420

Software Architecture: Principles and Practice

Software Architecture: Principles and Practice

Edited by
Colt McGarry

Larsen & Keller
www.larsen-keller.com

Software Architecture: Principles and Practice
Edited by Colt McGarry
ISBN: 978-1-63549-261-3 (Hardback)

© 2017 Larsen & Keller

 Larsen & Keller

Published by Larsen and Keller Education,
5 Penn Plaza,
19th Floor,
New York, NY 10001, USA

Cataloging-in-Publication Data

Software architecture : principles and practice / edited by Colt McGarry.
   p. cm.
Includes bibliographical references and index.
ISBN 978-1-63549-261-3
1. Software architecture. 2. Computer architecture. I. McGarry, Colt.
QA76.754 .S56 2017
005.3--dc23

The publisher's policy is to use permanent paper from mills that operate a sustainable forestry policy. Furthermore, the publisher ensures that the text paper and cover boards used have met acceptable environmental accreditation standards.

Printed and bound in the United States of America.

For more information regarding Larsen and Keller Education and its products, please visit the publisher's website www.larsen-keller.com

Table of Contents

Preface

Software architecture is a subfield of software development process and is also referred to as architectural decisions. It deals with the development, design, construction, deployment, maintenance, and production of structures which are the part of software systems. It includes software elements, their interrelation and their properties. This book is compiled in such a manner, that it will provide in-depth knowledge about the theory and practice of software architecture. Some of the diverse topics covered in it address the varied branches that fall under this category. This textbook is a complete source of knowledge on the present status of this important field. It is meant for those who are seeking a comprehensive analysis of the present status of this field.

A foreword of all Chapters of the book is provided below:

Chapter 1 - Software architecture studies the design and creation of software structures. Through software architecture, various elements are merged together to create a software system. The chapter on software architecture offers an insightful focus, keeping in mind the subject matter; **Chapter 2** - The types of architecture that have been explained in the following section are computer architecture and systems architecture. Computer architecture is the method or the rules that are used in describing the implementation and functionality of computer systems. The topics discussed in the section are of great importance to broaden the existing knowledge on architecture; **Chapter 3** - Software design is the technique used in creating software. It usually includes problem solving and planning a software solution. Some of the aspects explained in the chapter are requirements engineering, software architect, agent architecture, reference architecture, software system, architecture framework and view model. The major components of software architecture are discussed in this chapter; **Chapter 4** - Architectural pattern is a solution that is usually used as a solution for commonly occurring problems in software architecture. Blackboard system, database-centric architecture, service-oriented architecture and shared nothing architecture are the features that have been elucidated in the following chapter; **Chapter 5** - A software design pattern is a solution that is used for a problem that usually happens in software design. Design patterns are practices that programmers use for solving problems when they are designing a system or an application. Façade pattern, active record pattern, flyweight pattern, builder pattern, composite pattern and specification pattern are some of the patterns discussed in the following chapter; **Chapter 6** - Architecture description language is used in a number of disciplines such as systems engineering and enterprise modelling and engineering. The other architecture description languages used are Darwin, DUALLy, EAST-ADL, ERIL and Wright. This section helps the readers in understanding the different architecture description languages; **Chapter 7** - Component-based software engineering is an important branch of software engineering. It is used to define and is also used in implementing independent components into a system. Component-based scalable logical architecture, composition over inheritance, common component architecture, component object model and distributed component object model are some of the topics discussed in the following chapter; **Chapter 8** - Value stream mapping is a method that is used in analyzing the current state and also in analyzing and then designing a future state of the various stages that a product goes through from manufacture to distriburtion. The other software development practices used are kanban, queueing theory, test-driven development, node graph architecture and software architectural model. The aspects explained in this section are of vital importance and provide a better understanding of software development practices.

I would like to thank the entire editorial team who made sincere efforts for this book and my family who supported me in my efforts of working on this book. I take this opportunity to thank all those who have been a guiding force throughout my life.

Editor

Introduction to Software Architecture

Software architecture studies the design and creation of software structures. Through software architecture, various elements are merged together to create a software system. The chapter on software architecture offers an insightful focus, keeping in mind the subject matter.

Software architecture refers to the fundamental structures of a software system, the discipline of creating such structures, and the documentation of these structures. These structures are needed to reason about the software system. Each structure comprises software elements, relations among them, and properties of both elements and relations, along with rationale for the introduction and configuration of each element. The *architecture* of a software system is a metaphor, analogous to the architecture of a building.

Software architecture is about making fundamental structural choices which are costly to change once implemented. Software architecture choices, also called architectural decisions, include specific structural options from possibilities in the design of software. For example, the systems that controlled the space shuttle launch vehicle had the requirement of being very fast and very reliable. Therefore, an appropriate real-time computing language would need to be chosen. Additionally, to satisfy the need for reliability the choice could be made to have multiple redundant and independently produced copies of the program, and to run these copies on independent hardware while cross-checking results.

Documenting software architecture facilitates communication between stakeholders, captures decisions about the architecture design, and allows reuse of design components between projects.

Scope

Opinions vary as to the scope of software architectures:

- *Overall, macroscopic system structure*; this refers to architecture as a higher level abstraction of a software system that consists of a collection of computational *components* together with *connectors* that describe the interaction between these components.

- *The important stuff—whatever that is*; this refers to the fact that software architects should concern themselves with those decisions that have high impact on the system and its stakeholders.

- *That which is fundamental to understanding a system in its environment*; in this definition, the environment is characterized by *stakeholder concerns*, technical constraints, and various dimensions of project context.

- *Things that people perceive as hard to change*; since designing the architecture often takes place at the beginning of a software system's lifecycle, the architect should focus on decisions that "have to" be right the first time. Following this line of thought, architectural design issues may become non-architectural once their irreversibility can be overcome.

- *A set of architectural design decisions*; software architecture should not be considered merely a set of models or structures, but should include the decisions that lead to these particular structures, and the rationale behind them (e.g., justifications, answers to "why" questions)). This insight has led to substantial research into software architecture knowledge management.

There is no sharp distinction between software architecture versus design and requirements engineering. They are all part of a "chain of intentionality" from high-level intentions to low-level details. This duality is also referred to as the "twin peaks" of software engineering.

Characteristics

Software architecture exhibits the following:

Multitude of stakeholders: software systems have to cater to a variety of stakeholders such as business managers, application owners, developers, end users and infrastructure operators. These stakeholders all have their own concerns with respect to the system. Balancing these concerns and demonstrating how they are addressed is part of designing the system. This implies that architecture involves dealing with a broad variety of concerns and stakeholders, and has a multidisciplinary nature. Software architect require non-technicals skills such as communication and negotiation competencies.

Separation of concerns: the established way for architects to reduce complexity is to separate the concerns that drive the design. Architecture documentation shows that all stakeholder concerns are addressed by modeling and describing the architecture from separate points of view associated with the various stakeholder concerns. These separate descriptions are called architectural views (see for example the 4+1 Architectural View Model).

Quality-driven: classic software design approaches (e.g. Jackson Structured Programming) were driven by required functionality and the flow of data through the system, but the current insight is that the architecture of a software system is more closely related to its quality attributes such as fault-tolerance, backward compatibility, extensibility, reliability, maintainability, availability, security, usability, and other such –il-ities. Stakeholder concerns often translate into requirements and constraints on these quality attributes, which are variously called non-functional requirements, extra-functional requirements, behavioral requirements, or quality attribute requirements.

Recurring styles: like building architecture, the software architecture discipline has developed standard ways to address recurring concerns. These "standard ways" are called by various names at various levels of abstraction. Common terms for recurring solutions are architectural style, principle, tactic, reference architecture and architectural pattern.

Conceptual integrity: a term introduced by Fred Brooks in The Mythical Man-Month to denote the idea that the architecture of a software system represents an overall vision of what it should do and how it should do it. This vision should be separated from its implementation. The architect assumes the role of "keeper of the vision", making sure that additions to the system are in line with the architecture, hence preserving conceptual integrity.

Motivation

Software architecture is an "intellectually graspable" abstraction of a complex system. This abstraction provides a number of benefits:

- *It gives a basis for analysis of software systems' behavior before the system has been built*. The ability to verify that a future software system fulfills its stakeholders' needs without actually having to build it represents substantial cost-saving and risk-mitigation. A number of techniques have been developed in academia and practice to perform such analyses, for instance ATAM, ARID and TARA.

- *It provides a basis for re-use of elements and decisions*. A complete software architecture or parts of it, like individual architectural strategies and decisions, can be re-used across multiple systems whose stakeholders require similar quality attributes or functionality, saving design costs and mitigating the risk of design mistakes (assuming that the project contexts match).

- *It supports early design decisions that impact a system's development, deployment, and maintenance life*. Getting the early, high-impact decisions right is important to prevent schedule and budget overruns. On the other hand, a principle of lean software development is to defer decisions until the last responsible moment (M. and T. Poppendieck); however, it is not always clear when the this moment for a particular subset of decisions has come.

- *It facilitates communication with stakeholders, contributing to a system that better fulfills their needs*. Communicating about complex systems from the point of view of stakeholders helps them understand the consequences of their stated requirements and the design decisions based on them. Architecture gives the ability to communicate about design decisions before the system is implemented, when they are still relatively easy to adapt.

- *It helps in risk management.* Software architecture helps to reduce risks and chance of failure.

- *It enables cost reduction.* Software architecture is a means to manage risk and costs in complex IT projects.

History

The comparison between software design and (civil) architecture was first drawn in the late 1960s , but the term *software architecture* became prevalent only in the 1990s. The field of computer science had encountered problems associated with complexity since its formation. Earlier problems of complexity were solved by developers by choosing the right data structures, developing algorithms, and by applying the concept of separation of concerns. Although the term "software architecture" is relatively new to the industry, the fundamental principles of the field have been applied sporadically by software engineering pioneers since the mid-1980s. Early attempts to capture and explain software architecture of a system were imprecise and disorganized, often characterized by a set of box-and-line diagrams.

Software architecture as a concept has its origins in the research of Edsger Dijkstra in 1968 and David Parnas in the early 1970s. These scientists emphasized that the structure of a software system matters and getting the structure right is critical. During the 1990s there was a concerted effort to define and codify fundamental aspects of the discipline, with research work concentrating on architectural styles (patterns), architecture description languages, and architecture documentation. Research institutions have played a prominent role in furthering software architecture as a discipline. For instance, Mary Shaw and David Garlan of Carnegie Mellon wrote a book titled *Software Architecture: Perspectives on an Emerging Discipline* in 1996, which promoted software architecture concepts such as components, connectors, and styles.

IEEE 1471-2000, *Recommended Practice for Architecture Description of Software-Intensive Systems*, was the first formal standard in the area of software architecture. It was adopted in 2007 by ISO as ISO/IEC 42010:2007. In November 2011, IEEE 1471–2000 was superseded by ISO/IEC/IEEE 42010:2011, *Systems and software engineering — Architecture description* (jointly published by IEEE and ISO). While in IEEE 1471, software architecture was about the architecture of "software-intensive systems", defined as "any system where software contributes essential influences to the design, construction, deployment, and evolution of the system as a whole", the 2011 edition goes a step further by including the ISO/IEC 15288 and ISO/IEC 12207 definitions of a system, which embrace not only hardware and software, but also "humans, processes, procedures, facilities, materials and naturally occurring entities".

Architecture Activities

There are many activities that a software architect performs. A software architect typically works with project managers, discusses architecturally significant requirements with stakeholders, designs a software architecture, evaluates a design, communicates with designers and stakeholders, documents the architectural design and more. There are four core activities in software architecture design. These core architecture activities are performed iteratively and at different stages of the initial software development life-cycle, as well as over the evolution of a system.

Architectural Analysis is the process of understanding the environment in which a proposed system or systems will operate and determining the requirements for the system. The input or requirements to the analysis activity can come from any number of stakeholders and include items such as:

- what the system will do when operational (the functional requirements)

- how well the system will perform runtime non-functional requirements such as reliability, operability, performance efficiency, security, compatibility defined in ISO/IEC 25010:2011 standard

- development-time non-functional requirements such as maintainability and transferability defined in ISO 25010:2011 standard

- business requirements and environmental contexts of a system that may change over time, such as legal, social, financial, competitive, and technology concerns

The outputs of the analysis activity are those requirements that have a measurable impact on a software system's architecture, called architecturally significant requirements.

Architectural Synthesis or design is the process of creating an architecture. Given the architecturally significant requirements determined by the analysis, the current state of the design and the results of any evaluation activities, the design is created and improved.

Architecture Evaluation is the process of determining how well the current design or a portion of it satisfies the requirements derived during analysis. An evaluation can occur whenever an architect is considering a design decision, it can occur after some portion of the design has been completed, it can occur after the final design has been completed or it can occur after the system has been constructed. Some of the available software architecture evaluation techniques include Architecture Tradeoff Analysis Method (ATAM) and TARA. Frameworks for comparing the techniques are discussed in and.

Architecture Evolution is the process of maintaining and adapting an existing software architecture to meet requirement and environmental changes. As software architecture provides a fundamental structure of a software system, its evolution and maintenance would necessarily impact its fundamental structure. As such, architecture evolution is concerned with adding new functionality as well as maintaining existing functionality and system behaviour, for instance, via architectural refactoring.

Architecture requires critical supporting activities. These supporting activities take place throughout the core software architecture process. They include knowledge management and communication, design reasoning and decision making, and documentation.

Architecture Supporting Activities

Software architecture supporting activities are carried out during core software architecture activities. These supporting activities assist a software architect to carry out analysis, synthesis, evaluation and evolution. For instance, an architect has to gather knowledge, make decisions and document during the analysis phase.

- Knowledge Management and Communication is the activity of exploring and managing knowledge that is essential to designing a software architecture. A software architect does not work in isolation. They get inputs, functional and non-functional requirements and design contexts, from various stakeholders; and provides outputs to stakeholders. Software architecture knowledge is often tacit and is retained in the heads of stakeholders. Software Architecture Knowledge Management (AKM) is about finding, communicating, and retaining knowledge. As software architecture design issues are intricate and interdependent, a knowledge gap in design reasoning can lead to incorrect software architecture design. Examples of AKM and communication activities include searching for design patterns, prototyping, asking experienced developers and architects, evaluating the designs of similar systems, sharing knowledge with other designers and stakeholders.

- Design Reasoning and Decision Making is the activity of evaluating design decisions. This activity is fundamental to all three core software architecture activities. It entails gathering and associating decision contexts, formulating design decision problems, finding solution options and evaluating tradeoffs before making decisions. This process occurs at different levels of decision granularity, while evaluating significant architectural requirements and software architecture decisions, and software architecture analysis, synthesis, and evaluation. Examples of reasoning activities include understanding the impacts of a requirement or a design on quality attributes, questioning the issues that a design might cause, assessing possible solution options, and evaluating the tradeoffs between solutions.

- Documentation is the activity of recording the design generated during the software architecture process. A system design is described using several views that frequently include a static view showing the code structure of the system, a dynamic view showing the actions of the system during execution, and a deployment view showing how a system is placed on hardware for execution. Kruchten's 4+1 view suggests a description of commonly used views for documenting software architecture; Documenting Software Architectures: Views and Beyond has descriptions of the kinds of notations that could be used within the view description. Examples of documentation activities are writing a specification, recording a system design model, documenting a design rationale, developing a viewpoint, documenting views. Software engineering methods such as the OpenUP and architecture design methods such as The Process of Software Architecting (P. Eeles, P. Cripps) suggest artifact (a.k.a. work product) types and templates for these documentation activities; ISO/IEC/IEEE 42010:2011 is accompanied by a documentation template as well.

Software Architecture Topics

Software Architecture Description

Software architecture description involves the principles and practices of modeling and representing architectures, using mechanisms such as: architecture description languages, architecture viewpoints, and architecture frameworks.

Architecture Description Languages

An architecture description language (ADL) is any means of expression used to describe a software architecture (ISO/IEC/IEEE 42010). Many special-purpose ADLs have been developed since the 1990s, including ArchiMate, AADL (SAE standard), Wright (developed by Carnegie Mellon), Acme (developed by Carnegie Mellon), xADL (developed by UCI), Darwin (developed by Imperial College London), DAOP-ADL (developed by University of Málaga), SBC-ADL (developed by National Sun Yat-Sen University), and ByADL (University of L'Aquila, Italy).

ADLs have not yet succeeded on a broad scale in practice; UML, often profiled, and Informal Rich Pictures (IPRs) a.k.a. box-and-line diagrams dominate. Usage of UML has been criticized by some thought leaders, but successes have also been reported. Simon Brown's Context, Containers, Components, Classes (C4) model is a recent adid-iton to the architect's notation toolbox.

According to Gregor Hohpe, architects should stop drawing diagrams, in whatever notation, and start communicating.

Architecture Viewpoints

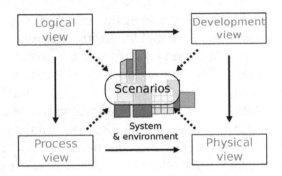

4+1 Architectural View Model.

Software architecture descriptions are commonly organized into views, which are analogous to the different types of blueprints made in building architecture. Each view addresses a set of system concerns, following the conventions of its *viewpoint*, where a viewpoint is a specification that describes the notations, modeling and analysis techniques to use in a view that express the architecture in question from the perspective of a given set of stakeholders and their concerns (ISO/IEC/IEEE 42010). The viewpoint specifies not only the concerns framed (i.e., to be addressed) but the presentation, model kinds used, conventions used and any consistency (correspondence) rules to keep a view consistent with other views.

Popular viewpoint models include the 4+1 views on software architecture, the viewpoints and perspectices catalog by Nick Rozanski and Eoin Woods, and the IBM ADS viewpoint model by Phlippe Spaas et al.

Architecture Frameworks

An architecture framework captures the "conventions, principles and practices for the description of architectures established within a specific domain of application and/or community of stakeholders" (ISO/IEC/IEEE 42010). A framework is usually implemented in terms of one or more viewpoints or ADLs.

Architecture Design Methods

Methods define process models (activities performed by roles) and specify artifacts to be created and delivered; they may also suggest technqiues and practices that assist practitioners when performing the activities and producing the artifacts defined in the method. Five such methods are compared and consolidated in.

Software Architecture and Agile Development

The importance of architecture was stated in the early works on Agile; for instance, Ken Schwaber's original Scrum paper from OOPSLA '97 has the notion of a pregame, in which a high-level system architecture is established. However, there are also concerns that software architecture leads to too much Big Design Up Front, especially among proponents of Agile software development. A number of methods have been developed to balance the trade-offs of up-front design and agility, including the agile method DSDM which mandates a "Foundations" phase during which "just enough" architectural foundations are laid. IEEE Software devoted a special issue to the interaction between agility and architec-ture. P. Kruchten, one of the creators of the Unified Process (UP) and the original 4+1 views on software architecture, summarizes the synergetic relationship in a December 2013 blog post called "Agile architecture".

Architectural Styles and Patterns

An architectural pattern is a general, reusable solution to a commonly occurring problem in software architecture within a given context. Architectural patterns are often documented as software design patterns.

Following traditional building architecture, a 'software architectural style' is a specific method of construction, characterized by the features that make it notable" (Architectural style). "An architectural style defines: a family of systems in terms of a pattern of structural organization; a vocabulary of components and connectors, with constraints on how they can be combined." "Architectural styles are reusable 'packages' of design decisions and constraints that are applied to an architecture to induce chosen desirable qualities."

There are many recognized architectural patterns and styles, among them:

- Blackboard
- Client-server (2-tier, 3-tier, n-tier, cloud computing exhibit this style)
- Component-based
- Data-centric
- Event-driven (or Implicit invocation)
- Layered (or Multilayered architecture)
- Monolithic application
- Peer-to-peer (P2P)
- Pipes and filters

- Plug-ins

- Representational state transfer (REST)

- Rule-based

- Service-oriented architecture and microservices as its implementation approach

- Shared nothing architecture

- Space-based architecture

Some software architects treat architectural patterns and architectural styles as the same, Others treat styles as compositions of patterns combined with architectural principles that jointly address a particular *intent*. These two positions have in common that both patterns and styles are idioms for architects to use; they "provide a common language" or "vocabulary" with which to describe classes of systems.

Software Architecture Erosion

Software architecture erosion (or "decay") refers to the gap observed between the planned and actual architecture of a software system as realized in its implementation. Software architecture erosion occurs when implementation decisions either do not fully achieve the architecture-as-planned or otherwise violate constraints or principles of that architecture. The gap between planned and actual architectures is sometimes understood in terms of the notion of technical debt.

As an example, consider a strictly layered system, where each layer can only use services provided by the layer immediately below it. Any source code component that does not observe this constraint represents an architecture violation. If not corrected, such violations can transform the architecture into a monolithic block, with adverse effects on understandability, maintainability, and evolvability.

Various approaches have been proposed to address erosion. "These approaches, which include tools, techniques and processes, are primarily classified into three generic categories that attempt to minimise, prevent and repair architecture erosion. Within these broad categories, each approach is further broken down reflecting the high-level strategies adopted to tackle erosion. These are: process-oriented architecture conformance, architecture evolution management, architecture design enforcement, architecture to implementation linkage, self-adaptation and architecture restoration techniques consisting of recovery, discovery and reconciliation."

There are two major techniques to detect architectural violations: reflexion models and domain-specific languages. Reflexion model (RM) techniques compare a high-level model provided by the system's architects with the source code implementation. Examples of commercial RM-based tools include the Bauhaus Suite (developed by Axivion), SAVE (developed by Fraunhofer IESE) and Structure-101 (developed by Headway Software). There are also domain-specific languages with focus on specifying and checking architectural constraints, including .QL (developed by Semmle Limited) and DCL (from Federal University of Minas Gerais).

Software Architecture Recovery

Software architecture recovery (or reconstruction, or reverse engineering) includes the methods, techniques and processes to uncover a software system's architecture from available information, including its implementation and documentation. Architecture recovery is often necessary to make informed decisions in the face of obsolete or out-of-date documentation and architecture erosion: implementation and maintenance decisions diverging from the envisioned architecture.

Related Fields

Design

Architecture is design but not all design is architectural. In practice, the architect is the one who draws the line between software architecture (architectural design) and detailed design (non-architectural design). There are no rules or guidelines that fit all cases, although there have been attempts to formalize the distinction. According to the *Intension/Locality Hypothesis*, the distinction between architectural and detailed design is defined by the *Locality Criterion*, according to which a statement about software design is non-local (architectural) if and only if a program that satisfies it can be expanded into a program that does not. For example, the client–server style is architectural (strategic) because a program that is built on this principle can be expanded into a program that is not client–server—for example, by adding peer-to-peer nodes.

Requirements Engineering

Requirements engineering and software architecture can be seen as complementary approaches: while software architecture targets the 'solution space' or the 'how', requirements engineering addresses the 'problem space' or the 'what'. Requirements engineering entails the elicitation, negotiation, specification, validation, documentation and management of requirements. Both requirements engineering and software architecture revolve around stakeholder concerns, needs and wishes.

There is considerable overlap between requirements engineering and software architecture, as evidenced for example by a study into five industrial software architecture methods that concludes that *"the inputs (goals, constrains, etc.) are usually ill-defined, and only get discovered or better understood as the architecture starts to emerge"* and that while *"most architectural concerns are expressed as requirements on the system, they can also include mandated design decisions"*. In short, the choice of required behavior given a particular problem impacts the architecture of the solution that addresses that problem, while at the same time the architectural design may impact the problem and introduce new requirements. Approaches such as the Twin Peaks model aim to exploit the synergistic relation between requirements and architecture.

Other Types of 'Architecture'

Computer architecture

Computer architecture targets the internal structure of a computer system, in terms of collaborating hardware components such as the CPU – or processor – the bus and the memory.

Systems architecture

The term systems architecture has originally been applied to the architecture of systems that consists of both hardware and software. The main concern addressed by the systems architecture, also known as IT architecture, is then the integration of software and hardware in a complete, correctly working device. In another common – much broader – meaning, the term applies to the architecture of any complex system which may be of technical, sociotechnical or social nature.

Enterprise architecture

The goal of enterprise architecture is to "translate business vision and strategy into effective enterprise". Enterprise architecture frameworks, such as TOGAF and the Zachman Framework, usually distinguish between different enterprise architecture layers. Although terminology differs from framework to framework, many include at least a distinction between a *business layer*, an *application* (or *information*) *layer*, and a *technology layer*. Enterprise architecture addresses among others the alignment between these layers, usually in a top-down approach. Continuing the building architecture metaphor for software architecture, enterprise architecture is analogous to city-level planning.

References

- Bass, Len; Paul Clements; Rick Kazman (2012). Software Architecture In Practice, Third Edition. Boston: Addison-Wesley. ISBN 978-0-321-81573-6.

- Jansen, A.; Bosch, J. (2005). "Software Architecture as a Set of Architectural Design Decisions". 5th Working IEEE/IFIP Conference on Software Architecture (WICSA'05). p. 109. doi:10.1109/WICSA.2005.61. ISBN 0-7695-2548-2.

- Architecture Knowledge Management. Dordrecht Heidelberg London New York: Springer. ISBN 978-3-642-02373-6.

- Brooks, Jr., Frederick P. (1975). The Mythical Man-Month - Essays on Software Engineering. Addison-Wesley. ISBN 0-201-00650-2.

- Babar, M.A.; Dingsøyr, T.; Lago, P.; Vliet, H. van (2009). Software Architecture Knowledge Management:Theory and Practice (eds.), First Edition. Springer. ISBN 978-3-642-02373-6.

- Shaw, Mary; Garlan, David (1996). Software architecture: perspectives on an emerging discipline. Prentice Hall. ISBN 978-0-13-182957-2.

- Torres, F. (2015). "Design – Context is King - What's Your Software's Operating Range?". IEEE Software. 32 (5): 9–12. doi:10.1109/MS.2015.121.

- Muller, Gerrit (August 20, 2007). "A Reference Architecture Primer" (PDF). Gaudi site. Retrieved November 13, 2015.

- Obbink, H.; Kruchten, P.; Kozaczynski, W.; Postema, H.; Ran, A.; Dominick, L.; Kazman, R.; Hilliard, R.; Tracz, W.; Kahane, E. (Feb 6, 2002). "Software Architecture Review and Assessment (SARA) Report" (PDF). Retrieved November 1, 2015.

- Zimmermann, Olaf (2015). "Architectural Refactoring: A Task-Centric View on Software Evolution". IEEE Software. 32 (2): 26–29. doi:10.1109/MS.2015.37.

- Poort, Eltjo; van Vliet, Hans (September 2012). "RCDA: Architecting as a risk- and cost management discipline". The Journal of Systems and Software. Elsevier. 85 (9): 1995–2013. doi:10.1016/j.jss.2012.03.071.

- Chen, Lianping; Ali Babar, Muhammad; Nuseibeh, Bashar (2013). "Characterizing Architecturally Significant Requirements". IEEE Software. 30 (2): 38–45. doi:10.1109/MS.2012.174.

- Naur, Peter; Randell, Brian, eds. (1969). "Software Engineering: Report of a conference sponsored by the NATO Science Committee, Garmisch, Germany, 7–11 Oct. 1968." (PDF). Brussels: NATO, Scientific Affairs Division,. Retrieved 2012-11-16.

- P. Kruchten, H. Obbink & J. Stafford (2006). "The past, present and future of software architecture". Retrieved 2012-11-12.

- ISO/IEC (2011). "ISO/IEC 25010:2011 Systems and software engineering – Systems and software Quality Requirements and Evaluation (SQuaRE) – System and software quality models". Retrieved 2012-10-08.

- Woods, E. (2012). "Industrial architectural assessment using TARA". Journal of Systems and Software. 85 (9): 2034–2047. doi:10.1016/j.jss.2012.04.055.

## 2

Types of Software Architecture

The types of architecture that have been explained in the following section are computer architecture and systems architecture. Computer architecture is the method or the rules that are used in describing the implementation and functionality of computer systems. The topics discussed in the section are of great importance to broaden the existing knowledge on architecture.

Computer Architecture

Pipelined implementation of MIPS architecture. Pipelining is a key concept in computer architecture.

In computer engineering, computer architecture is a set of rules and methods that describe the functionality, organization, and implementation of computer systems. Some definitions of architecture define it as describing the capabilities and programming model of a computer but not a particular implementation. In other definitions computer architecture involves instruction set architecture design, microarchitecture design, logic design, and implementation.

History

The first documented computer architecture was in the correspondence between Charles Babbage and Ada Lovelace, describing the analytical engine. When building the computer Z1 in 1936, Konrad Zuse described in two patent applications for his future projects that machine instructions could be stored in the same storage used for data, i.e. the stored-program concept. Two other early and important examples were:

- John von Neumann's 1945 paper, First Draft of a Report on the EDVAC, which described an organization of logical elements; and

- Alan Turing's more detailed *Proposed Electronic Calculator* for the Automatic Computing Engine, also 1945 and which cited von Neumann's paper.

The term "architecture" in computer literature can be traced to the work of Lyle R. Johnson, Mohammad Usman Khan and Frederick P. Brooks, Jr., members in 1959 of the Machine Organization department in IBM's main research center. Johnson had the opportunity to write a proprietary research communication about the Stretch, an IBM-developed supercomputer for Los Alamos National Laboratory (at the time known as Los Alamos Scientific Laboratory). To describe the level of detail for discussing the luxuriously embellished computer, he noted that his description of formats, instruction types, hardware parameters, and speed enhancements were at the level of "system architecture" – a term that seemed more useful than "machine organization."

Subsequently, Brooks, a Stretch designer, started Chapter 2 of a book (Planning a Computer System: Project Stretch, ed. W. Buchholz, 1962) by writing,

Computer architecture, like other architecture, is the art of determining the needs of the user of a structure and then designing to meet those needs as effectively as possible within economic and technological constraints.

Brooks went on to help develop the IBM System/360 (now called the IBM zSeries) line of computers, in which "architecture" became a noun defining "what the user needs to know". Later, computer users came to use the term in many less-explicit ways.

The earliest computer architectures were designed on paper and then directly built into the final hardware form. Later, computer architecture prototypes were physically built in the form of a transistor–transistor logic (TTL) computer—such as the prototypes of the 6800 and the PA-RISC—tested, and tweaked, before committing to the final hardware form. As of the 1990s, new computer architectures are typically "built", tested, and tweaked—inside some other computer architecture in a computer architecture simulator; or inside a FPGA as a soft microprocessor; or both—before committing to the final hardware form.

Subcategories

The discipline of computer architecture has three main subcategories:

1. *Instruction Set Architecture*, or ISA. The ISA defines the machine code that a processor reads and acts upon as well as the word size, memory address modes, processor registers, and data type.

2. *Microarchitecture*, or *computer organization* describes how a particular processor will implement the ISA. The size of a computer's CPU cache for instance, is an issue that generally has nothing to do with the ISA.

3. *System Design* includes all of the other hardware components within a computing system. These include:

1. Data processing other than the CPU, such as direct memory access (DMA)

2. Other issues such as virtualization, multiprocessing, and software features.

There are other types of computer architecture. The following types are used in bigger companies like Intel, and count for 1% of all of computer architecture

- Macroarchitecture: architectural layers more abstract than microarchitecture

- Assembly Instruction Set Architecture (ISA): A smart assembler may convert an abstract assembly language common to a group of machines into slightly different machine language for different implementations

- Programmer Visible Macroarchitecture: higher level language tools such as compilers may define a consistent interface or contract to programmers using them, abstracting differences between underlying ISA, UISA, and microarchitectures. E.g. the C, C++, or Java standards define different Programmer Visible Macroarchitecture.

- UISA (Microcode Instruction Set Architecture)—a group of machines with different hardware level microarchitectures may share a common microcode architecture, and hence a UISA.

- Pin Architecture: The hardware functions that a microprocessor should provide to a hardware platform, e.g., the x86 pins A20M, FERR/IGNNE or FLUSH. Also, messages that the processor should emit so that external caches can be invalidated (emptied). Pin architecture functions are more flexible than ISA functions because external hardware can adapt to new encodings, or change from a pin to a message. The term "architecture" fits, because the functions must be provided for compatible systems, even if the detailed method changes.

Roles

Definition

The purpose is to design a computer that maximizes performance while keeping power consumption in check, costs low relative to the amount of expected performance, and is also very reliable. For this, many aspects are to be considered which includes Instruction Set Design, Functional Organization, Logic Design, and Implementation. The implementation involves Integrated Circuit Design, Packaging, Power, and Cooling. Optimization of the design requires familiarity with Compilers, Operating Systems to Logic Design and Packaging.

Instruction Set Architecture

An instruction set architecture (ISA) is the interface between the computer's software and hardware and also can be viewed as the programmer's view of the machine. Computers do not understand high level languages such as Java, C++, or most programming languages used. A processor only understands instructions encoded in some numerical fashion, usually as binary numbers. Software tools, such as compilers, translate those high level languages into instructions that the processor can understand.

Besides instructions, the ISA defines items in the computer that are available to a program—e.g. data types, registers, addressing modes, and memory. Instructions locate these available items with register indexes (or names) and memory addressing modes.

The ISA of a computer is usually described in a small instruction manual, which describes how the instructions are encoded. Also, it may define short (vaguely) mnemonic names for the instructions. The names can be recognized by a software development tool called an assembler. An assembler is a computer program that translates a human-readable form of the ISA into a computer-readable form. Disassemblers are also widely available, usually in debuggers and software programs to isolate and correct malfunctions in binary computer programs.

ISAs vary in quality and completeness. A good ISA compromises between programmer convenience (how easy the code is to understand), size of the code (how much code is required to do a specific action), cost of the computer to interpret the instructions (more complexity means more space needed to disassemble the instructions), and speed of the computer (with larger disassemblers comes longer disassemble time). For example, single-instruction ISAs like an ISA that subtracts one from a value and if the value is zero then the value returns to a higher value are both inexpensive, and fast, however ISAs like that are not convenient or helpful when looking at the size of the ISA. Memory organization defines how instructions interact with the memory, and how memory interacts with itself.

During design emulation software (emulators) can run programs written in a proposed instruction set. Modern emulators can measure size, cost, and speed to determine if a particular ISA is meeting its goals.

Computer Organization

Computer organization helps optimize performance-based products. For example, software engineers need to know the processing power of processors. They may need to optimize software in order to gain the most performance for the lowest price. This can require quite detailed analysis of the computer's organization. For example, in a SD card, the designers might need to arrange the card so that the most data can be processed in the fastest possible way.

Computer organization also helps plan the selection of a processor for a particular project. Multimedia projects may need very rapid data access, while virtual machines may need fast interrupts. Sometimes certain tasks need additional components as well. For example, a computer capable of running a virtual machine needs virtual memory hardware so that the memory of different virtual computers can be kept separated. Computer organization and features also affect power consumption and processor cost.

Implementation

Once an instruction set and micro-architecture are designed, a practical machine must be developed. This design process is called the *implementation*. Implementation is usually not considered architectural design, but rather hardware design engineering. Implementation can be further broken down into several steps:

- Logic Implementation designs the circuits required at a logic gate level

- Circuit Implementation does transistor-level designs of basic elements (gates, multiplexers, latches etc.) as well as of some larger blocks (ALUs, caches etc.) that may be implemented at the log gate level, or even at the physical level if the design calls for it.

- Physical Implementation draws physical circuits. The different circuit components are placed in a chip floorplan or on a board and the wires connecting them are created.

- Design Validation tests the computer as a whole to see if it works in all situations and all timings. Once the design validation process starts, the design at the logic level are tested using logic emulators. However, this is usually too slow to run realistic test. So, after making corrections based on the first test, prototypes are constructed using Field-Programmable Gate-Arrays (FPGAs). Most hobby projects stop at this stage. The final step is to test prototype integrated circuits. Integrated circuits may require several redesigns to fix problems.

For CPUs, the entire implementation process is organized differently and is often referred to as CPU design.

Design Goals

The exact form of a computer system depends on the constraints and goals. Computer architectures usually trade off standards, power versus performance, cost, memory capacity, latency (latency is the amount of time that it takes for information from one node to travel to the source) and throughput. Sometimes other considerations, such as features, size, weight, reliability, and expandability are also factors.

The most common scheme does an in depth power analysis and figures out how to keep power consumption low, while maintaining adequate performance.

Performance

Modern computer performance is often described in IPC (instructions per cycle). This measures the efficiency of the architecture at any clock frequency. Since a faster rate can make a faster computer, this is a useful measurement. Older computers had IPC counts as low as 0.1 instructions per cycle. Simple modern processors easily reach near 1. Superscalar processors may reach three to five IPC by executing several instructions per clock cycle. Multicore and vector processing CPUs can multiply this further by acting on a lot of data per instruction,since they have several CPU cores executing in parallel.

Counting machine language instructions would be misleading because they can do varying amounts of work in different ISAs. The "instruction" in the standard measurements is not a count of the ISA's actual machine language instructions, but a unit of measurement, usually based on the speed of the VAX computer architecture.

Many people used to measure a computer's speed by the clock rate (usually in MHz or GHz). This refers to the cycles per second of the main clock of the CPU. However, this metric is somewhat misleading, as a machine with a higher clock rate may not necessarily have greater performance. As a result, manufacturers have moved away from clock speed as a measure of performance.

Other factors influence speed, such as the mix of functional units, bus speeds, available memory, and the type and order of instructions in the programs.

In a typical home computer, the simplest, most reliable way to speed performance is usually to add random access memory (RAM). More RAM increases the likelihood that needed data or a program is stored in the RAM—so the system is less likely to need to move memory data from the disk. The reason why RAM is important is because in a HDD (Hard disk drive) you have physical moving parts that you would need to move to access certain parts of a memory. SSD (Solid state drive) are faster than HDD but they still are much slower than the read/write speed of RAM.

There are two main types of speed: latency and throughput. Latency is the time between the start of a process and its completion. Throughput is the amount of work done per unit time. Interrupt latency is the guaranteed maximum response time of the system to an electronic event (like when the disk drive finishes moving some data).

Performance is affected by a very wide range of design choices — for example, pipelining a processor usually makes latency worse, but makes throughput better. Computers that control machinery usually need low interrupt latencies. These computers operate in a real-time environment and fail if an operation is not completed in a specified amount of time. For example, computer-controlled anti-lock brakes must begin braking within a predictable, short time after the brake pedal is sensed or else failure of the brake will occur.

Benchmarking takes all these factors into account by measuring the time a computer takes to run through a series of test programs. Although benchmarking shows strengths, it shouldn't be how you choose a computer. Often the measured machines split on different measures. For example, one system might handle scientific applications quickly, while another might render video games more smoothly. Furthermore, designers may target and add special features to their products, through hardware or software, that permit a specific benchmark to execute quickly but don't offer similar advantages to general tasks.

Power Consumption

Power consumption is another measurement that is important in modern computers. Power efficiency can often be traded for speed or lower cost. The typical measurement when referring to power consumption in Computer Architecture is MIPS/W (millions of instructions per second per watt).

Modern circuits have less power required per transistor as the number of transistors per chip grows. This is because each transistor that is in a new chip requires its own power supply. Therefore, power efficiency has increased in importance over time. Recent processor designs such as Intel's Haswell (microarchitecture), put more emphasis on increasing power efficiency. Also, in the world of embedded computing, power efficiency has long been and remains an important goal next to throughput and latency.

Shifts in Market Demand

Increases in publicly released refresh rates have grown slowly over the past few years, with respect to vast leaps in power consumption reduction and miniaturization demand. Compared to the processing speed increase of 3 GHz to 4 GHz (2006 to 2014), a new demand for more battery life and reductions in size is the current focus because of the mobile technology being produced. This change in focus can be shown by the significant reductions in power consumption, as much as 50%, that were reported by Intel in their release of the Haswell (microarchitecture); where they dropped their benchmark down to 10-20 watts vs. 30-40 watts in the previous model.

Systems Architecture

A system architecture or systems architecture is the conceptual model that defines the structure, behavior, and more views of a system. An architecture description is a formal description and representation of a system, organized in a way that supports reasoning about the structures and behaviors of the system.

A system architecture can comprise system components, the expand systems developed, that will work together to implement the overall system. There have been efforts to formalize languages to describe system architecture, collectively these are called architecture description languages (ADLs).

Overview

Various organizations can define systems architecture in different ways, including:

- The fundamental organization of a system, embodied in its components, their relationships to each other and to the environment, and the principles governing its design and evolution.

- A representation of a system, including a mapping of functionality onto hardware and software components, a mapping of the software architecture onto the hardware architecture, and human interaction with these components.

- An allocated arrangement of physical elements which provides the design solution for a consumer product or life-cycle process intended to satisfy the requirements of the functional architecture and the requirements baseline.

- An architecture comprises the most important, pervasive, top-level, strategic inventions, decisions, and their associated rationales about the overall structure (i.e., essential elements and their relationships) and associated characteristics and behavior.

- A description of the design and contents of a computer system. If documented, it may include information such as a detailed inventory of current hardware, software and networking capabilities; a description of long-range plans and priorities for future purchases, and a plan for upgrading and/or replacing dated equipment and software.

- A formal description of a system, or a detailed plan of the system at component level to guide its implementation.

- The composite of the design architectures for products and their life-cycle processes.

- The structure of components, their interrelationships, and the principles and guidelines governing their design and evolution over time.

One can think of system architecture as a set of representations of an existing (or future) system. These representations initially describe a general, high-level functional organization, and are progressively refined to more detailed and concrete descriptions.

System architecture conveys the informational content of the elements comprising a system, the relationships among those elements, and the rules governing those relationships. The architectural components and set of relationships between these components that an architecture description may consist of hardware, software, documentation, facilities, manual procedures, or roles played by organizations or people.

A system architecture primarily concentrates on the internal interfaces among the system's components or subsystems, and on the interface(s) between the system and its external environment, especially the user. (In the specific case of computer systems, this latter, special, interface is known as the computer human interface, *AKA* human computer interface, or CHI; formerly called the man-machine interface.)

One can contrast a system architecture with system architecture engineering (SAE) - the method and discipline for effectively implementing the architecture of a system:

- SAE is a *method* because a sequence of steps is prescribed to produce or to change the architecture of a system within a set of constraints.

- SAE is a *discipline* because a body of knowledge is used to inform practitioners as to the most effective way to architect the system within a set of constraints.

History

Systems architecture depends heavily on practices and techniques which were developed over thousands of years in many other fields, perhaps the most important being civil architecture.

- Prior to the advent of digital computers, the electronics and other engineering disciplines used the term "system" as it is still commonly used today. However, with the arrival of digital computers and the development of software engineering as a separate discipline, it was often necessary to distinguish among engineered hardware artifacts, software artifacts, and the combined artifacts. A programmable hardware artifact, or computing machine, that lacks its computer program is impotent; even as a software artifact, or program, is equally impotent unless it can be used to alter the sequential states of a suitable (hardware) machine. However, a hardware machine and its programming can be designed to perform an almost illimitable number of abstract and physical tasks. Within the computer and software engineering disciplines (and, often, other engineering disciplines, such as communications), then, the term system came to be defined as containing all of the elements necessary (which generally includes both hardware and software) to perform a useful function.

- Consequently, within these engineering disciplines, a system generally refers to a programmable hardware machine and its included program. And a systems engineer is defined as one concerned with the complete device, both hardware and software and, more particularly, all of the interfaces of the device, including that between hardware and software, and especially between the complete device and its user (the CHI). The hardware engineer deals (more or less) exclusively with the hardware device; the software engineer deals (more or less) exclusively with the computer program; and the systems engineer is responsible for seeing that the program is capable of properly running within the hardware device, and that the system composed of the two entities is capable of properly interacting with its external environment, especially the user, and performing its intended function.

- A systems architecture makes use of elements of both software and hardware and is used to enable design of such a composite system. A good architecture may be viewed as a 'partitioning scheme,' or algorithm, which partitions all of the system's present and foreseeable requirements into a workable set of cleanly bounded subsystems with nothing left over. That is, it is a partitioning scheme which is exclusive, inclusive, and exhaustive. A major purpose of the partitioning is to arrange the elements in the sub systems so that there is a minimum of interdependencies needed among them. In both software and hardware, a good sub system tends to be seen to be a meaningful "object". Moreover, a good architecture provides for an easy mapping to the user's requirements and the validation tests of the user's requirements. Ideally, a mapping also exists from every least element to every requirement and test.

Types

Several types of systems architectures (underlain by the same fundamental principles) have been identified as follows:

- Hardware architecture

- Software architecture

- Enterprise architecture

- Collaborative systems architectures(such as the Internet, intelligent transportation systems, and joint air defense systems)

- Manufacturing systems architectures

- Strategic systems architecture

References

- Laplante, Phillip A. (2001). Dictionary of Computer Science, Engineering, and Technology. CRC Press. pp. 94–95. ISBN 0-8493-2691-5.

## 3

Key Concepts of Software Architecture

Software design is the technique used in creating software. It usually includes problem solving and planning a software solution. Some of the aspects explained in the chapter are requirements engineering, software architect, agent architecture, reference architecture, software system, architecture framework and view model. The major components of software architecture are discussed in this chapter.

Software Design

Software design is the process by which an agent creates a specification of a software artifact, intended to accomplish goals, using a set of primitive components and subject to constraints. Software design may refer to either "all the activity involved in conceptualizing, framing, implementing, commissioning, and ultimately modifying complex systems" or "the activity following requirements specification and before programming, as ... [in] a stylized software engineering process."

Software design usually involves problem solving and planning a software solution. This includes both a low-level component and algorithm design and a high-level, architecture design.

Overview

Software design is the process of implementing software solutions to one or more sets of problems. One of the main components of software design is the software requirements analysis (SRA). SRA is a part of the software development process that lists specifications used in software engineering. If the software is "semi-automated" or user centered, software design may involve user experience design yielding a storyboard to help determine those specifications. If the software is completely automated (meaning no user or user interface), a software design may be as simple as a flow chart or text describing a planned sequence of events. There are also semi-standard methods like Unified Modeling Language and Fundamental modeling concepts. In either case, some documentation of the plan is usually the product of the design. Furthermore, a software design may be platform-independent or platform-specific, depending upon the availability of the technology used for the design.

The main difference between software analysis and design is that the output of a software analysis consists of smaller problems to solve. Additionally, the analysis should not be designed very differently across different team members or groups. In contrast, the design focuses on capabilities, and thus multiple designs for the same problem can and will exist. Depending on the environment, the design often varies, whether it is created from reliable frameworks or implemented with suitable design patterns. Design examples include operation systems, webpages, mobile devices or even the new cloud computing paradigm.

Software design is both a process and a model. The design process is a sequence of steps that enables the designer to describe all aspects of the software for building. Creative skill, past experience, a sense of what makes "good" software, and an overall commitment to quality are examples of critical success factors for a competent design. It is important to note, however, that the design process is not always a straightforward procedure; the design model can be compared to an architect's plans for a house. It begins by representing the totality of the thing that is to be built (e.g., a three-dimensional rendering of the house); slowly, the thing is refined to provide guidance for constructing each detail (e.g., the plumbing layout). Similarly, the design model that is created for software provides a variety of different views of the computer software. Basic design principles enable the software engineer to navigate the design process. Davis [DAV95] suggests a set of principles for software design, which have been adapted and extended in the following list:

- The design process should not suffer from "tunnel vision." A good designer should consider alternative approaches, judging each based on the requirements of the problem, the resources available to do the job.

- The design should be traceable to the analysis model. Because a single element of the design model can often be traced back to multiple requirements, it is necessary to have a means for tracking how requirements have been satisfied by the design model.

- The design should not reinvent the wheel. Systems are constructed using a set of design patterns, many of which have likely been encountered before. These patterns should always be chosen as an alternative to reinvention. Time is short and resources are limited; design time should be invested in representing truly new ideas and integrating patterns that already exist when applicable.

- The design should "minimize the intellectual distance" between the software and the problem as it exists in the real world. That is, the structure of the software design should, whenever possible, mimic the structure of the problem domain.

- The design should exhibit uniformity and integration. A design is uniform if it appears fully coherent. In order to achieve this outcome, rules of style and format should be defined for a design team before design work begins. A design is integrated if care is taken in defining interfaces between design components.

- The design should be structured to accommodate change. The design concepts discussed in the next section enable a design to achieve this principle.

- The design should be structured to degrade gently, even when aberrant data, events, or operating conditions are encountered. Well-designed software should never "bomb"; it should be designed to accommodate unusual circumstances, and if it must terminate processing, it should do so in a graceful manner.

- Design is not coding, coding is not design. Even when detailed procedural designs are created for program components, the level of abstraction of the design model is higher than the source code. The only design decisions made at the coding level should address the small implementation details that enable the procedural design to be coded.

- The design should be assessed for quality as it is being created, not after the fact. A variety of design concepts and design measures are available to assist the designer in assessing quality throughout the development process.

- The design should be reviewed to minimize conceptual (semantic) errors. There is sometimes a tendency to focus on minutiae when the design is reviewed, missing the forest for the trees. A design team should ensure that major conceptual elements of the design (omissions, ambiguity, inconsistency) have been addressed before worrying about the syntax of the design model.

Design Concepts

The design concepts provide the software designer with a foundation from which more sophisticated methods can be applied. A set of fundamental design concepts has evolved. They are as follows:

1. Abstraction - Abstraction is the process or result of generalization by reducing the information content of a concept or an observable phenomenon, typically in order to retain only information which is relevant for a particular purpose.

2. Refinement - It is the process of elaboration. A hierarchy is developed by decomposing a macroscopic statement of function in a step-wise fashion until programming language statements are reached. In each step, one or several instructions of a given program are decomposed into more detailed instructions. Abstraction and Refinement are complementary concepts.

3. Modularity - Software architecture is divided into components called modules.

4. Software Architecture - It refers to the overall structure of the software and the ways in which that structure provides conceptual integrity for a system. Good software architecture will yield a good return on investment with respect to the desired outcome of the project, e.g. in terms of performance, quality, schedule and cost.

5. Control Hierarchy - A program structure that represents the organization of a program component and implies a hierarchy of control.

6. Structural Partitioning - The program structure can be divided both horizontally and vertically. Horizontal partitions define separate branches of modular hierarchy for each major program function. Vertical partitioning suggests that control and work should be distributed top down in the program structure.

7. Data Structure - It is a representation of the logical relationship among individual elements of data.

8. Software Procedure - It focuses on the processing of each module individually.

9. Information Hiding - Modules should be specified and designed so that information contained within a module is inaccessible to other modules that have no need for such information.

In his object model, Grady Booch mentions Abstraction, Encapsulation, Modularisation, and Hierarchy as fundamental design principles. The acronym PHAME (Principles of Hierarchy, Abstraction, Modularisation, and Encapsulation) is sometimes used to refer to these four fundamental principles.

Design Considerations

There are many aspects to consider in the design of a piece of software. The importance of each consideration should reflect the goals and expectations that the software is being created to meet. Some of these aspects are:

- Compatibility - The software is able to operate with other products that are designed for interoperability with another product. For example, a piece of software may be backward-compatible with an older version of itself.

- Extensibility - New capabilities can be added to the software without major changes to the underlying architecture.

- Modularity - the resulting software comprises well defined, independent components which leads to better maintainability. The components could be then implemented and tested in isolation before being integrated to form a desired software system. This allows division of work in a software development project.

- Fault-tolerance - The software is resistant to and able to recover from component failure.

- Maintainability - A measure of how easily bug fixes or functional modifications can be accomplished. High maintainability can be the product of modularity and extensibility.

- Reliability (Software durability) - The software is able to perform a required function under stated conditions for a specified period of time.

- Reusability - The ability to use some or all of the aspects of the preexisting software in other projects with little to no modification.

- Robustness - The software is able to operate under stress or tolerate unpredictable or invalid input. For example, it can be designed with a resilience to low memory conditions.

- Security - The software is able to withstand and resist hostile acts and influences.

- Usability - The software user interface must be usable for its target user/audience. Default values for the parameters must be chosen so that they are a good choice for the majority of the users.

- Performance - The software performs its tasks within a time-frame that is acceptable for the user, and does not require too much memory.

- Portability - The software should be usable across a number of different conditions and environments.

- Scalability - The software adapts well to increasing data or number of users.

Modeling Language

A modeling language is any artificial language that can be used to express information, knowledge or systems in a structure that is defined by a consistent set of rules. These rules are used for interpretation of the components within the structure. A modeling language can be graphical or textual. Examples of graphical modeling languages for software design are:

- Architecture description language (ADL) is a language used to describe and represent the software architecture of a software system.

- Business Process Modeling Notation (BPMN) is an example of a Process Modeling language.

- EXPRESS and EXPRESS-G (ISO 10303-11) is an international standard general-purpose data modeling language.

- Extended Enterprise Modeling Language (EEML) is commonly used for business process modeling across a number of layers.

- Flowchart is a schematic representation of an algorithm or step-wise process.

- Fundamental Modeling Concepts (FMC) is modeling language for software-intensive systems.

- IDEF is a family of modeling languages, the most notable of which include IDEF0 for functional modeling, IDEF1X for information modeling, and IDEF5 for modeling ontologies.

- Jackson Structured Programming (JSP) is a method for structured programming based on correspondences between data stream structure and program structure.

- LePUS3 is an object-oriented visual Design Description Language and a formal specification language that is suitable primarily for modeling large object-oriented (Java, C++, C#) programs and design patterns.

- Unified Modeling Language (UML) is a general modeling language to describe software both structurally and behaviorally. It has a graphical notation and allows for extension with a Profile (UML).

- Alloy (specification language) is a general purpose specification language for expressing complex structural constraints and behavior in a software system. It provides a concise language base on first-order relational logic.

- Systems Modeling Language (SysML) is a new general-purpose modeling language for systems engineering.

- Service-oriented modeling framework (SOMF)

Design Patterns

A software designer or architect may identify a design problem which has been visited and perhaps even solved by others in the past. A template or pattern describing a solution to a common problem is known as a design pattern. The reuse of such patterns can help speed up the software development process.

Technique

The difficulty of using the term "design" in relation to software is that in some senses, the source code of a program *is* the design for the program that it produces. To the extent that this is true, "software design" refers to the design of the design. Edsger W. Dijkstra referred to this layering of semantic levels as the "radical novelty" of computer programming, and Donald Knuth used his experience writing TeX to describe the futility of attempting to design a program prior to implementing it:

TEX would have been a complete failure if I had merely specified it and not participated fully in its initial implementation. The process of implementation constantly led me to unanticipated questions and to new insights about how the original specifications could be improved.

Usage

Software design documentation may be reviewed or presented to allow constraints, specifications and even requirements to be adjusted prior to computer programming. Redesign may occur after review of a programmed simulation or prototype. It is possible to design software in the process of programming, without a plan or requirement analysis, but for more complex projects this would not be considered feasible. A separate design prior to programming allows for multidisciplinary designers and Subject Matter Experts (SMEs) to collaborate with highly skilled programmers for software that is both useful and technically sound.

Requirements Engineering

Requirements engineering (RE) refers to the process of defining, documenting and maintaining requirements to the sub-fields of systems engineering and software engineering concerned with this process.

The first use of the term *requirements engineering* was probably in 1979 in a TRW technical report but did not come into general use until the 1990s with the publication of an IEEE Computer Society tutorial and the establishment of a conference series on requirements engineering that has evolved into the current International Requirements Engineering Conference.

In the waterfall model, requirements engineering is presented as the first phase of the development process. Later software development methods, including the Rational Unified Process (RUP), extreme programming (XP) and Scrum assume that requirements engineering continues through the lifetime of a system.

Alan M. Davis maintains an extensive bibliography of requirements engineering.

Requirement management which is a sub-function of Systems Engineering practices are also indexed in the INCOSE (International Council on Systems Engineering) manuals.

Requirements Engineering Activities

The activities involved in requirements engineering vary widely, depending on the type of system being developed and the specific practices of the organization(s) involved. These may include:

1.   Requirements inception or requirements elicitation -

2. Requirements identification - identifying new requirements

3. Requirements analysis and negotiation - checking requirements and resolving stakeholder conflicts

4. Requirements specification (e.g., software requirements specification; SRS) - documenting the requirements in a requirements document

5. Systems modeling - deriving models of the system, often using a notation such as the Unified Modeling Language (UML) or the Lifecycle Modeling Language (LML)

6. Requirements validation - checking that the documented requirements and models are consistent and meet stakeholder needs

7. Requirements management - managing changes to the requirements as the system is developed and put into use

These are sometimes presented as chronological stages although, in practice, there is considerable interleaving of these activities.

Problems

One limited study in Germany presented possible problems in implementing requirements engineering and asked respondents whether they agreed that they were actual problems. The results were not presented as being generalizable but suggested that the principal perceived problems were incomplete requirements, moving targets, and time boxing, with lesser problems being communications flaws, lack of traceability, terminological problems, and unclear responsibilities.

Criticism

Some recent research suggests that software requirements are often an illusion misrepresenting design decisions as requirements in situations where no real requirements are evident.

Software Architect

A software architect is a software expert who makes high-level design choices and dictates technical standards, including software coding standards, tools, and platforms. The leading expert is referred to as the *chief architect*.

History

With the popularity of multi-tier application development extend this to a list to include even very recent trends, the choices of how an application can be built have also increased. Given that expansion, the risk that a software development project may inadvertently create a "new" end product that, in essence, already existed has grown markedly. A new 'software architect' role has become necessary during software development.

The software architect concept began to take hold when object-oriented programming (OOP) was coming into more widespread use (in the late 1990s and early years of the 21st century). OOP allowed ever-larger and more complex applications to be built, which in turn required increased high-level application and system oversight.

Responsibilities

The main responsibilities of a software architect include:

- Limit choices available during development by
    - choosing a standard way of pursuing application development
    - creating, defining, or choosing an application framework for the application
- Recognize potential reuse in the organization or in the application by
    - observing and understanding the broader system environment
    - creating the component design
    - having knowledge of other applications in the organization
- Subdivide a complex application, during the design phase, into smaller, more manageable pieces
- Grasp the functions of each component within the application
- Understand the interactions and dependencies among components
- Communicate these concepts to developers

In order to perform these responsibilities effectively, software architects often use tools or standardized model and symbol sets such as Unified Modeling Language(UML) and OOP to represent systems or develop artifacts. UML has become an important tool for software architects to use in communicating the overall system design to developers and other team members, comparable to the drawings made by building architects.

Duties

The role of software architect generally has certain common traits:

Architects make high-level design choices much more often than low-level choices. In addition, the architect may sometimes dictate technical standards, including coding standards, tools, or platforms.

Software architects may also be engaged in the design of the architecture of the hardware environment, or may focus entirely on the design methodology of the code.

Architects can use various software architectural models that specialize in communicating architecture.

Other Types of IT-related Architects

The enterprise architect handles the interaction between the business and IT sides of an organization and is principally involved with determining the AS-IS and TO-BE states from a business and IT process perspective. Unfortunately Dubious - discuss many organizations are bundling the software architect duties within the role of Enterprise Architecture. This is primarily done as an effort to "up-sell" the role of a software architect and/or to merge two disparate business-related disciplines to avoid overhead.

An application architect works with a single software application.

Other similar titles in use, but without consensus on their exact meaning, include:

- Solution architect, which may refer to a person directly involved in advancing a particular business solution needing interactions between multiple applications. May also refer to an application architect.

- System architect (singular), which is often used as a synonym for application architect. However, if one subscribes to Systems theory and the idea that an enterprise can be a system, then System Architect could also mean Enterprise Architect.

- Systems architect (plural), which is often used as a synonym for enterprise architect or solution architect.

The table below indicates many of the differences between various kinds of software architects:

Architect type	Strategic thinking	System interactions	Communication	Design
enterprise architect	across projects	highly abstracted	across organization	minimal, high level
solutions architect	focused on solution	very detailed	multiple teams	detailed
application architect	component re-use, maintainability	centered on single application	single project	very detailed

In the software industry, as the table above suggests, the various versions of architect do not always have the same goals.

Agent Architecture

Agent architecture in computer science is a blueprint for software agents and intelligent control systems, depicting the arrangement of components. The architectures implemented by intelligent agents are referred to as cognitive architectures.

Kinds of Agent Architectures

Reactive Architectures

- Subsumption

Deliberative Reasoning Architectures

- Procedural Reasoning System (PRS)

Layered/Hybrid Architectures

- 3T
- AuRA
- Brahms
- GAIuS
- GRL
- ICARUS
- InteRRaP
- TinyCog
- TouringMachines

Cognitive Architectures

- ASMO
- Soar
- ACT-R

- Brahms

- LIDA

- PreAct

- Cougaar

- PRODIGY

- FORR

Reference Architecture

A reference architecture in the field of software architecture or enterprise architecture provides a template solution for an architecture for a particular domain. It also provides a common vocabulary with which to discuss implementations, often with the aim to stress commonality. A software reference architecture is a software architecture where the structures and respective elements and relations provide templates for concrete architectures in a particular domain or in a family of software systems.

A reference architecture often consists of a list of functions and some indication of their interfaces (or APIs) and interactions with each other and with functions located outside of the scope of the reference architecture.

Reference architectures can be defined at different levels of abstraction. A highly abstract one might show different pieces of equipment on a communications network, each providing different functions. A lower level one might demonstrate the interactions of procedures (or methods) within a computer program defined to perform a very specific task.

A reference architecture provides a template, often based on the generalization of a set of solutions. These solutions may have been generalized and structured for the depiction of one or more architecture structures based on the harvesting of a set of patterns that have been observed in a number of successful implementations. Further it shows how to compose these parts together into a solution. Reference Architectures will be instantiated for a particular domain or for specific projects.

Adopting a reference architecture within an organization accelerates delivery through the re-use of an effective solution and provides a basis for governance to ensure the consistency and applicability of technology use within an organization. In the field of software architecture, many empirical studies have shown the following common benefits and drawbacks from adopting a software reference architecture within organizations: (a) improvement of the interoperability of the software systems by establishing a standard solution and common mechanisms for information exchange; (b) reduction of the development costs of software projects through the reuse of common assets;

(c) improvement of the communication inside the organization because stakeholders share the same architectural mindset; and, (d) influencing the learning curve of developers due to the need of learning its features.

Examples

- The Java Platform, Enterprise Edition (Java EE) architecture is a layered reference architecture which provides a template solution for many enterprise systems developed in Java.

- The IBM Insurance Application Architecture is a reference architecture for the Insurance domain.

- AUTOSAR is a component-based reference architecture for automotive software architectures.

Time-triggered Architecture

Time-triggered architecture (abbreviated as TTA), also known as a time-triggered system, is a computer system that executes one or more sets of tasks according to a pre-determined task schedule. Implementation of a TT system will typically involve use of a single interrupt that is linked to the periodic overflow of a timer. This interrupt may drive a task scheduler (a restricted form of real-time operating system). The scheduler will—in turn—release the system tasks at predetermined points in time.

History and Development

Because they have highly deterministic timing behaviour, TT systems have been used for many years to develop safety-critical aerospace and related systems.

Use of TT systems was popularised by the publication of *Patterns for Time-Triggered Embedded Systems* (PTTES) in 2001 and the related introductory book *Embedded C* in 2002. The PTTES book also introduced the concepts of time-triggered hybrid schedulers (an architecture for time-triggered systems that require task pre-emption) and shared-clock schedulers (an architecture for distributed time-triggered systems involving multiple, synchronised, nodes).

Since publication of PTTES, extensive research work on TT systems has been carried out.

Current Applications

Time-triggered systems are now commonly associated with international safety standards such as IEC 61508 (industrial systems), ISO 26262 (automotive systems), IEC 62304 (medical systems) and IEC 60730 (household goods).

Alternatives

Time-triggered systems can be viewed as a subset of a more general event-triggered (ET) system architecture.

Implementation of an ET system will typically involve use of multiple interrupts, each associated with specific periodic events (such as timer overflows) or aperiodic events (such as the arrival of messages over a communication bus at random points in time). ET designs are traditionally associated with the use of what is known as a real-time operating system (or RTOS), though use of such a software platform is not a defining characteristic of an ET architecture.

Software System

A software system is a system of intercommunicating components based on software forming part of a computer system (a combination of hardware and software). It "*consists of a number of separate programs, configuration files, which are used to set up these programs, system documentation, which describes the structure of the system, and user documentation, which explains how to use the system*".

While a computer program is a set of instructions (source, or object code) a software system has many more components such as specification, test results, end-user documentation, maintenance records, etc.

Overview

The term "software system" should be distinguished from the terms "computer program" and "software". The term computer program generally refers to a set of instructions (source, or object code) that perform a specific task. However, a software system generally refers to a more encompassing concept with many more components such as specification, test results, end-user documentation, maintenance records, etc.

The use of the term software system is at times related to the application of systems theory approaches in the context of software engineering. A software system consists of several separate computer programs and associated configuration files, documentation, etc., that operate together. The concept is used in the study of large and complex software, because it focuses on the major *components* of software and their *interactions*. It is also related to the field of software architecture.

Software systems are an active area of research for groups interested in software engineering in particular and systems engineering in general. Academic journals like the *Journal of Systems and Software* (published by Elsevier) are dedicated to the subject.

The ACM *Software System Award* is an annual award that honors people or an organization *"for developing a software system that has had a lasting influence, reflected in contributions to concepts, in commercial acceptance, or both"*. It has been awarded by the Association for Computing Machinery (ACM) since 1983, with a cash prize sponsored by IBM.

Categories

Major categories of software systems include those based on application software, programming software and system software, although the distinction can sometimes be difficult. Examples of software systems include operating systems, computer reservations systems, air traffic control systems, military command and control systems, telecommunication networks, content management systems, database management systems, expert systems, embedded systems etc.

Software Architecture Description

Software architecture description is the set of practices for expressing, communicating and analysing software architectures (also called architectural rendering), and the result of applying such practices through a work product expressing a software architecture (ISO/IEC/IEEE 42010).

Architecture descriptions (ADs) are also sometimes referred to as *architecture representations, architecture specifications* or *software architecture documentation*.

Concepts

Architecture description defines the practices, techniques and types of representations used by software architects to record a software architecture. Architecture description is largely a modeling activity (Software architectural model). Architecture models can take various forms, including text, informal drawings, diagrams or other formalisms (modeling language). An architecture description will often employ several different *model kinds* to effectively address a variety of audiences, the *stakeholders* (such as end users, system owners, software developers, system engineers, program managers) and a variety of architectural *concerns* (such as functionality, safety, delivery, reliability, scalability).

Often, the models of an architecture description are organized into *multiple views* of the architecture such that "each [view] addresses specific concerns of interest to different stakeholders of the system". An *architecture viewpoint* is a way of looking at a system (RM_ODP). Each view in an architecture description should have a viewpoint documenting the concerns and stakeholders it is addressed to, and the model kinds, notations and modeling conventions it utilizes (ISO/IEC/IEEE 42010).

The use of multiple views, while effective for communicating with diverse stakeholders and recording and analyzing diverse concerns, does raise potential problems: since views are typically not independent, the potential for overlap means there may be redundancy or inconsistency between views of a single system. Various mechanisms can be used to define and manage *correspondences* between views to share detail, to reduce redundancy and to enforce consistency.

A common misunderstanding about architecture descriptions is that ADs only discuss "technical issues", but ADs need to address issues of relevance to many stakeholders. Some issues are technical; many issues are not: ADs are used to help architects, their clients and others manage cost, schedule and process. A related misunderstanding is that ADs only address the *structural* aspects of a system. However, this rarely satisfies the stakeholders, whose concerns often include structural, behavioral, aesthetic, and other "extra-functional" concerns.

History

The earliest architecture descriptions used informal pictures and diagrams and associated text. Informal descriptions remain the most widely used representations in industry. Influences on architecture description came from the areas of Software Engineering (such as data abstraction and programming in the large) and from system design (such as SARA).

Work on programming in the large, such as module interconnection languages (MILs) focused on the expression of the large-scale properties of software: modules (including programs, libraries, subroutines and subsystems) and module-relationships (dependencies and interconnections between modules). This work influenced both architectural thinking about programming languages (e.g., Ada), and design and architecture notations (such as Buhr diagrams and use case maps and codified in architectural features of UML: packages, subsystems, dependences) and much of the work on architecture description languages. In addition to MILs, under the influence of mature work in the areas of Requirements and Design within Software Engineering, various kinds of models were "lifted" from software engineering and design to be applied to the description of architectures. These included function and activity models from Structured Analysis SADT, data modeling techniques (entity-relation) and object-oriented techniques.

Perry and Wolf cited the precedent of building architecture for the role of multiple views: "A building architect works with the customer by means of a number of different views in which some particular aspect of the building is emphasized."

Perry and Wolf posited that the representation of architectures should include: { *elements, form and rationale* }, distinguishing three kinds of elements (and therefore three kinds of views):

- processing: how the data is transformed;

- data: information that is used and transformed;

- connecting: glue holding the other elements together;

Perry and Wolf identified four objectives or uses for architecture descriptions (called "architecture specifications" in their paper):

- prescribe architectural constraints without overspecifying solutions

- separate aesthetics from engineering

- express different aspects of the architecture each in an appropriate manner

- conduct architecture analysis, particularly dependency and consistency analyses

Following the Perry and Wolf paper, two schools of thought on software architecture description emerged:

- Multiple views school

- Structuralist school

Mechanisms for Architecture Description

There are several common mechanisms used for architecture description. These mechanisms facilitate reuse of successful styles of description so that they may be applied to many systems:

- architecture viewpoints

- architecture description languages

- architecture frameworks

Architecture Viewpoints

Software architecture descriptions are commonly organized into views, which are analogous to the different types of blueprints made in building architecture. Each view addresses a set of system concerns, following the conventions of its *viewpoint*, where a viewpoint is a specification that describes the notations, modeling techniques to be used in a view to express the architecture in question from the perspective of a given set of stakeholders and their concerns (ISO/IEC 42010). The viewpoint specifies not only the concerns framed (i.e., to be addressed) but the presentation, model kinds used, conventions used and any consistency (correspondence) rules to keep a view consistent with other views.

Examples of viewpoints include:

- Functional viewpoint

- Logical viewpoint

- Information/Data viewpoint

- Module viewpoint

- Component-and-connector viewpoint

- Requirements viewpoint

- Developer/Implementation viewpoint

- Concurrency/process/runtime/thread/execution viewpoint

- Performance viewpoint

- Security viewpoint

- Physical/Deployment/Installation viewpoint

- User action/feedback viewpoint

The term *viewtype* is used to refer to categories of similar views sharing a common set of elements and relations.

Architecture Description Languages

An architecture description language (ADL) is any means of expression used to describe a software architecture (ISO/IEC/IEEE 42010). Many special-purpose ADLs have been developed since the 1990s, including AADL (SAE standard), Wright (developed by Carnegie Mellon), Acme (developed by Carnegie Mellon), xADL (developed by UCI), Darwin (developed by Imperial College London), DAOP-ADL (developed by University of Málaga), and ByADL (University of L'Aquila, Italy). Early ADLs emphasized modeling systems in terms of their components, connectors and configurations. More recent ADLs (such as ArchiMate and SysML) have tended to be "wide-spectrum" languages capable of expressing not only components and connectors but a variety of concerns through multiple sub-languages. In addition to special-purpose languages, existing languages such as the UML can be used as ADLs *"for analysis, design, and implementation of software-based systems as well as for modeling business and similar processes."*

Architecture Frameworks

An architecture framework captures the "conventions, principles and practices for the description of architectures established within a specific domain of application and/

or community of stakeholders" (ISO/IEC/IEEE 42010). A framework is usually implemented in terms of one or more viewpoints or ADLs. Frameworks of interest in software architecture include:

- 4+1

- RM-ODP (Reference Model of Open Distributed Processing)

- TOGAF

Multiple Views

Represented in Kruchten's very influential 1995 paper on the "4+1 view model", this approach emphasized the varying stakeholders and concerns to be modeled.

Structuralism

Second, reflected in work of CMU and elsewhere, the notion that architecture was the high level organization of a system at run-time and that architecture should be described in terms of their components and connectors: "the architecture of a software system defines that system in terms of computational components and interactions among those components".

During the 1990s-2000s, much of the academic work on ADLs took place within the paradigm of components and connectors. However, these ADLs have had very little impact in industry. Since the 1990s, there has been a convergence in approaches toward architecture description, with IEEE 1471 in 2000 codifying best practices: supporting, but not requiring, multiple viewpoints in an AD.

Architecture Description Via Decisions

Elaborating on the rationale aspect of Perry and Wolf's original formula, a third school of thought has emerged, documenting the decisions and reasons for decisions as an essential way of conceiving and expressing a software architecture. This approach treats decisions as first-class elements of the architecture description, making explicit what was often implicit in earlier representations.

Uses of Architecture Descriptions

Architecture descriptions serve a variety of purposes including (ISO/IEC/IEEE 42010):

- to guide system construction and maintenance

- to aid system planning, costing and evolution

- to serve as a medium for analysis, evaluation or comparison of architectures

- to facilitate communication among system stakeholders regarding the architecture and the system

- to document architectural knowledge beyond the scope of individual projects (such as software product lines and product families, and reference architectures)

- to capture reusable architectural idioms (such as architectural styles and patterns)

Architecture Framework

The ISO/IEC/IEEE 42010 Conceptual Model of Architecture Description defines the term architecture framework as:

"An architecture framework establishes a common practice for creating, interpreting, analyzing and using architecture descriptions within a particular domain of application or stakeholder community. Examples of Architecture Frameworks: MODAF, TOGAF, Kruchten's 4+1 View Model, RM-ODP."

Especially the domain within a company or other organisation is covered by enterprise architecture frameworks.

The Survey of Architecture Frameworks lists some of the available architecture frameworks.

View Model

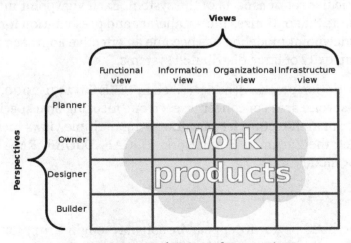

The TEAF Matrix of Views and Perspectives.

A view model or viewpoints framework in systems engineering, software engineering, and enterprise engineering is a framework which defines a coherent set of *views* to be used in the construction of a system architecture, software architecture, or enterprise architecture. A *view* is a representation of a whole system from the perspective of a related set of concerns.

Since the early 1990s there have been a number of efforts to prescribe approaches for describing and analyzing system architectures. These recent efforts define a set of views (or viewpoints). They are sometimes referred to as architecture frameworks or enterprise architecture frameworks, but are not usually called "view models".

Usually a *view* is a work product that presents specific architecture data for a given system. However, the same term is sometimes used to refer to a view *definition*, including the particular viewpoint and the corresponding guidance that defines each concrete view. The term *view model* is related to view definitions.

Overview

The purpose of views and viewpoints is to enable humans to comprehend very complex systems, to organize the elements of the problem and the solution around domains of expertise and to separate concerns. In the engineering of physically intensive systems, viewpoints often correspond to capabilities and responsibilities within the engineering organization.

Most complex system specifications are so extensive that no single individual can fully comprehend all aspects of the specifications. Furthermore, we all have different interests in a given system and different reasons for examining the system's specifications. A business executive will ask different questions of a system make-up than would a system implementer. The concept of viewpoints framework, therefore, is to provide separate viewpoints into the specification of a given complex system in order to facilitate communication with the stakeholders. Each viewpoint satisfies an audience with interest in a particular set of aspects of the system. Each viewpoint may use a specific *viewpoint language* that optimizes the vocabulary and presentation for the audience of that viewpoint. Viewpoint modeling has become an effective approach for dealing with the inherent complexity of large distributed systems.

Architecture description practices, as described in IEEE Std 1471-2000, utilize multiple views to address several areas of concerns, each one focusing on a specific aspect of the system. Examples of architecture frameworks using multiple views include Kruchten's "4+1" view model, the Zachman Framework, TOGAF, DoDAF, RM-ODP, and Hamdaqa's "5+1" view model.

History

In the 1970s, methods began to appear in software engineering for modeling with multiple views. Douglas T. Ross and K.E. Schoman in 1977 introduce the constructs context, viewpoint, and vantage point to organize the modeling process in systems requirements definition. According to Ross and Schoman, a viewpoint "makes clear what aspects are considered relevant to achieving ... the overall purpose [of the model]" and determines *How do we look at [a subject being modelled]?*

As examples of viewpoints, the paper offers: Technical, Operational and Economic viewpoints. In 1992, Anthony Finkelstein and others published a very important paper on viewpoints. In that work: "A viewpoint can be thought of as a combination of the idea of a "actor", "knowledge source", "role" or "agent" in the development process and the idea of a "view" or "perspective" which an actor maintains." An important idea in this paper was to distinguish "a *representation style*, the scheme and notation by which the viewpoint expresses what it can see" and "a *specification*, the statements expressed in the viewpoint's style describing particular domains". Subsequent work, such as IEEE 1471, preserved this distinction by utilizing two separate terms: viewpoint and view, respectively.

Since the early 1990s there have been a number of efforts to codify approaches for describing and analyzing system architectures. These are often terms architecture frameworks or sometimes *viewpoint sets*. Many of these have been funded by the United States Department of Defense, but some have sprung from international or national efforts in ISO or the IEEE. Among these, the IEEE Recommended Practice for Architectural Description of Software-Intensive Systems (IEEE Std 1471-2000) established useful definitions of view, viewpoint, stakeholder and concern and guidelines for documenting a system architecture through the use of multiple views by applying viewpoints to address stakeholder concerns.

IEEE 1471 (now ISO/IEC/IEEE 42010:2011, *Systems and software engineering — Architecture description*) prescribes the contents of architecture descriptions and describes their creation and use under a number of scenarios, including precedented and unprecedented design, evolutionary design, and capture of design of existing systems. In all of these scenarios the overall process is the same: identify stakeholders, elicit concerns, identify a set of viewpoints to be used, and then apply these viewpoint specifications to develop the set of views relevant to the system of interest. Rather than define a particular set of viewpoints, the standard provides uniform mechanisms and requirements for architects and organizations to define their own viewpoints. In 1996 the ISO Reference Model for Open Distributed Processing (RM-ODP) was published to provide a useful framework for describing the architecture and design of large-scale distributed systems.

View Model Topics

View

A view of a system is a representation of the system from the perspective of a viewpoint. This viewpoint on a system involves a perspective focusing on specific concerns regarding the system, which suppresses details to provide a simplified model having only those elements related to the concerns of the viewpoint. For example, a security viewpoint focuses on security concerns and a security viewpoint model contains those elements that are related to security from a more general model of a system.

A view allows a user to examine a portion of a particular interest area. For example, an Information View may present all functions, organizations, technology, etc. that use a particular piece of information, while the Organizational View may present all functions, technology, and information of concern to a particular organization. In the Zachman Framework views comprise a group of work products whose development requires a particular analytical and technical expertise because they focus on either the "what," "how," "who," "where," "when," or "why" of the enterprise. For example, Functional View work products answer the question "how is the mission carried out?" They are most easily developed by experts in functional decomposition using process and activity modeling. They show the enterprise from the point of view of functions. They also may show organizational and information components, but only as they relate to functions.

Viewpoints

In systems engineering, a viewpoint is a partitioning or restriction of concerns in a system. Adoption of a viewpoint is usable so that issues in those aspects can be addressed separately. A good selection of viewpoints also partitions the design of the system into specific areas of expertise.

Viewpoints provide the conventions, rules, and languages for constructing, presenting and analysing views. In ISO/IEC 42010:2007 (IEEE-Std-1471-2000) a viewpoint is a specification for an individual view. A view is a representation of a whole system from the perspective of a viewpoint. A view may consist of one or more architectural models. Each such architectural model is developed using the methods established by its associated architectural system, as well as for the system as a whole.

Modeling Perspectives

Modeling perspectives is a set of different ways to represent pre-selected aspects of a system. Each perspective has a different focus, conceptualization, dedication and visualization of what the model is representing.

In information systems, the traditional way to divide modeling perspectives is to distinguish the structural, functional and behavioral/processual perspectives. This together with rule, object, communication and actor and role perspectives is one way of classifying modeling approaches

Viewpoint Model

In any given viewpoint, it is possible to make a model of the system that contains only the objects that are visible from that viewpoint, but also captures all of the objects, relationships and constraints that are present in the system and relevant to that viewpoint. Such a model is said to be a viewpoint model, or a view of the system from that viewpoint.

A given view is a specification for the system at a particular level of abstraction from a given viewpoint. Different levels of abstraction contain different levels of detail. Higher-level views allow the engineer to fashion and comprehend the whole design and identify and resolve problems in the large. Lower-level views allow the engineer to concentrate on a part of the design and develop the detailed specifications.

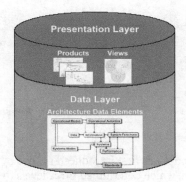

Illustration of the views, products and data in Architecture Framework.

In the system itself, however, all of the specifications appearing in the various viewpoint models must be addressed in the realized components of the system. And the specifications for any given component may be drawn from many different viewpoints. On the other hand, the specifications induced by the distribution of functions over specific components and component interactions will typically reflect a different partitioning of concerns than that reflected in the original viewpoints. Thus additional viewpoints, addressing the concerns of the individual components and the bottom-up synthesis of the system, may also be useful.

Architecture Description

An architecture description is a representation of a system architecture, at any time, in terms of its component parts, how those parts function, the rules and constraints under which those parts function, and how those parts relate to each other and to the environment. In an architecture description the *architecture data* is shared across several views and products.

At the data layer are the architecture data elements and their defining attributes and relationships. At the presentation layer are the products and views that support a visual means to communicate and understand the purpose of the architecture, what it describes, and the various architectural analyses performed. Products provide a way for visualizing architecture data as graphical, tabular, or textual representations. Views provide the ability to visualize architecture data that stem across products, logically organizing the data for a specific or holistic perspective of the architecture.

Types of System View Models

Three Schema Approach

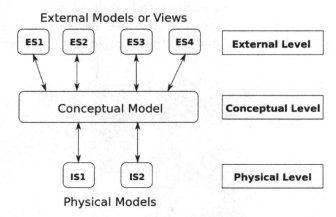

The notion of a three-schema model was first introduced in 1977 by the ANSI/X3/SPARC three level architecture, which determined three levels to model data.

The Three schema approach for data modeling, introduced in 1977, can be considered one of the first view models. It is an approach to building information systems and systems information management, that promotes the conceptual model as the key to achieving data integration. The Three schema approach defines three schemas and views:

- External schema for user views

- Conceptual schema integrates external schemata

- Internal schema that defines physical storage structures

At the center, the conceptual schema defines the ontology of the concepts as the users think of them and talk about them. The physical schema describes the internal formats of the data stored in the database, and the external schema defines the view of the data presented to the application programs. The framework attempted to permit multiple data models to be used for external schemata.

Over the years, the skill and interest in building information systems has grown tremendously. However, for the most part, the traditional approach to building systems has only focused on defining data from two distinct views, the "user view" and the "computer view". From the user view, which will be referred to as the "external schema," the definition of data is in the context of reports and screens designed to aid individuals in doing their specific jobs. The required structure of data from a usage view changes with the business environment and the individual preferences of the user. From the computer view, which will be referred to as the "internal schema," data is defined in terms of file structures for storage and retrieval. The required structure of data for computer storage depends upon the specific computer technology employed and the need for efficient processing of data.

4+1 View Model of Architecture

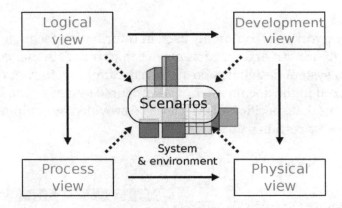

Illustration of the 4+1 view model or architecture.

4+1 is a view model designed by Philippe Kruchten in 1995 for describing the architecture of software-intensive systems, based on the use of multiple, concurrent views. The views are used to describe the system in the viewpoint of different stakeholders, such as end-users, developers and project managers. The four views of the model are logical, development, process and physical view:

The four views of the model are concerned with :

- *Logical view* : is concerned with the functionality that the system provides to end-users.

- *Development view* : illustrates a system from a programmers perspective and is concerned with software management.

- *Process view* : deals with the dynamic aspect of the system, explains the system processes and how they communicate, and focuses on the runtime behavior of the system.

- *Physical view* : depicts the system from a system engineer›s point of view. It is concerned with the topology of software components on the physical layer, as well as communication between these components.

In addition selected use cases or scenarios are utilized to illustrate the architecture. Hence the model contains 4+1 views.

Types of Enterprise Architecture View

Enterprise Architecture framework defines how to organize the structure and views associated with an Enterprise Architecture. Because the discipline of Enterprise Architecture and Engineering is so broad, and because enterprises can be large and complex, the models associated with the discipline also tend to be large and complex. To manage this scale and complexity, an Architecture Framework provides tools and methods that can bring the task into focus and allow valuable artifacts to be produced when they are most needed.

Architecture Frameworks are commonly used in Information technology and Information system governance. An organization may wish to mandate that certain models be produced before a system design can be approved. Similarly, they may wish to specify certain views be used in the documentation of procured systems - the U.S. Department of Defense stipulates that specific DoDAF views be provided by equipment suppliers for capital project above a certain value.

Zachman Framework

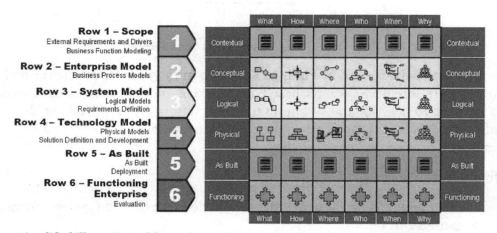

Simplified illustration of the Zachman Framework with an explanation of the rows. The original framework is more advanced.

The Zachman Framework, originally conceived by John Zachman at IBM in the 1987, is a framework for enterprise architecture, which provides a formal and highly structured way of viewing and defining an enterprise.

The Framework is used for organizing architectural "artifacts" in a way that takes into account both who the artifact targets (for example, business owner and builder) and what particular issue (for example, data and functionality) is being addressed. These artifacts may include design documents, specifications, and models.

The Zachman Framework is often referenced as a standard approach for expressing the basic elements of enterprise architecture. The Zachman Framework has been recognized by the U.S. Federal Government as having "... received worldwide acceptance as an integrated framework for managing change in enterprises and the systems that support them."

RM-ODP Views

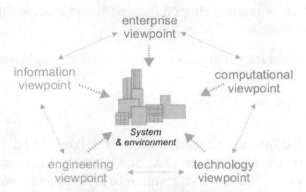

The RM-ODP view model, which provides five generic and complementary viewpoints on the system and its environment.

The International Organization for Standardization (ISO) Reference Model for Open Distributed Processing (RM-ODP) specifies a set of viewpoints for partitioning the design of a distributed software/hardware system. Since most integration problems arise in the design of such systems or in very analogous situations, these viewpoints may prove useful in separating integration concerns. The RMODP viewpoints are:

- the *enterprise viewpoint*, which is concerned with the purpose and behaviors of the system as it relates to the business objective and the business processes of the organization

- the *information viewpoint*, which is concerned with the nature of the information handled by the system and constraints on the use and interpretation of that information

- the *computational viewpoint*, which is concerned with the functional decomposition of the system into a set of components that exhibit specific behaviors and interact at interfaces

- the *engineering viewpoint*, which is concerned with the mechanisms and functions required to support the interactions of the computational components

- the *technology viewpoint*, which is concerned with the explicit choice of technologies for the implementation of the system, and particularly for the communications among the components

RMODP further defines a requirement for a design to contain specifications of consistency between viewpoints, including:

- the use of enterprise objects and processes in defining information units

- the use of enterprise objects and behaviors in specifying the behaviors of computational components, and use of the information units in defining computational interfaces

- the association of engineering choices with computational interfaces and behavior requirements

- the satisfaction of information, computational and engineering requirements in the chosen technologies

DoDAF Views

The Department of Defense Architecture Framework (DoDAF) defines a standard way to organize an enterprise architecture (EA) or systems architecture into complementary and consistent views. It is especially suited to large systems with complex integration and interoperability challenges, and is apparently unique in its use of "operational views" detailing the external customer's operating domain in which the developing system will operate.

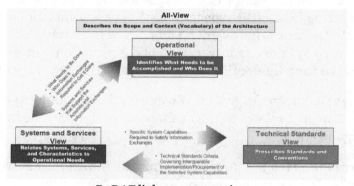

DoDAF linkages among views.

The DoDAF defines a set of products that act as mechanisms for visualizing, understanding, and assimilating the broad scope and complexities of an architecture description through graphic, tabular, or textual means. These products are organized under four views:

- Overarching All View (AV),

- Operational View (OV),

- Systems View (SV), and the

- Technical Standards View (TV).

Each view depicts certain perspectives of an architecture as described below. Only a subset of the full DoDAF viewset is usually created for each system development. The figure represents the information that links the operational view, systems and services view, and technical standards view. The three views and their interrelationships driven – by common architecture data elements – provide the basis for deriving measures such as interoperability or performance, and for measuring the impact of the values of these metrics on operational mission and task effectiveness.

Federal Enterprise Architecture Views

In the US Federal Enterprise Architecture enterprise, segment, and solution architecture provide different business perspectives by varying the level of detail and addressing related but distinct concerns. Just as enterprises are themselves hierarchically organized, so are the different views provided by each type of architecture. The Federal Enterprise Architecture Practice Guidance (2006) has defined three types of architecture:

Level	Scope	Detail	Impact	Audience
Enterprise Architecture	Agency/ Organization	Low	Strategic Outcomes	All Stakeholders
Segment Architecture	Line of Business	Medium	Business Outcomes	Business Owners
Solution Architecture	Function/ Process	High	Operational Outcomes	Users and Developers

Federal Enterprise Architecture levels and attributes

- Enterprise architecture,

- Segment architecture, and

- Solution architecture.

By definition, Enterprise Architecture (EA) is fundamentally concerned with identifying common or shared assets – whether they are strategies, business processes, investments, data, systems, or technologies. EA is driven by strategy; it helps an agency identify whether its resources are properly aligned to the agency mission and strategic goals and objectives. From an investment perspective, EA is used to drive decisions about the IT investment portfolio as a whole. Consequently, the primary stakeholders of the EA are the senior managers and executives tasked with ensuring the agency fulfills its mission as effectively and efficiently as possible.

By contrast, segment architecture defines a simple roadmap for a core mission area, business service, or enterprise service. Segment architecture is driven by business management and delivers products that improve the delivery of services to citizens and agency staff. From an investment perspective, segment architecture drives decisions for a business case or group of business cases supporting a core mission area or common or shared service. The primary stakeholders for segment architecture are business owners and managers. Segment architecture is related to EA through three principles: structure, reuse, and alignment. First, segment architecture inherits the framework used by the EA, although it may be extended and specialized to meet the specific needs of a core mission area or common or shared service. Second, segment architecture reuses important assets defined at the enterprise level including: data; common business processes and investments; and applications and technologies. Third, segment architecture aligns with elements defined at the enterprise level, such as business strategies, mandates, standards, and performance measures.

Nominal Set of Views

In search of "Framework for Modeling Space Systems Architectures" Peter Shames and Joseph Skipper (2006) defined a "nominal set of views", Derived from CCSDS RASDS, RM-ODP, ISO 10746 and compliant with IEEE 1471.

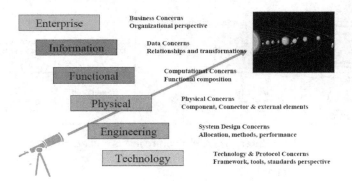

Illustration of the "Nominal set of views".

This "set of views", as described below, is a listing of possible modeling viewpoints. Not all of these views may be used for any one project and other views may be defined as necessary. Note that for some analyses elements from multiple viewpoints may be combined into a new view, possibly using a layered representation.

In a latter presentation this nominal set of views was presented as an Extended RASDS Semantic Information Model Derivation. Hereby RASDS stands for Reference Architecture for Space Data Systems. see second image.

Enterprise Viewpoint

- Organization view – Includes organizational elements and their structures and relationships. May include agreements, contracts, policies and organizational interactions.

- Requirements view – Describes the requirements, goals, and objectives that drive the system. Says what the system must be able to do.

- Scenario view – Describes the way that the system is intended to be used, see scenario planning. Includes user views and descriptions of how the system is expected to behave.

Information viewpoint

- Metamodel view – An abstract view that defines information model elements and their structures and relationships. Defines the classes of data that are created and managed by the system and the data architecture.

- Information view – Describes the actual data and information as it is realized and manipulated within the system. Data elements are defined by the metamodel view and they are referred to by functional objects in other views.

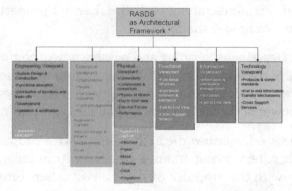

Reference Architecture for Space Data Systems.

Functional viewpoint

- Functional Dataflow view – An abstract view that describes the functional elements in the system, their interactions, behavior, provided services, constraints and data flows among them. Defines which functions the system is capable of performing, regardless of how these functions are actually implemented.

- Functional Control view – Describes the control flows and interactions among functional elements within the system. Includes overall system control interactions, interactions between control elements and sensor / effector elements and management interactions.

Physical viewpoint

- Data System view – Describes instruments, computers, and data storage components, their data system attributes and the communications connectors (busses, networks, point to point links) that are used in the system.

- Telecomm view – Describes the telecomm components (antenna, transceiver), their attributes and their connectors (RF or optical links).

- Navigation view – Describes the motion of the major elements within the system (trajectory, path, orbit), including their interaction with external elements and forces that are outside of the control of the system, but that must be modeled with it to understand system behavior (planets, asteroids, solar pressure, gravity)

- Structural view – Describes the structural components in the system (s/c bus, struts, panels, articulation), their physical attributes and connectors, along with the relevant structural aspects of other components (mass, stiffness, attachment)

- Thermal view – Describes the active and passive thermal components in the system (radiators, coolers, vents) and their connectors (physical and free space radiation) and attributes, along with the thermal properties of other components (i.e. antenna as sun shade)

- Power view – Describes the active and passive power components in the system (solar panels, batteries, RTGs) within the system and their connectors, along with the power properties of other components (data system and propulsion elements as power sinks and structural panels as grounding plane)

- Propulsion view – Describes the active and passive propulsion components in the system (thrusters, gyros, motors, wheels) within the system and their connectors, along with the propulsive properties of other components

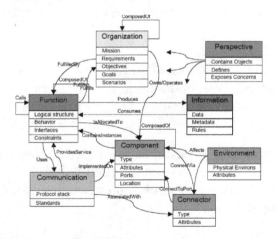

MBED Top Level Ontology based on the Nominal set of views.

Engineering viewpoint

- Allocation view – Describes the allocation of functional objects to engineered

physical and computational components within the system, permits analysis of performance and used to verify satisfaction of requirements

- Software view - Describes the software engineering aspects of the system, software design and implementation of functionality within software components, select languages and libraries to be used, define APIs, do the engineering of abstract functional objects into tangible software elements. Some functional elements, described using a software language, may actually be implemented as hardware (FPGA, ASIC)

- Hardware views – Describes the hardware engineering aspects of the system, hardware design, selection and implementation of all of the physical components to be assembled into the system. There may be many of these views, each specific to a different engineering discipline.

- Communications Protocol view – Describes the end to end design of the communications protocols and related data transport and data management services, shows the protocol stacks as they are implemented on each of the physical components of the system.

- Risk view – Describes the risks associated with the system design, processes, and technologies, assigns additional risk assessment attributes to other elements described in the architecture

- Control Engineering view - Analyzes system from the perspective of its controllability, allocation of elements into system under control and control system

- Integration and Test view – Looks at the system from the perspective of what must be done to assemble, integrate and test system and sub-systems, and assemblies. Includes verification of proper functionality, driven by scenarios, in satisfaction of requirements.

- IV&V view – independent validation and verification of functionality and proper operation of the system in satisfaction of requirements. Does system as designed and developed meet goals and objectives.

Technology viewpoint

- Standards view – Defines the standards to be adopted during design of the system (e.g. communication protocols, radiation tolerance, soldering). These are essentially constraints on the design and implementation processes.

- Infrastructure view – Defines the infrastructure elements that are to support the engineering, design, and fabrication process. May include data system elements (design repositories, frameworks, tools, networks) and hardware elements (chip fabrication, thermal vacuum facility, machine shop, RF testing lab)

- Technology Development & Assessment view – Includes description of technology development programs designed to produce algorithms or components that may be included in a system development project. Includes evaluation of properties of selected hardware and software components to determine if they are at a sufficient state of maturity to be adopted for the mission being designed.

In contrast to the previous listed view models, this "nominal set of views" lists a whole range of views, possible to develop powerful and extensible approaches for describing a general class of software intensive system architectures.

Agile Software Development

Agile software development describes a set of principles for software development under which requirements and solutions evolve through the collaborative effort of self-organizing cross-functional teams. It advocates adaptive planning, evolutionary development, early delivery, and continuous improvement, and it encourages rapid and flexible response to change. These principles support the definition and continuing evolution of many software development methods.

The term *agile* was first coined for this in 2001, in the *Manifesto for Agile Software Development* (Agile Manifesto), and although originally written as *Agile* (with a capital *A*) this is progressively becoming deprecated.

History

Incremental software development methods can be traced back to 1957. Evolutionary project management and adaptive software development emerged in the early 1970s. During the 1990s, a number of *lightweight* software development methods evolved in reaction to the prevailing *heavyweight* methods that critics described as heavily regulated, regimented, and micro-managed. These included: from 1991, rapid application development; from 1994, unified process and dynamic systems development method (DSDM); from 1995, Scrum; from 1996, Crystal Clear and extreme programming (XP); and from 1997, feature-driven development. Although these originated before the publication of the Agile Manifesto in 2001, they are now collectively referred to as agile methods.

The Manifesto for Agile Software Development

In February 2001, 17 software developers met at the Snowbird resort in Utah to discuss lightweight development methods. They published the *Manifesto for Agile Software Development*, in which they shared that through their combined experience of developing software and helping others to do it they had come to value:

- *Individuals and interactions* over processes and tools
- *Working software* over comprehensive documentation
- *Customer collaboration* over contract negotiation
- *Responding to change* over following a plan

While the secondary concerns were important the primary concerns were more critical to success.

By these terms, they meant:

Individuals and interactions

> Self-organization and motivation are important, as are interactions like co-location and pair programming.

Working software

> Working software is more useful and welcome than just presenting documents to clients in meetings.

Customer collaboration

> Requirements cannot be fully collected at the beginning of the software development cycle, therefore continuous customer or stakeholder involvement is very important.

Responding to change

> Agile methods are focused on quick responses to change and continuous development.

Some of the authors formed the Agile Alliance, a non-profit organization that promotes software development according to the manifesto's values and principles. Introducing the manifesto on behalf of the Agile Alliance, Jim Highsmith said,

The Agile movement is not anti-methodology, in fact many of us want to restore credibility to the word methodology. We want to restore a balance. We embrace modeling, but not in order to file some diagram in a dusty corporate repository. We embrace documentation, but not hundreds of pages of never-maintained and rarely-used tomes. We plan, but recognize the limits of planning in a turbulent environment. Those who would brand proponents of XP or SCRUM or any of the other Agile Methodologies as "hackers" are ignorant of both the methodologies and the original definition of the term hacker.

—Jim Highsmith, History: The Agile Manifesto

Agile Principles

The Agile Manifesto is based on twelve principles:

1. Customer satisfaction by early and continuous delivery of valuable software

2. Welcome changing requirements, even in late development

3. Working software is delivered frequently (weeks rather than months)

4. Close, daily cooperation between business people and developers

5. Projects are built around motivated individuals, who should be trusted

6. Face-to-face conversation is the best form of communication (co-location)

7. Working software is the principal measure of progress

8. Sustainable development, able to maintain a constant pace

9. Continuous attention to technical excellence and good design

10. Simplicity—the art of maximizing the amount of work not done—is essential

11. Best architectures, requirements, and designs emerge from self-organizing teams

12. Regularly, the team reflects on how to become more effective, and adjusts accordingly

Evolutions

Later, Ken Schwaber with others founded the Scrum Alliance and created the Certified Scrum Master programs and its derivatives. Schwaber left the Scrum Alliance in the fall of 2009, and founded Scrum.org.

In 2005, a group headed by Alistair Cockburn and Jim Highsmith wrote an addendum of project management principles, the Declaration of Interdependence, to guide software project management according to agile software development methods.

In 2009, a movement by Robert C Martin wrote an extension of software development principles, the Software Craftsmanship Manifesto, to guide agile software development according to professional conduct and mastery.

In 2011 the original Agile Alliance created the Guide to Agile Practices, an evolving open-source compendium of the working definitions of agile practices, terms, and elements, along with interpretations and experience guidelines from the worldwide community of agile practitioners.

Related disciplines, including project management (PRINCE2 and PMI) and business analysis (IIBA) have extended or updated their bodies of knowledge and certifications to embrace working with agile methods.

Overview

Pair programming, an agile development technique used by XP. Note information radiators in the background.

There are many specific agile development methods. Most promote teamwork, collaboration, and process adaptability throughout the product development life-cycle.

Iterative, Incremental and Evolutionary

Most agile development methods break product development work into small increments that minimize the amount of up-front planning and design. Iterations are short time frames (timeboxes) that typically last from one to four weeks. Each iteration involves a cross-functional team working in all functions: planning, analysis, design, coding, unit testing, and acceptance testing. At the end of the iteration a working product is demonstrated to stakeholders. This minimizes overall risk and allows the product to adapt to changes quickly. An iteration might not add enough functionality to warrant a market release, but the goal is to have an available release (with minimal bugs) at the end of each iteration. Multiple iterations might be required to release a product or new features.

Working software is the primary measure of progress.

Efficient and Face-to-face Communication

No matter which development method is followed, every team should include a customer representative (*product owner* in Scrum). This person is agreed by stakeholders to act on their behalf and makes a personal commitment to being available for developers to answer questions throughout the iteration. At the end of each iteration, stakeholders and the customer representative review progress and re-evaluate priorities with a view to optimizing the return on investment (ROI) and ensuring alignment with customer needs and company goals.

In agile software development, an *information radiator* is a (normally large) physical display located prominently near the development team, where passers-by can see it. It presents an up-to-date summary of the product development status. A build light indicator may also be used to inform a team about the current status of their product development.

Very Short Feedback Loop and Adaptation Cycle

A common characteristic in agile development is the daily stand-up (also known as the *daily scrum)*. In a brief session, team members report to each other what they did the previous day toward their team's iteration goal, what they intend to do today toward the goal, and any roadblocks or impediments they can see to the goal.

Quality Focus

Specific tools and techniques, such as continuous integration, automated unit testing, pair programming, test-driven development, design patterns, domain-driven design, code refactoring and other techniques are often used to improve quality and enhance product development agility.

Philosophy

Compared to traditional software engineering, agile software development mainly targets complex systems and product development with dynamic, non-deterministic and non-linear characteristics, where accurate estimates, stable plans, and predictions are often hard to get in early stages—and big up-front designs and arrangements would probably cause a lot of waste, i.e., are not economically sound. These basic arguments and previous industry experiences, learned from years of successes and failures, have helped shape agile development's favor of adaptive, iterative and evolutionary development.

Adaptive Vs. Predictive

Development methods exist on a continuum from *adaptive* to *predictive*. Agile methods lie on the *adaptive* side of this continuum. One key of adaptive development methods is a "Rolling Wave" approach to schedule planning, which identifies milestones but leaves flexibility in the path to reach them, and also allows for the milestones themselves to change. Adaptive methods focus on adapting quickly to changing realities. When the needs of a project change, an adaptive team changes as well. An adaptive team has difficulty describing exactly what will happen in the future. The further away a date is, the more vague an adaptive method is about what will happen on that date. An adaptive team cannot report exactly what tasks they will do next week, but only which features they plan for next month. When asked about a release six months from now, an adaptive team might be able to report only the mission statement for the release, or a statement of expected value vs. cost.

Predictive methods, in contrast, focus on analysing and planning the future in detail and cater for known risks. In the extremes, a predictive team can report exactly what features and tasks are planned for the entire length of the development process. Predictive methods rely on effective early phase analysis and if this goes very wrong, the project may have difficulty changing direction. Predictive teams often institute a change control board to ensure they consider only the most valuable changes.

Risk analysis can be used to choose between adaptive (*agile* or *value-driven*) and predictive (*plan-driven*) methods. Barry Boehm and Richard Turner suggest that each side of the continuum has its own *home ground*, as follows:

Home grounds of different development methods		
Agile methods	Plan-driven methods	Formal methods
Low criticality	High criticality	Extreme criticality
Senior developers	Junior developers(?)	Senior developers
Requirements change often	Requirements do not change often	Limited requirements, limited features see Wirth's law
Small number of developers	Large number of developers	Requirements that can be modeled
Culture that responds to change	Culture that demands order	Extreme quality

Iterative vs. Waterfall

One of the differences between agile and waterfall is the approach to quality and testing. In the waterfall model, there is always a separate *testing phase* after a *build phase*; however, in agile development testing is completed in the same iteration as programming.

Because testing is done in every iteration—which develops a small piece of the software—users can frequently use those new pieces of software and validate the value.

After the users know the real value of the updated piece of software, they can make better decisions about the software's future. Having a value retrospective and software re-planning session in each iteration—Scrum typically has iterations of just two weeks—helps the team continuously adapt its plans so as to maximize the value it delivers.

This iterative approach supports a *product* rather than a *project* mindset. This provides greater flexibility throughout the development process; whereas on projects the requirements are defined and locked down from the very beginning, making it difficult to change them later. Iterative product development allows the software to evolve in response to changes in business environment or market requirements.

Because of the short iteration style of agile software development, it also has strong connections with the lean startup concept.

Code vs. Documentation

In a letter to *IEEE Computer*, Steven Rakitin expressed cynicism about agile development, calling it "yet another attempt to undermine the discipline of software engineering" and translating "Working software over comprehensive documentation" as "We want to spend all our time coding. Remember, real programmers don't write documentation."

This is disputed by proponents of agile software development, who state that developers should write documentation if that's the best way to achieve the relevant goals, but that there are often better ways to achieve those goals than writing static documentation. Scott Ambler states that documentation should be "Just Barely Good Enough" (JBGE), that too much or comprehensive documentation would usually cause waste, and developers rarely trust detailed documentation because it's usually out of sync with code, while too little documentation may also cause problems for maintenance, communication, learning and knowledge sharing. Alistair Cockburn wrote of the *Crystal Clear* method:

Crystal considers development a series of co-operative games, and intends that the documentation is enough to help the next win at the next game. The work products for Crystal include use cases, risk list, iteration plan, core domain models, and design notes to inform on choices...however there are no templates for these documents and descriptions are necessarily vague, but the objective is clear, just enough documentation for the next game. I always tend to characterize this to my team as: what would you want to know if you joined the team tomorrow.

—Alistair Cockburn.

Agile Methods

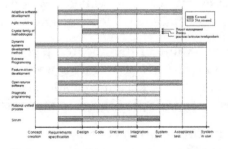

Software development life-cycle support

Agile methods support a broad range of the software development life cycle. Some focus on the practices (e.g., XP, pragmatic programming, agile modeling), while some focus on managing the flow of work (e.g., Scrum, Kanban). Some support activities for requirements specification and development (e.g., FDD), while some seek to cover the full development life cycle (e.g., DSDM, RUP).

Popular agile software development frameworks include (but are not limited to):

- Adaptive software development (ASD)
- Agile modeling
- Agile Unified Process (AUP)
- Crystal Clear methods
- Disciplined agile delivery
- Dynamic systems development method (DSDM)
- Extreme programming (XP)
- Feature-driven development (FDD)
- Lean software development
- Kanban
- Scrum
- Scrumban
- RAD(Rapid Application Development)

Agile Practices

Agile development is supported by a number of concrete practices, covering areas like requirements, design, modelling, coding, testing, planning, risk management, process, quality, etc. Some notable agile practices include:

- Acceptance test-driven development (ATDD)
- Agile modeling
- Backlogs (Product and Sprint)
- Behavior-driven development (BDD)
- Business analyst designer method (BADM)
- Cross-functional team
- Continuous integration (CI)
- Domain-driven design (DDD)
- Information radiators (scrum board, task board, visual management board,

burndown chart)

- Iterative and incremental development (IID)

- Pair programming

- Planning poker

- Refactoring

- Scrum events (sprint planning, daily scrum, sprint review and retrospective)

- Test-driven development (TDD)

- Agile testing

- Timeboxing

- User story

- Story-driven modeling

- Retrospective

- Velocity tracking

- User Story Mapping

The Agile Alliance has provided a comprehensive online guide to applying agile these and other practices.

Method Tailoring

In the literature, different terms refer to the notion of method adaptation, including 'method tailoring', 'method fragment adaptation' and 'situational method engineering'. Method tailoring is defined as:

A process or capability in which human agents determine a system development approach for a specific project situation through responsive changes in, and dynamic interplays between contexts, intentions, and method fragments.

—*Mehmet Nafiz Aydin et al., An Agile Information Systems Development Method in use*

Potentially, almost all agile methods are suitable for method tailoring. Even the DSDM method is being used for this purpose and has been successfully tailored in a CMM context. Situation-appropriateness can be considered as a distinguishing characteristic between agile methods and traditional software development methods, with the latter being relatively much more rigid and prescriptive. The practical implication is that agile methods allow product development teams to adapt working practices according to the needs of individual products. Practices are concrete activities and products that are part of a method framework. At a more extreme level, the philosophy behind the method, consisting of a number of principles, could be adapted (Aydin, 2004).

Some approaches, such as Scrum and extreme programming, make the need for method adaptation explicit. With these less-prescriptive frameworks, one of the principles is that no single process fits every product development, but rather that practices should be tailored to the needs of the product. Mehdi Mirakhorli proposes a tailoring practice that provides a sufficient road-map and guidelines for adapting all the practices. RDP Practice is designed for customizing XP. This practice, first proposed as a long research paper in the APSO workshop at the ICSE 2008 conference, is currently the only proposed and applicable method for customizing XP. Although it is specifically a solution for XP, this practice has the capability of extending to other methodologies. At first glance, this practice seems to be in the category of static method adaptation but experiences with RDP Practice says that it can be treated like dynamic method adaptation. The distinction between static method adaptation and dynamic method adaptation is subtle.

Scrum isn't designed for method tailoring. Schwaber notes that "Scrum is not a methodology that needs enhancing. That is how we got into trouble in the first place, thinking that the problem was not having a perfect methodology. Effort centers on the changes in the enterprise that is needed." Bas Vodde reinforces this statement, suggesting that Scrum isn't like traditional, large methodologies that require you to "pick and choose" elements. It is the basics on top of which you add additional elements to localise and contextualise its use.

Comparison with Other Methods

RAD

Agile methods have much in common with the Rapid Application Development techniques from the 1980/90s as espoused by James Martin and others. In addition to technology-focused methods, customer-and-design-centered methods, such as Visualization-Driven Rapid Prototyping developed by Brian Willison, work to engage customers and end users to facilitate agile software development.

Further, James M. Kerr and Richard Hunter wrote a book on the subject that presented a day-by-day diary of a real RAD development. It covered work right from inception through to production and contains many of the techniques that forge the backbone of, and are very much present in, today's agile product development approaches.

CMMI

In 2008 the Software Engineering Institute (SEI) published the technical report "CMMI or Agile: Why Not Embrace Both" to make clear that the Capability Maturity Model Integration and agile methods can co-exist. Modern CMMI-compatible development processes are also iterative. The CMMI Version 1.3 includes tips for implementing CMMI and agile process improvement together.

DevOps

Organizations that adopt agile development see more frequent releases; which led to the concepts of continuous delivery and DevOps. While DevOps and agile software development both embody many Lean philosophies, such as collaboration and communication, they are distinct concepts. While agile principles represent a change in thinking, DevOps seeks to implement actual organizational cultural change.

Large-scale, Offshore and Distributed

Agile development has been widely seen as highly suited to certain types of environments, including small teams of experts working on greenfield projects, and the challenges and limitations encountered in the adoption of agile methods in a large organization with legacy infrastructure are well-documented and understood.

In response, a range of strategies and patterns has evolved for overcoming challenges with large-scale development efforts (>20 developers) or distributed (non-colocated) development teams, amongst other challenges; and there are now several recognised frameworks that seek to mitigate or avoid these challenges, including:

- Scaled Agile Framework (SAFe), Dean Leffingwell *inter alia*

- Disciplined agile delivery (DAD), Scott Ambler *inter alia*

- Large-scale scrum (LeSS), Craig Larman and Bas Vodde

- Nexus (scaled professional Scrum), Ken Schwaber

- Scrum at Scale, Jeff Sutherland, Alex Brown

- Enterprise Scrum, Mike Beedle

- Setchu (Scrum-based lightweight framework), Michael Ebbage

- Xscale

- Agile path

- Holistic Software Development

There are many conflicting viewpoints on whether all of these are effective or indeed fit the definition of agile development, and this remains an active and ongoing area of research.

When agile software development is applied in a distributed setting (with teams dispersed across multiple business locations), it is commonly referred to as distributed agile development. The goal is to leverage the unique benefits offered by each approach. Distributed development allow organizations to build software by strategically setting up teams in different parts of the globe, virtually building software round-the-clock (more commonly referred to as follow-the-sun model). On the other hand, agile development provides increased transparency, continuous feedback and more flexibility when responding to changes.

Regulated Domains

Agile methods were initially seen as best suitable for non-critical product developments, thereby excluded from use in regulated domains such as medical devices, pharmaceutical, financial, nuclear systems, automotive, and avionics sectors, etc. However, in the last several years, there have been several initiatives for the adaptation of agile methods for these domains.

There are numerous standards that may apply in regulated domains, including ISO 26262, ISO 9000, ISO 9001, and ISO/IEC 15504. A number of key concerns are of particular importance in regulated domains which may conflict with the use of agile methods:

- Quality Assurance (QA): Systematic and inherent quality management underpinning a controlled professional process and reliability and correctness of product.

- Safety and Security: Formal planning and risk management to mitigate safety risks for users and securely protecting users from unintentional and malicious misuse.

- Traceability: Documentation providing auditable evidence of regulatory compliance and facilitating traceability and investigation of problems.

- Verification and Validation (V&V): Embedded throughout the software development process (e.g. user requirements specification, functional specification, design specification, code review, unit tests, integration tests, system tests).

The Scrum framework in particular has received considerable attention. Two derived methods have been defined: R-Scrum (Regulated Scrum) and SafeScrum.

Agile Coaching

Teams and organizations choosing to adopt more agile ways of working typically undertake an *agile transformation* with the support of one or more agile coaches. The agile coach guides teams through the transformation. There are typically two styles of agile coaching: push based and pull-based agile coaching.

Experience and Adoption

Agile methods were first used by technology early adopters such as Tektronix. Although agile methods can be used with any programming paradigm or language in practice, they were originally closely associated with object-oriented environments such as Smalltalk and Lisp and later Java. The initial adopters of agile methods were usually small to medium-sized teams working on unprecedented systems with requirements that were difficult to finalize and likely to change as the system was being developed. This section describes common problems that organizations encounter when they try to adopt agile methods as well as various techniques to measure the quality and performance of agile teams.

Common Agile Pitfalls

Organizations and teams implementing agile development often face difficulties transitioning from more traditional methods such as waterfall development, such as teams having an agile process forced on them. These are often termed *agile anti-patterns* or more commonly *agile smells*. Below are some common examples:

Lack of Overall Product Design

A goal of agile software development is to focus more on producing working software and less on documentation. This is in contrast to waterfall models where the process is often highly controlled and minor changes to the system require significant revision of supporting documentation. However, this does not justify completely doing without any analysis or design at all. Failure to pay attention to design can cause a team to proceed rapidly at first but then to have significant rework required as they attempt to scale up the system. One of the key features of agile software development is that it is iterative. When done correctly design emerges as the system is developed and commonalities and opportunities for re-use are discovered.

Adding Stories to an Iteration in Progress

In agile software development, *stories* (similar to use case descriptions) are typically used to define requirements and an *iteration* is a short period of time during which the team commits to specific goals. Adding stories to an iteration in progress is detrimental to a good flow of work. These should be added to the product backlog and prioritized for a subsequent iteration or in rare cases the iteration could be cancelled.

This does not mean that a story cannot expand. Teams must deal with new information, which may produce additional tasks for a story. If the new information prevents the story from being completed during the iteration, then it should be carried over to a subsequent iteration. However, it should be prioritized against all remaining stories, as the new information may have changed the story's original priority.

Lack of Sponsor Support

Agile software development is often implemented as a grassroots effort in organizations by software development teams trying to optimize their development processes and ensure consistency in the software development life cycle. By not having sponsor support, teams may face difficulties and resistance from business partners, other development teams and management. Additionally, they may suffer without appropriate funding and resources. This increases the likelihood of failure.

Insufficient Training

A survey performed by Version One found respondents cited insufficient training as the most significant cause for failed agile implementations Teams have fallen into the trap of assuming the reduced processes of agile development compared to other methodologies such as waterfall means that there are no actual rules for agile development. Agile development is a set of prescribed methodologies, and training/practice is a requirement.

Product Owner Role is not Properly Filled

The product owner is responsible for representing the business in the development activity and is often the most demanding role.

A common mistake is to have the product owner role filled by someone from the development team. This requires the team to make its own decisions on prioritization without real feedback from the business. They try to solve business issues internally or delay work as they reach outside the team for direction. This often leads to distraction and a breakdown in collaboration.

Teams are not Focused

The agile process requires teams to meet product commitments, which means they should focus only on work for that product. However, team members who are seen as have spare capacity are often expected to take on other work, which means it is then difficult for them to help complete the work to which their team had commmited.

Excessive Preparation/Planning

Teams may fall into the trap of spending too much time preparing or planning. This is a common trap for teams less familiar with the agile process where the teams feel obligated to have a complete understanding and specification of all stories. Teams should be prepared to move forward only with those stories in which they have confidence, then during the iteration continue to discover and prepare work for subsequent iterations (often referred to as backlog refinement or grooming).

Problem-solving in the Daily Standup

A daily standup should be a focused, timely meeting where all team members disseminate information. If problem-solving occurs, it often can only involve certain team members and potentially is not the best use of the entire team's time. If during the daily standup the team starts diving into problem-solving, it should be tabled until a subteam can discuss, usually immediately after the standup completes.

Assigning Tasks

One of the intended benefits of agile development is to empower the team to make choices, as they are closest to the problem. Additionally, they should make choices as close to implementation as possible, to use more timely information in the decision. If team members are assigned tasks by others or too early in the process, the benefits of localized and timely decision making can be lost.

Being assigned work also constrains team members into certain roles (for example, team member A must always do the database work), which limits opportunities for cross-training. Team members themselves can choose to take on tasks that stretch their abilities and provide cross-training opportunities.

Scrum Master as a Contributor

Another common pitfall is for a scrum master to act as a contributor. While not prohibited by the Scrum methodology, the scrum master needs to ensure they have the capacity to act in the role of scrum master first and not working on development tasks. A scrum master's role is to facilitate the process rather than create the product.

Having the scrum master also multitasking may result in too many context switches to be productive. Additionally, as a scrum master is responsible for ensuring roadblocks are removed so that the team can make forward progress, the benefit gained by individual tasks moving forward may not outweigh roadblocks that are deferred due to lack of capacity.

Lack of Test Automation

Due to the iterative nature of agile development, multiple rounds of testing are often needed. Automated testing helps reduce the impact of repeated unit, integration, and regression tests and frees developers and testers to focus on higher value work.

Test automation also supports continued refactoring required by iterative software development. Allowing a developer to quickly run tests to confirm refactoring has not modified the functionality of the application may reduce the workload and increase confidence that cleanup efforts have not introduced new defects.

Allowing Technical Debt to Build Up

Focusing on delivering new functionality may result in increased technical debt. The team must allow themselves time for defect remediation and refactoring. Technical debt hinders planning abilities by increasing the amount of unscheduled work as production defects distract the team from further progress.

As the system evolves it is important to refactor as entropy of the system naturally increases. Over time the lack of constant maintenance causes increasing defects and development costs.

Attempting to take on too much in an Iteration

A common misconception is that agile development allows continuous change, however an iteration backlog is an agreement of what work can be completed during an iteration. Having too much work-in-progress (WIP) results in inefficiencies such as context-switching and queueing. The team must avoid feeling pressured into taking on additional work.

Fixed Time, Resources, Scope, and Quality

Agile development fixes time (iteration duration), quality, and ideally resources in advance (though maintaining fixed resources may be difficult if developers are often pulled away from tasks to handle production incidents), while the scope remains variable. The customer or product owner often pushes for a fixed scope for an iteration. However, teams should be reluctant to commit to locked time, resources and scope (commonly known as the project management triangle). Efforts to add scope to the fixed time and resources of agile development may result in decreased quality.

Measuring Agility

The best agile practitioners have always emphasized sound engineering principles. As a result, there are a number of agile best practices and tools for measuring the performance of product development and teams.

Internal Assessments

The *Agility Index Measurements* (AIM) scores product development against a number of agility factors to achieve a total. The similarly named *Agility Measurement Index*, scores developments against five dimensions of product development (duration, risk, novelty, effort, and interaction).

Other techniques are based on measurable goals and one study suggests that velocity can be used as a metric of agility.

There are also agile self-assessments to determine whether a team is using agile practices (Nokia test, Karlskrona test, 42 points test).

Public Surveys

One of the early studies reporting gains in quality, productivity, and business satisfaction by using agile methods was a survey conducted by Shine Technologies from November 2002 to January 2003.

A similar survey, the State of Agile, is conducted every year starting in 2006 with thousands of participants from around the software development community. This tracks trends on the benefits of agile, lessons learned, and good practices. Each survey has reported increasing numbers saying that agile development helps them deliver software faster; improves their ability to manage changing customer priorities; and increases their productivity. Surveys have also consistently shown better results with agile product development methods compared to classical project management. In balance, there are reports that some feel that agile development methods are still too young to enable extensive academic research of their success.

Criticism

Agile methodologies can be inefficient in large organizations and certain types of developments. Agile methods seem best for early-stage non-sequential product development. Many organizations believe that agile methodologies are too extreme and adopt a hybrid approach that mixes elements of agile and plan-driven approaches. Some methods, such as DSDM, have combined elements of agile and plan-driven approaches in a disciplined way, without sacrificing the fundamental principles that make agile work.

The term "agile" has also been criticized as being a management fad that simply describes existing good practices under new jargon, promotes a "one size fits all" mindset towards development strategies, and wrongly emphasizes method over results.

Alistair Cockburn organized a celebration of the 10th anniversary of the Agile Manifesto in Snowbird, Utah on 12 February 2011, gathering some 30+ people who had been involved at the original meeting and since. A list of about 20 elephants in the room ("undiscussable" agile topics/issues) were collected, including aspects: the alliances, failures and limitations of agile practices and context (possible causes: commercial interests, decontextualization, no obvious way to make progress based on failure, limited objective evidence, cognitive biases and reasoning fallacies), politics and culture. As Philippe Kruchten wrote:

The agile movement is in some ways a bit like a teenager: very self-conscious, checking constantly its appearance in a mirror, accepting few criticisms, only interested in being with its peers, rejecting en bloc all wisdom from the past, just because it is from the past, adopting fads and new jargon, at times cocky and arrogant. But I have no doubts that it will mature further, become more open to the outside world, more reflective, and also therefore more effective.

— Philippe Kruchten

Applications Outside Software Development

Agile Brazil 2014 conference

Agile methods have been extensively used for development of software products and some of them use certain characteristics of software, such as object technologies. However, these techniques can be applied to the development of non-software products, such as computers, motor vehicles, medical devices, food, clothing, and music; see Flexible product development. Agile methods have been used in non-development IT infrastructure deployments and migrations. Some of the wider principles of agile have also found application in general management (e.g., strategy, governance, risk, finance) under the terms business agility or agile business management.

Under an agile business management model, agile techniques, practices, principles and values are expressed across five domains.

1. Integrated customer engagement – to embed customers within any delivery process to share accountability for product/service delivery.

2. Facilitation-based management – adopting agile management models, like the role of Scrum Master, to facilitate the day-to-day operation of teams.

3. Agile work practices – adopting specific iterative and incremental work practices such as Scrum, Kanban, test-driven development or feature-driven development across all business functions (from sales, human resources, finance and Marketing).

4. An enabling organisational structure – with a focus on staff engagement, personal autonomy and outcomes based governance.

5. An education model that blends agile practices and philosophies to create micro-schools that emphasize collaborative culture creation and self-directed learning.

Agile development paradigms can be used in other areas of life such as raising children. Its success in child development might be founded on some basic management principles; communication, adaptation and awareness. Bruce Feiler has claimed that the basic agile development paradigms can be applied to household management and raising children. In his TED Talk "Agile programming – for your family", these paradigms brought significant changes to his household environment, such as the kids doing dishes, taking out the trash, and decreasing his children's emotional outbreaks, which inadvertently increased their emotional stability.

References

- Booch, Grady; et al. (2004). Object-Oriented Analysis and Design with Applications (3rd ed.). MA, USA: Addison Wesley. ISBN 0-201-89551-X. Retrieved 30 January 2015.

- Suryanarayana, Girish (November 2014). Refactoring for Software Design Smells. Morgan Kaufmann. p. 258. ISBN 978-0128013977. Retrieved 31 January 2015.

- Carroll, ed., John (1995). Scenario-Based Design: Envisioning Work and Technology in System Development. New York: John Wiley & Sons. ISBN 0471076597.

- Bell, Michael (2008). "Introduction to Service-Oriented Modeling". Service-Oriented Modeling: Service Analysis, Design, and Architecture. Wiley & Sons. ISBN 978-0-470-14111-3.

- Kotonya, Gerald; Sommerville, Ian (September 1998). Requirements Engineering: Processes and Techniques. John Wiley & Sons. ISBN 0-471-97208-8.

- Chemuturi, M. (2013). Requirements Engineering and Management for Software Development Projects. doi:10.1007/978-1-4614-5377-2. ISBN 978-1-4614-5376-5.

- Thayer, Richard H.; Dorfman, Merlin, eds. (March 1997). Software Requirements Engineering (2nd ed.). IEEE Computer Society Press. ISBN 0-8186-7738-4.

- Software Maintenance: Concepts and Practice by Penny Grubb and Armstrong A. Takang 2003 ISBN 981238426X pages 7-8

- Kerr, James M.; Hunter, Richard (1993). Inside RAD: How to Build a Fully Functional System in 90 Days or Less. McGraw-Hill. p. 3. ISBN 0-07-034223-7.

- Ambler, Scott (12 April 2002). Agile Modeling: Effective Practices for EXtreme Programming and the Unified Process. John Wiley & Sons. pp. 12, 164, 363. ISBN 978-0-471-20282-0.

- Jeffries, Ron; Anderson, Ann; Hendrickson, Chet (2001). Extreme Programming installed. Addison-Weslsy. pp. 72–147. ISBN 0201-70842-6.

- Larman, Craig (2004). Agile and Iterative Development: A Manager's Guide. Addison-Wesley. p. 27. ISBN 978-0-13-111155-4.

- Boehm, B.; R. Turner (2004). Balancing Agility and Discipline: A Guide for the Perplexed. Boston, MA: Addison-Wesley. ISBN 0-321-18612-5. Appendix A, pages 165–194

- Larman, Craig (2004). "Chapter 11: Practice Tips". Agile and Iterative Development: A Manager's Guide. p. 253. ISBN 9780131111554. Retrieved 14 October 2013.

- Sliger, Michele; Broderick, Stacia (2008). The Software Project Manager's Bridge to Agility. Addison-Wesley. p. 46. ISBN 0-321-50275-2.

- Boehm, B.; R. Turner (2004). Balancing Agility and Discipline: A Guide for the Perplexed. Boston, MA: Addison-Wesley. pp. 55–57. ISBN 0-321-18612-5.

- Kerr, James M.; Hunter, Richard (1993). Inside RAD: How to Build a Fully Functional System in 90 Days or Less. McGraw-Hill. ISBN 0-07-034223-7.

- Beck, K. (1999). Extreme Programming Explained: Embrace Change. Boston, MA: Addison-Wesley. ISBN 0-321-27865-8.

- Newton Lee (2014). "Getting on the Billboard Charts: Music Production as Agile Software Development," Digital Da Vinci: Computers in Music. Springer Science+Business Media. ISBN 978-1-4939-0535-5.

- Moran, Alan (2015). Managing Agile: Strategy, Implementation, Organisation and People. Springer Verlag. ISBN 978-3-319-16262-1.

Various Software Architectural Patterns

4

Architectural pattern is a solution that is usually used as a solution for commonly occurring problems in software architecture. Blackboard system, database-centric architecture, service-oriented architecture and shared nothing architecture are the features that have been elucidated in the following chapter.

Architectural Pattern

An architectural pattern is a general, reusable solution to a commonly occurring problem in software architecture within a given context. Architectural patterns are similar to software design pattern but have a broader scope. The architectural patterns address various issues in software engineering, such as computer hardware performance limitations, high availability and minimization of a business risk. Some architectural patterns have been implemented within software frameworks.

Definition

Even though an architectural pattern conveys an image of a system, it is not an architecture. An architectural pattern is a concept that solves and delineates some essential cohesive elements of a software architecture. Countless different architectures may implement the same pattern and share the related characteristics. Patterns are often defined as "strictly described and commonly available". When it is strictly described and commonly available, it is a pattern.

Architectural Style

Following traditional building architecture, a 'software architectural style' is a specific method of construction, characterized by the features that make it notable" (Architectural style). "An architectural style defines: a family of systems in terms of a pattern of structural organization; a vocabulary of components and connectors, with constraints on how they can be combined."

"An architectural style is a named collection of architectural design decisions that (1) are applicable in a given development context, (2) constrain architectural design decisions that are specific to a particular system within that context, and (3) elicit beneficial qualities in each resulting system."

Some treat architectural patterns and architectural styles as the same, some treat styles as specializations of patterns. What they have in common is both patterns and styles are idioms for architects to use, they "provide a common language" or "vocabulary" with which to describe classes of systems.

The main difference is that a pattern can be seen as a solution to a problem, while a style is more general and does not require a problem to solve for its appearance.

Examples

Here is a list of architecture patterns, and corresponding design patterns and solution patterns.

Sub-Domain Area	Architecture Pattern Name	Design Patterns	Solution Patterns	Related Patterns
Data Integration/SOA	• ETL (Data Extraction Transformation & Loading)	• Change Data Capture • Near Real-Time ETL • Batch ETL • Data Discovery	• Error handling • Job scheduling • Data validation • Slowly Changing Dimensions Load	• EAI • Master Data Hub • Operational Data Store (ODS) • Data Mart • Data Warehouse
	• MFT			
	• EAI/ESB	• Publish/subscribe • Request/reply • Message Exchange Patterns	• One-Way • Synchronous Request/Response • Basic Callback • Claim Check	• SOA

Data Architecture	• Transaction Data Stores (TDS/ OLTP) • Master Data Store • Operational Data Store • Data Mart • Data Warehouse	• Custom Applications Databases • Packaged Application Databases		• ETL • EAI • SOA
Business Intelligence	• Transactional Reporting • Operational Reporting • Analytical Reporting	• Transactional Reporting Data Access • Operational Reporting Data Access • Analytical Reporting Data Access • Analytical Dashboard Data Access • Operational Dashboard Data Access • Data Mining	• Real-Time Dashboards • In-Memory Analytics • Statistical Analysis • Predictive analytics	• ETL • EAI • TDS • Operational Data Store • Data Mart

Master data management	• Master Data Hub	• Master Data Replication • Master Data Services • Master Data Synchronization		• Change Data Capture • EAI • STD
Data Modeling	• Dimensional Data Modeling • E-R Data Modeling	• Modeling Standards • Naming Conventions		

Some additional examples of architectural patterns:

- Blackboard system

- Broker Pattern

- Event-driven architecture

- Implicit invocation

- Layers

- Microservices

- Model-view-controller, Presentation-abstraction-control, Model-view-presenter, and Model-view-viewmodel

- Multitier architecture (often three-tier or n-tier)

- Naked objects

- Operational Data Store (ODS)

- Peer-to-peer

- Pipe and filter architecture

- Service-oriented architecture

Blackboard System

A blackboard system is an artificial intelligence approach based on the blackboard architectural model, where a common knowledge base, the "blackboard", is iteratively updated by a diverse group of specialist knowledge sources, starting with a problem specification and ending with a solution. Each knowledge source updates the blackboard with a partial solution when its internal constraints match the blackboard state. In this way, the specialists work together to solve the problem. The blackboard model was originally designed as a way to handle complex, ill-defined problems, where the solution is the sum of its parts.

Metaphor

The following scenario provides a simple metaphor that gives some insight into how a blackboard functions:

A group of specialists are seated in a room with a large blackboard. They work as a team to brainstorm a solution to a problem, using the blackboard as the workplace for cooperatively developing the solution.

The session begins when the problem specifications are written onto the blackboard. The specialists all watch the blackboard, looking for an opportunity to apply their expertise to the developing solution. When someone writes something on the blackboard that allows another specialist to apply their expertise, the second specialist records their contribution on the blackboard, hopefully enabling other specialists to then apply their expertise. This process of adding contributions to the blackboard continues until the problem has been solved.

Components

A blackboard-system application consists of three major components

1. The software specialist modules, which are called knowledge sources (KSs). Like the human experts at a blackboard, each knowledge source provides specific expertise needed by the application.

2. The blackboard, a shared repository of problems, partial solutions, suggestions, and contributed information. The blackboard can be thought of as a dynamic "library" of contributions to the current problem that have been recently "published" by other knowledge sources.

3. The control shell, which controls the flow of problem-solving activity in the system. Just as the eager human specialists need a moderator to prevent them from trampling each other in a mad dash to grab the chalk, KSs need a mechanism to

organize their use in the most effective and coherent fashion. In a blackboard system, this is provided by the control shell.

Implementations

Famous examples of early academic blackboard systems are the Hearsay II speech recognition system and Douglas Hofstadter's Copycat and Numbo projects.

More recent examples include deployed real-world applications, such as the PLAN component of the Mission Control System for RADARSAT-1, an Earth observation satellite developed by Canada to monitor environmental changes and Earth's natural resources.

GTXImage CAD software by GTX Corporation was developed in the early 1990s using a set of rulebases and neural networks as specialists operating on a blackboard system.

Adobe Acrobat Capture (now discontinued) used a Blackboard system to decompose and recognize image pages to understand the objects, text, and fonts on the page. This function is currently built into the retail version of Adobe Acrobat as "OCR Text Recognition". Details of a similar OCR blackboard for Farsi text are in the public domain.

Blackboard systems are used routinely in many military C4ISTAR systems for detecting and tracking objects.

Criticism

Blackboard systems were popular before the AI Winter and, along with most symbolic AI models, fell out of fashion during that period. Along with other models it was realised that initial successes on toy problems did not scale well to real problems on the available computers of the time. Most problems using blackboards are inherently NP-hard, so resist tractable solution by any algorithm in the large size limit. During the same period, statistical pattern recognition became dominant, most notably via simple Hidden Markov Models outperforming symbolic approaches such as Hearsay-II in the domain of speech recognition.

Recent Developments

Blackboard-like systems have been constructed within modern Bayesian machine learning settings, using agents to add and remove Bayesian network nodes. In these 'Bayesian Blackboard' systems, the heuristics can acquire more rigorous probabilistic meanings as proposal and acceptances in Metropolis Hastings sampling though the space of possible structures. Conversely, using these mappings, existing Metropolis-Hastings samplers over structural spaces may now thus be viewed as forms of blackboard systems even when not named as such by the authors. Such samplers are commonly found in musical transcription algorithms for example.

Database-centric Architecture

Database-centric Architecture or data-centric architecture has several distinct meanings, generally relating to software architectures in which databases play a crucial role. Often this description is meant to contrast the design to an alternative approach. For example, the characterization of an architecture as "database-centric" may mean any combination of the following:

- using a standard, general-purpose relational database management system, as opposed to customized in-memory or file-based data structures and access methods. With the evolution of sophisticated DBMS software, much of which is either free or included with the operating system, application developers have become increasingly reliant on standard database tools, especially for the sake of rapid application development.

- using dynamic, table-driven logic, as opposed to logic embodied in previously compiled programs. The use of table-driven logic, i.e. behavior that is heavily dictated by the contents of a database, allows programs to be simpler and more flexible. This capability is a central feature of dynamic programming languages. Control tables for tables that are normally coded and embedded within programs as data structures (i.e. not compiled statements) but could equally be read in from a flat file, database or even retrieved from a spreadsheet.

- using stored procedures that run on database servers, as opposed to greater reliance on logic running in middle-tier application servers in a multi-tier architecture. The extent to which business logic should be placed at the backend versus another tier is a subject of ongoing debate. For example, Toon Koppelaars presents a detailed analysis of alternative Oracle-based architectures that vary in the placement of business logic, concluding that a database-centric approach has practical advantages from the standpoint of ease of development and maintainability.

- using a shared database as the basis for communicating between parallel processes in distributed computing applications, as opposed to direct inter-process communication via message passing functions and message-oriented middleware. A potential benefit of database-centric architecture in distributed applications is that it simplifies the design by utilizing DBMS-provided transaction processing and indexing to achieve a high degree of reliability, performance, and capacity. For example, Base One describes a database-centric distributed computing architecture for grid and cluster computing, and explains how this design provides enhanced security, fault-tolerance, and scalability.

Representational State Transfer

Representational state transfer (REST) or RESTful web services are one way of providing interoperability between computer systems on the Internet. REST-compliant web services allow requesting systems to access and manipulate textual representations of web resources using a uniform and predefined set of stateless operations. Other forms of web service exist, which expose their own arbitrary sets of operations such as WSDL and SOAP. "Web resources" were first defined on the World Wide Web as documents or files identified by their URLs, but today they have a much more generic and abstract definition encompassing every thing or entity that can be identified, named, addressed or handled, in any way whatsoever, on the web. In a REST web service, requests made to a resource's URI will elicit a response that may be in XML, HTML, JSON or some other defined format. The response may confirm that some alteration has been made to the stored resource, and it may provide hypertext links to other related resources or collections of resources. Using HTTP, as is most common, the kind of operations available include those predefined by the HTTP verbs GET, POST, PUT, DELETE and so on. By making use of a stateless protocol and standard operations REST systems aim for fast performance, reliability, and the ability to grow, by using reused components that can be managed and updated without affecting the system as a whole, even while it is running.

The term *representational state transfer* was introduced and defined in 2000 by Roy Fielding in his doctoral dissertation. Fielding used REST to design HTTP 1.1 and Uniform Resource Identifiers (URI). The term is intended to evoke an image of how a well-designed web application behaves: It is a network of web resources (a virtual state-machine) where the user progresses through the application by selecting links, such as /user/tom, and operations such as GET or DELETE (state transitions), resulting in the next resource (representing the next state of the application) being transferred to the user for their use.

History

REST was defined by Roy Thomas Fielding in his 2000 PhD dissertation "Architectural Styles and the Design of Network-based Software Architectures" at UC Irvine. Fielding developed the REST architectural style in parallel with HTTP 1.1 of 1996–1999, based on the existing design of HTTP 1.0 of 1996.

In a retrospective look at the development of REST, Roy Fielding said:

Throughout the HTTP standardization process, I was called on to defend the design choices of the Web. That is an extremely difficult thing to do within a process that accepts proposals from anyone on a topic that was rapidly becoming the center of an entire industry. I had comments from well over 500 developers, many of whom were distinguished engineers with decades of experience, and I had to explain everything from the most abstract notions of Web interaction to the finest details of HTTP syntax. That process honed my model down to a core set of principles, properties, and constraints that are now called REST.

Architectural Properties

The architectural properties affected by the constraints of the REST architectural style are:

- Performance - component interactions can be the dominant factor in user-perceived performance and network efficiency

- Scalability to support large numbers of components and interactions among components. Roy Fielding, one of the principal authors of the HTTP specification, describes REST's effect on scalability as follows:

- REST's client–server separation of concerns simplifies component implementation, reduces the complexity of connector semantics, improves the effectiveness of performance tuning, and increases the scalability of pure server components. Layered system constraints allow intermediaries—proxies, gateways, and firewalls—to be introduced at various points in the communication without changing the interfaces between components, thus allowing them to assist in communication translation or improve performance via large-scale, shared caching. REST enables intermediate processing by constraining messages to be self-descriptive: interaction is stateless between requests, standard methods and media types are used to indicate semantics and exchange information, and responses explicitly indicate cacheability.

- Simplicity of a Uniform Interface

- Modifiability of components to meet changing needs (even while the application is running)

- Visibility of communication between components by service agents

- Portability of components by moving program code with the data

- Reliability is the resistance to failure at the system level in the presence of failures within components, connectors, or data

Architectural Constraints

There are six guiding constraints that define a RESTful system. These constraints restrict the ways that the server may process and respond to client requests so that, by operating within these constraints, the service gains desirable non-functional properties, such as performance, scalability, simplicity, modifiability, visibility, portability, and reliability. If a service violates any of the required constraints, it cannot be considered RESTful.

The formal REST constraints are as follows:

Client-server

The first constraints added to our hybrid style are those of the client-server architectural style, described in Section 3.4.1. Separation of concerns is the principle behind the client-server constraints. By separating the user interface concerns from the data storage concerns, we improve the portability of the user interface across multiple platforms and improve scalability by simplifying the server components. Perhaps most significant to the Web, however, is that the separation allows the components to evolve independently, thus supporting the Internet-scale requirement of multiple organizational domains.

Stateless

The client–server communication is constrained by no client context being stored on the server between requests. Each request from any client contains all the information necessary to service the request, and session state is held in the client. The session state can be transferred by the server to another service such as a database to maintain a persistent state for a period and allow authentication. The client begins sending requests when it is ready to make the transition to a new state. While one or more requests are outstanding, the client is considered to be *in transition*. The representation of each application state contains links that may be used the next time the client chooses to initiate a new state-transition.

Cacheable

As on the World Wide Web, clients and intermediaries can cache responses. Responses must therefore, implicitly or explicitly, define themselves as cacheable, or not, to prevent clients from reusing stale or inappropriate data in response to further requests. Well-managed caching partially or completely eliminates some client–server interactions, further improving scalability and performance.

Layered System

A client cannot ordinarily tell whether it is connected directly to the end server, or to an intermediary along the way. Intermediary servers may improve system scalability by enabling load balancing and by providing shared caches. They may also enforce security policies.

Code on Demand (Optional)

Servers can temporarily extend or customize the functionality of a client by the transfer of executable code. Examples of this may include compiled components such as Java applets and client-side scripts such as JavaScript.

Uniform Interface

The uniform interface constraint is fundamental to the design of any REST service. The uniform interface simplifies and decouples the architecture, which enables each part to evolve independently. The four constraints for this uniform interface are

Identification of resources

> Individual resources are identified in requests, for example using URIs in web-based REST systems. The resources themselves are conceptually separate from the representations that are returned to the client. For example, the server may send data from its database as HTML, XML or JSON, none of which are the server's internal representation.

Manipulation of resources through representations

> When a client holds a representation of a resource, including any metadata attached, it has enough information to modify or delete the resource.

Self-descriptive messages

> Each message includes enough information to describe how to process the message. For example, which parser to invoke may be specified by an Internet media type (previously known as a MIME type).

Hypermedia as the engine of application state (HATEOAS)

> Having accessed an initial URI for the REST application—analogous to a human web user accessing the home page of a website—a REST client should then be able to use server-provided links dynamically to discover all the available actions and resources it needs. As access proceeds, the server responds with text that includes hyperlinks to other actions that are currently available. There is no need for the client to be hard-coded with information regarding the structure or dynamics of the REST service.

Applied to Web Services

Web service APIs that adhere to the REST architectural constraints are called RESTful APIs. HTTP-based RESTful APIs are defined with the following aspects:

- base URL, such as http://api.example.com/resources/

- an internet media type that defines state transition data elements (e.g., Atom, microformats, application/vnd.collection+json, etc.) The current representation tells the client how to compose requests for transitions to all the next available application states. This could be as simple as a URL or as complex as a java applet.

- standard HTTP methods (e.g., OPTIONS, GET, PUT, POST, and DELETE)

Relationship between URL and HTTP Methods

The following table shows how HTTP methods are typically used in a RESTful API:

Uniform Resource Locator (URL)	HTTP methods			
	GET	PUT	POST	DELETE
Collection, such as http://api.example.com/resources/	List the URIs and perhaps other details of the collection's members.	Replace the entire collection with another collection.	Create a new entry in the collection. The new entry's URI is assigned automatically and is usually returned by the operation.	Delete the entire collection.
Element, such as http://api.example.com/resources/item17	Retrieve a representation of the addressed member of the collection, expressed in an appropriate Internet media type.	Replace the addressed member of the collection, or if it does not exist, create it.	Not generally used. Treat the addressed member as a collection in its own right and create a new entry within it.	Delete the addressed member of the collection.

The GET method is a safe method (or *nullipotent*), meaning that calling it produces no side-effects: retrieving or accessing a record does not change it. The PUT and DELETE methods are idempotent, meaning that the state of the system exposed by the API is unchanged no matter how many times the same request is repeated.

Unlike SOAP-based web services, there is no "official" standard for RESTful web APIs. This is because REST is an architectural style, while SOAP is a protocol. REST is not a standard in itself, but RESTful implementations make use of standards, such as HTTP, URI, JSON, and XML.

Service-Oriented Architecture

A service-oriented architecture (SOA) is a style of software design where services are provided to the other components by application components, through a communication protocol over a network. The basic principles of service oriented architecture are independent of vendors, products and technologies. A service is a discrete unit of functionality that can be accessed remotely and acted upon and updated independently, such as retrieving a credit card statement online.

A service has four properties according to one of many definitions of SOA:

1. It logically represents a business activity with a specified outcome.

2. It is self-contained.

3. It is a black box for its consumers.

4. It may consist of other underlying services.

Different services can be used in conjunction to provide the functionality of a large software application. Service-oriented architecture makes it easier for software components to communicate and cooperate over the network, without requiring any human interaction or changes in the underlying program, so that service candidates can be redesigned before their implementation.

Overview

In SOA, services use protocols which describe how they pass and parse messages using description metadata, this metadata describes both the functional characteristics of the service and quality-of-service characteristics. Service-oriented architecture aims to allow users to combine large chunks of functionality to form applications which are built purely from existing services and combining them in an ad hoc manner. A service presents a simple interface to the requester that abstracts away the underlying complexity acting as a black box, Further users can also access these independent services without any knowledge of their internal implementation.

Defining Concepts

The related buzzword service-orientation promotes *loose coupling* between services. SOA separates functions into distinct units, or services, which developers make accessible over a network in order to allow users to combine and reuse them in the production of applications. These services and their corresponding consumers communicate with each other by passing data in a well-defined, shared format, or by coordinating an activity between two or more services.

A manifesto was published for service-oriented architecture in October, 2009. This came up with six core values which are listed as follows

1. Business value is given more importance than technical strategy.

2. Strategic goals is given more importance than project-specific benefits.

3. Intrinsic inter-operability is given more importance than custom integration.

4. Shared services is given more importance than specific-purpose implementations.

5. Flexibility is given more importance than optimization.

6. Evolutionary refinement is given more importance than pursuit of initial perfection.

SOA can be seen as part of the continuum which ranges from the older concept of distributed computing and modular programming, through SOA, and on to current practices of mashups, SaaS, and cloud computing.

Principles

There are no industry standards relating to the exact composition of a service-oriented architecture, although many industry sources have published their own principles. Some of these include the following:

Standardized service contract

> Services adhere to a standard communications agreements, as defined collectively by one or more service-description documents within a given set of services.

Service reference autonomy (an aspect of loose coupling)

> The relationship between services is minimized to the level that they are only aware of their existence.

Service location transparency (an aspect of loose coupling)

> Services can be called from anywhere within the network that it is located no matter where it is present.

Service abstraction

> The services act as black boxes, that is their inner logic is hidden from the consumers.

Service autonomy

> Services are independent and control the functionality they encapsulate, from a Design-time and a run-time perspective.

Service statelessness

> Services are stateless that is either return the requested value or a give an exception hence minimizing resource use.

Service granularity

A principle to ensure services have an adequate size and scope. The functionality provided by the service to the user must be relevant.

Service normalization

Services are decomposed or consolidated (normalized) to minimize redundancy. In some, this may not be done, These are the cases where performance optimization, access, and aggregation are required.

Service composability

Services can be used to compose other services.

Service discovery

Services are supplemented with communicative meta data by which they can be effectively discovered and interpreted.

Service re usability

Logic is divided into various services, to promote re use of code.

Service encapsulation

Many services which were not initially planned under SOA, may get encapsulated or become a part of SOA.

Patterns

Each SOA building block can play any of the three roles:

Service provider

It creates a web service and provides its information to the service registry. Each provider debates upon a lot of hows and whys likes which service to expose, whom to give more importance: security or easy availability, what price to offer the service for and many more. The provider also has to decide what category the service should be listed in for a given broker service and what sort of trading partner agreements are required to use the service.

Service broker, service registry or service repository

Its main functionality is to make the information regarding the web service available to any potential requester. Whoever implements the broker decides the scope of the broker. Public brokers are available anywhere and everywhere but private brokers are only available to a limited amount of public. UDDI was an early, no longer actively supported attempt to provide Web services discovery.

Service requester/consumer

It locates entries in the broker registry using various find operations and then binds to the service provider in order to invoke one of its web services. Whichever service the service-consumers need, they have to take it into the brokers, bind it with respective service and then use it. They can access multiple services if the service provides multiple services.

The service consumer-provider relationship is governed by a service contract, which has a business part, a functional part and a technical part.

Possible first-class service composition patterns are two sides of the same coin. These patterns are generally event-driven:

- Orchestration is usually implemented and executed centrally through a Enterprise service bus

- Choreography is enacted by all participants and could be implemented with workflow management system

Lower level Enterprise Integration Patterns that are not bound to a particular architectural style continue to be relevant and eligible in SOA design.

Implementation Approaches

Service-oriented architecture can be implemented with Web services. This is done to make the functional building-blocks accessible over standard Internet protocols that are independent of platforms and programming languages. These services can represent either new applications or just wrappers around existing legacy systems to make them network-enabled.

Implementers commonly build SOAs using web services standards (for example, SOAP) that have gained broad industry acceptance after recommendation of Version 1.2 from the W3C (World Wide Web Consortium) in 2003. These standards (also referred to as web service specifications) also provide greater interoperability and some protection from lock-in to proprietary vendor software. One can, however, implement SOA using any service-based technology, such as Jini, CORBA or REST.

Architectures can operate independently of specific technologies and can therefore be implemented using a wide range of technologies, including:

- Web services based on WSDL and SOAP

- Messaging, e.g., with ActiveMQ, JMS, RabbitMQ

- RESTful HTTP, with Representational state transfer (REST) constituting its own constraints-based architectural style

- OPC-UA

- WCF (Microsoft's implementation of Web services, forming a part of WCF)

- Apache Thrift

- SORCER

Implementations can use one or more of these protocols and, for example, might use a file-system mechanism to communicate data following a defined interface specification between processes conforming to the SOA concept. The key is independent services with defined interfaces that can be called to perform their tasks in a standard way, without a service having foreknowledge of the calling application, and without the application having or needing knowledge of how the service actually performs its tasks. SOA enables the development of applications that are built by combining loosely coupled and interoperable services.

These services inter-operate based on a formal definition (or contract, e.g., WSDL) that is independent of the underlying platform and programming language. The interface definition hides the implementation of the language-specific service. SOA-based systems can therefore function independently of development technologies and platforms (such as Java, .NET, etc.). Services written in C# running on .NET platforms and services written in Java running on Java EE platforms, for example, can both be consumed by a common composite application (or client). Applications running on either platform can also consume services running on the other as web services that facilitate reuse. Managed environments can also wrap COBOL legacy systems and present them as software services.

High-level programming languages such as BPEL and specifications such as WS-CDL and WS-Coordination extend the service concept by providing a method of defining and supporting orchestration of fine-grained services into more coarse-grained business services, which architects can in turn incorporate into workflows and business processes implemented in composite applications or portals

Service-oriented modeling is an SOA framework that identifies the various disciplines that guide SOA practitioners to conceptualize, analyze, design, and architect their service-oriented assets. The Service-oriented modeling framework (SOMF) offers a modeling language and a work structure or "map" depicting the various components that contribute to a successful service-oriented modeling approach. It illustrates the major elements that identify the "what to do" aspects of a service development scheme. The model enables practitioners to craft a project plan and to identify the milestones of a service-oriented initiative. SOMF also provides a common modeling notation to address alignment between business and IT organizations.

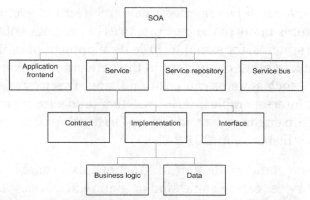

Elements of SOA, by Dirk Krafzig, Karl Banke, and Dirk Slama

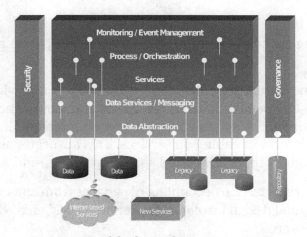

SOA meta-model, The Linthicum Group, 2007

Organizational Benefits

Some enterprise architects believe that SOA can help businesses respond more quickly and more cost-effectively to changing market conditions. This style of *architecture* promotes reuse at the macro (service) level rather than micro (classes) level. It can also simplify interconnection to—and usage of—existing IT (legacy) assets.

With SOA, the idea is that an organization can look at a problem holistically. A business has more overall control. Theoretically there would not be a mass of developers using whatever tool sets might please them. But rather they would be coding to a standard that is set within the business. They can also develop enterprise-wide SOA that encapsulates a business-oriented infrastructure. SOA has also been illustrated as a highway system providing efficiency for car drivers. The point being that if everyone had a car, but there was no highway anywhere, things would be limited and disorganized, in any attempt to get anywhere quickly or efficiently. IBM Vice President of Web Services Michael Liebow says that SOA "builds highways".

In some respects, SOA could be regarded as an architectural evolution rather than as a revolution. It captures many of the best practices of previous software architectures. In communications systems, for example, little development of solutions that use truly static bindings to talk to other equipment in the network has taken place. By embracing a SOA approach, such systems can position themselves to stress the importance of well-defined, highly inter-operable interfaces. Other predecessors of SOA include Component-based software engineering and Object-Oriented Analysis and Design (OOAD) of remote objects, for instance, in CORBA.

A service comprises a stand-alone unit of functionality available only via a formally defined interface. Services can be some kind of "nano-enterprises" that are easy to produce and improve. Also services can be "mega-corporations" constructed as the coordinated work of subordinate services. A mature rollout of SOA effectively defines the API of an organization.

Reasons for treating the implementation of services as separate projects from larger projects include:

1. Separation promotes the concept to the business that services can be delivered quickly and independently from the larger and slower-moving projects common in the organization. The business starts understanding systems and simplified user interfaces calling on services. This advocates agility. That is to say, it fosters business innovations and speeds up time-to-market.

2. Separation promotes the decoupling of services from consuming projects. This encourages good design insofar as the service is designed without knowing who its consumers are.

3. Documentation and test artifacts of the service are not embedded within the detail of the larger project. This is important when the service needs to be reused later.

SOA promises to simplify testing indirectly. Services are autonomous, stateless, with fully documented interfaces, and separate from the cross-cutting concerns of the implementation. If an organization possesses appropriately defined test data, then a corresponding stub is built that reacts to the test data when a service is being built. A full set of regression tests, scripts, data, and responses is also captured for the service. The service can be tested as a 'black box' using existing stubs corresponding to the services it calls. Test environments can be constructed where the primitive and out-of-scope services are stubs, while the remainder of the mesh is test deployments of full services. As each interface is fully documented with its own full set of regression test documentation, it becomes simple to identify problems in test services. Testing evolves to merely validate that the test service operates according to its documentation, and finds gaps in documentation and test cases of all services within the environment. Managing the data state of idempotent services is the only complexity.

Examples may prove useful to aid in documenting a service to the level where it becomes useful. The documentation of some APIs within the Java Community Process provide good examples. As these are exhaustive, staff would typically use only important subsets. The 'ossjsa.pdf' file within JSR-89 exemplifies such a file.

Criticisms

SOA has been conflated with Web services.; however, Web services are only one option to implement the patterns that comprise the SOA style. In the absence of native or binary forms of remote procedure call (RPC), applications could run more slowly and require more processing power, increasing costs. Most implementations do incur these overheads, but SOA can be implemented using technologies (for example, Java Business Integration (JBI), Windows Communication Foundation (WCF) and data distribution service (DDS)) that do not depend on remote procedure calls or translation through XML. At the same time, emerging open-source XML parsing technologies (such as VTD-XML) and various XML-compatible binary formats promise to significantly improve SOA performance. Services implemented using JSON instead of XML do not suffer from this performance concern.

Stateful services require both the consumer and the provider to share the same consumer-specific context, which is either included in or referenced by messages exchanged between the provider and the consumer. This constraint has the drawback that it could reduce the overall scalability of the service provider if the service-provider needs to retain the shared context for each consumer. It also increases the coupling between a service provider and a consumer and makes switching service providers more difficult. Ultimately, some critics feel that SOA services are still too constrained by applications they represent.

A primary challenge faced by service-oriented architecture is managing of metadata. Environments based on SOA include many services which communicate among each other to perform tasks. Due to the fact that the design may involve multiple services working in conjunction, an Application may generate millions of messages. Further services may belong to different organizations or even competing firms creating a huge trust issue. Thus SOA governance comes into the scheme of things.

Another major problem faced by SOA is the lack of a uniform testing framework. There are no tools that provide the required features for testing these services in a Service Oriented Architecture. The major causes of difficulty are:

- Heterogeneity and complexity of solution.

- Huge set of testing combinations due to integration of autonomous services.

- Inclusion of services from different and competing vendors.

- Platform is continuously changing due to availability of new features and services.

See for additional challenges, partial solutions and research roadmap ionput regarding software service engineering

Extensions and Variants

Web 2.0

Tim O'Reilly coined the term "Web 2.0" to describe a perceived, quickly growing set of web-based applications. A topic that has experienced extensive coverage involves the relationship between Web 2.0 and service-oriented architectures.

SOA is the philosophy of encapsulating application logic in services with a uniformly defined interface and making these publicly available via discovery mechanisms. The notion of complexity-hiding and reuse, but also the concept of loosely coupling services has inspired researchers to elaborate on similarities between the two philosophies, SOA and Web 2.0, and their respective applications. Some argue Web 2.0 and SOA have significantly different elements and thus can not be regarded "parallel philosophies", whereas others consider the two concepts as complementary and regard Web 2.0 as the global SOA.

The philosophies of Web 2.0 and SOA serve different user needs and thus expose differences with respect to the design and also the technologies used in real-world applications. However, as of 2008, use-cases demonstrated the potential of combining technologies and principles of both Web 2.0 and SOA.

Microservices

Microservices are a modern interpretation of service-oriented architectures used to build distributed software systems. Services in a microservice architecture are processes that communicate with each other over the network in order to fulfill a goal. These services use technology agnostic protocols, which aid in encapsulating choice of language and frameworks, making their choice a concern internal to the service. Microservices is a new realisation and implementation approach to SOA, which has become popular since 2014 (and after the introduction of DevOps), which also emphasizes continuous deployment and other agile practices.

Shared Nothing Architecture

A shared nothing architecture (SN) is a distributed computing architecture in which each node is independent and self-sufficient, and there is no single point of contention across the system. More specifically, none of the nodes share memory or disk storage.

People typically contrast SN with systems that keep a large amount of centrally-stored state information, whether in a database, an application server, or any other similar single point of contention.

The advantages of SN architecture versus a central entity that controls the network (a controller-based architecture) include eliminating any single point of failure, allowing self-healing capabilities and providing an advantage with offering non-disruptive upgrade.

History

While SN is best known in the context of web development, the concept predates the web: Michael Stonebraker at the University of California, Berkeley used the term in a 1986 database paper. In it he mentions existing commercial implementations of the architecture (although none are named explicitly). Teradata, which delivered its first system in 1983, was probably one of those commercial implementations. Tandem Computers officially released NonStop SQL, a shared nothing database, in 1984.

Applications

Shared nothing is popular for web development because of its scalability. As Google has demonstrated, a pure SN system can scale almost infinitely simply by adding nodes in the form of inexpensive computers, since there is no single bottleneck to slow the system down. Google calls this *sharding*. A SN system typically partitions its data among many nodes on different databases (assigning different computers to deal with different users or queries), or may require every node to maintain its own copy of the application's data, using some kind of coordination protocol. This is often referred to as *database sharding*.

There is some doubt about whether a web application with many independent web nodes but a single, shared database (clustered or otherwise) should be counted as SN. One of the approaches to achieve SN architecture for stateful applications (which typically maintain state in a centralized database) is the use of a data grid, also known as distributed caching. This still leaves the centralized database as a single point of failure.

Shared nothing architectures have become prevalent in the data warehousing space. There is much debate as to whether the shared nothing approach is superior to shared Disk with sound arguments presented by both camps. Shared nothing architectures certainly take longer to respond to queries that involve joins over large data sets from different partitions (machines). However, the potential for scaling is huge.

What is Shared?

While there is no single point of contention within the software/hardware components of SN systems, information from disparate nodes may still need to be reintegrated at some point. Such points occur wherever an information system that is outside the SN architecture queries information from disparate nodes within the SN architecture for a single purpose. Examples of such external nodes might be:

1. persons (minds) who look at two SN nodes and decide that they hold or process data about the same thing (simply recognising that two nodes belong to the same SN system would be sufficient)

2. any software/hardware system that is written to query different nodes within the SN architecture

Space-Based Architecture

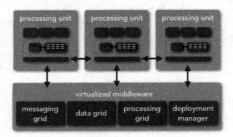

Space based architecture diagram

Space-based architecture (SBA) is a software architecture pattern for achieving linear scalability of stateful, high-performance applications using the tuple space paradigm. It follows many of the principles of representational state transfer (REST), service-oriented architecture (SOA) and event-driven architecture (EDA), as well as elements of grid computing. With a space-based architecture, applications are built out of a set of self-sufficient units, known as processing-units (PU). These units are independent of each other, so that the application can scale by adding more units. The SBA model is closely related to other patterns that have been proved successful in addressing the application scalability challenge, such as shared nothing architecture (SN), used by Google, Amazon.com and other well-known companies. The model has also been applied by many firms in the securities industry for implementing scalable electronic securities trading applications.

Components of Space-based Architecture

An application built on the principles of space-based architecture typically has the following components:

Processing unit

The unit of scalability and fail-over. Normally, a processing unit is built out of a POJO (Plain Old Java Object) container, such as that provided by the Spring Framework.

Virtual middleware

A common runtime and clustering model, used across the entire middleware stack. The core middleware components in a typical SBA architecture are:

Component	Description
Messaging grid	Handles the flow of incoming transaction as well as the communication between services
Data grid	Manages the data in distributed memory with options for synchronizing that data with an underlying database
Processing grid	Parallel processing component based on the master/worker pattern (also known as a blackboard pattern) that enables parallel processing of events among different services

POJO-driven services model

A lightweight services model that can take any standard Java implementation and turn it into a loosely coupled distributed service. The model is ideal for interaction with services that run within the same processing-unit.

SLA-driven container

The SLA-driven container enables the deployment of the application on a dynamic pool of machines based on Service Level Agreements. SLA definitions include the number of instances that need to run in order to comply with the application scaling and fail-over policies, as well as other policies.

Model–View–Adapter

Model–view–adapter (MVA) or mediating-controller MVC is a software architectural pattern and multitier architecture. In complex computer applications that present large amounts of data to users, developers often wish to separate data (model) and user interface (view) concerns so that changes to the user interface will not affect data handling and that the data can be reorganized without changing the user interface. MVA and traditional MVC both attempt to solve this same problem, but with two different styles of solution. Traditional MVC arranges model (e.g., data structures and storage), view (e.g., user interface), and controller (e.g., business logic) in a triangle, with model, view, and controller as vertices, so that some information flows between the model and views outside of the controller's direct control. The model–view–adapter solves this rather differently from the model–view–controller by arranging model, adapter or mediating controller and view linearly without any connections whatsoever directly between model and view.

View and Model do not Communicate Directly

The view is completely decoupled from the model such that view and the model can interact only via the mediating controller or adapter between the view and the model. Via this arrangement, only the adapter or mediating controller has knowledge of both the model and the view, because it is the responsibility of solely the adapter or mediating controller to adapt or mediate between the model and the view—hence the names adapter and mediator. The model and view are kept intentionally oblivious of each other. In traditional MVC, the model and view are made aware of each other, which might permit disadvantageous coupling of view (e.g., user interface) concerns into the model (e.g., database) and vice versa, when the architecture might have been better served by the schema of the database and the presentation of information in the user-interface are divorced entirely from each other and allowed to diverge from each other radically. For example, in a text editor, the model might best be a piece table (instead of, say, a gap buffer or a linked list of lines). But, the user interface should present the final resting state of the edits on the file, not some direct information-overload presentation of the piece-table's meticulous raw undo-redo deltas and incremental operations on that file since the current editing session began.

Model is Intentionally Oblivious of Views

This separation of concerns permits a wide variety of different views to indirectly access the same model either via exactly the same adapter or via the same class of adapters. For example, one underlying data-storage model and schema and technology could be accessed via a wide variety multiple different views—e.g., Qt GUI, Microsoft MFC GUI, GTK+ GUI, Microsoft .NET GUI, Java Swing GUI, Silverlight website, and AJAX website—where (unlike traditional MVC) the model is kept completely oblivious of what information flows toward these user interfaces. The adapter or class of adapters keeps the model completely oblivious that it is supporting multiple of the user interfaces and perhaps even supporting this variety concurrently. To the model, these multiple types of user interface would look like multiple instances of a generic user oblivious of type of technology.

View is Intentionally Oblivious of Models

Likewise, any one user interface can be kept intentionally oblivious of a wide variety of different models that may underlie the mediating controller or adapter. For example, the same website can be kept oblivious of the fact that it can be served by an SQL database server such as PostgreSQL, Sybase SQL Server, or Microsoft SQL Server that has business logic built into the database server via stored procedures and that has transactions that the server may roll back or B) by an SQL database server such as MySQL that lacks one or more of these capabilities, or C) by a nonSQL RDF database, because the website interacts only with the mediating controller or adapter and never directly with the model.

Multiple Adapters between the same Model-view Pair

Additionally, multiple adapters may be created to change the way one view presents data for a given model. For example, different governments (either among different states of the USA or different nation-states internationally) may impose different codes of law, that in turn impose different business logic for the same underlying database and for the same outwardly presented website. In this scenario, a class of various adapters or mediating controllers can represent the variations in business logic among these jurisdictions in between the same database model and the same website view.

Model–View–Presenter

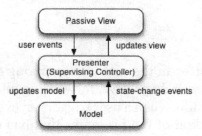

Diagram that depicts the Model View Presenter (MVP) GUI design pattern.

Model–view–presenter (MVP) is a derivation of the model–view–controller (MVC) architectural pattern, and is used mostly for building user interfaces.

In MVP the *presenter* assumes the functionality of the "middle-man". In MVP, all presentation logic is pushed to the presenter.

Pattern Description

MVP is a user interface architectural pattern engineered to facilitate automated unit testing and improve the separation of concerns in presentation logic:

- The *model* is an interface defining the data to be displayed or otherwise acted upon in the user interface.

- The *presenter* acts upon the model and the view. It retrieves data from repositories (the model), and formats it for display in the view.

- The *view* is a passive interface that displays data (the model) and routes user commands (events) to the presenter to act upon that data.

Normally, the view implementation instantiates the concrete presenter object, providing a reference to itself. The following C# code demonstrates a simple view constructor, where ConcreteDomainPresenter implements the IDomainPresenter interface:

```
public class DomainView : IDomainView

{

    private IDomainPresenter domainPresenter = null;


    ///<summary>Constructor</summary>

    public DomainView()

    {

        domainPresenter = new ConcreteDomainPresenter(this);

    }

}
```

The degree of logic permitted in the view varies among different implementations. At one extreme, the view is entirely passive, forwarding all interaction operations to the presenter. In this formulation, when a user triggers an event method of the view, it does nothing but invoke a method of the presenter that has no parameters and no return value. The presenter then retrieves data from the view through methods defined by the view interface. Finally, the presenter operates on the model and updates the view with the results of the operation. Other versions of model-view-presenter allow some latitude with respect to which class handles a particular interaction, event, or command. This is often more suitable for web-based architectures, where the view, which executes on a client's browser, may be the best place to handle a particular interaction or command.

From a layering point of view, the presenter class might be considered as belonging to the application layer in a multilayered architecture system, but it can also be seen as a presenter layer of its own between the application layer and the user interface layer.

Implementation in .NET

The .NET environment supports the MVP pattern much like any other development environment. The same model and presenter class can be used to support multiple interfaces, such as an ASP.NET Web application, a Windows Forms application, or a Silverlight application. The presenter gets and sets information from/to the view through an interface that can be accessed by the interface (view) component.

In addition to manually implementing the pattern, a model-view-presenter framework may be used to support the MVP pattern in a more automated fashion. Below is a list of such frameworks under the .NET platform.

NET Frameworks

- Claymore
- MVC# Framework
- Web Client Software Factory
- Evolution.Net MVP Framework
- ASP.NET Web Forms Model-View-Presenter (MVP)
- Nucleo.NET
- WinForms MVP

Implementation in Java

In a Java (AWT/Swing/SWT) application, the MVP pattern can be used by letting the user interface class implement a view interface.

The same approach can be used for Java web-based applications, since modern Java component-based Web frameworks allow development of client-side logic using the same component approach as thick clients.

Implementing MVP in Google Web Toolkit requires only that some component implement the view interface. The same approach is possible using Vaadin or the Echo2 Web framework.

MVP can be implemented in Java SE (AWT and Swing) applications using the Biscotti and MVP4J frameworks.

Java Frameworks

- JavaFX
- MVP4J
- Echo2
- Google Web Toolkit
- GWT-Platform
- JFace
- Swing
- Vaadin
- ZK

Implementation in PHP

As of PHP's flexible runtime environment, there are wide possibilities of approaches of an application logic. A great example of MVP pattern implementation is Nette Framework implementing rich presenter layer and view layer through templating system Latte (web template engine). Implementation of model layer is left on the end application programmer.

PHP Frameworks

- Nette Framework

- RhubarbPHP Framework

- Nano MVP Framework

History

The model-view-presenter software pattern originated in the early 1990s at Taligent, a joint venture of Apple, HP, and IBM, and was the underlying programming model for application development in Taligent's C++-based CommonPoint environment. The pattern was later migrated by Taligent to Java and popularized in a paper by Taligent CTO Mike Potel. After Taligent's demise in 1997, Andy Bower and Blair McGlashan of Dolphin Smalltalk adapted the MVP pattern to form the basis for their Smalltalk user interface framework. In 2006, Microsoft began incorporating MVP into their documentation and examples for user interface programming in the .NET framework. The evolution and multiple variants of the MVP pattern, including the relationship of MVP to other design patterns such as MVC, is discussed in detail in an article by Martin Fowler and another by Derek Greer

Model–View–Viewmodel

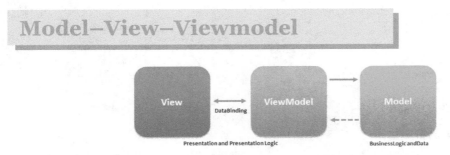

Model–view–view-model (MVVM) is a software architectural pattern.

MVVM facilitates a separation of development of the graphical user interface – be it via a markup language or GUI code – from development of the business logic or back-end logic (the *data model*). The *view model* of MVVM is a value converter; meaning the view model is responsible for exposing (converting) the data objects from the model in such a way that objects are easily managed and presented. In this respect, the view model is more model than view, and handles most if not all of the view's display logic. The view model may implement a mediator pattern, organizing access to the back-end logic around the set of use cases supported by the view.

MVVM is a variation of Martin Fowler's Presentation Model design pattern. MVVM abstracts a view's state and behavior in the same way, but a Presentation Model abstracts a view (creates a *view model*) in a manner *not* dependent on a specific user-interface platform. MVVM and Presentation Model both derive from the model–view–controller pattern (MVC).

MVVM was developed by Microsoft architects Ken Cooper and Ted Peters specifically to simplify event-driven programming of user interfaces—by exploiting features of Windows Presentation Foundation (WPF) (Microsoft's .NET graphics system) and Silverlight (WPF's Internet application derivative). John Gossman, one of Microsoft's WPF and Silverlight architects, announced MVVM on his blog in 2005.

Model–view–viewmodel is also referred to as model–view–binder, especially in implementations not involving the .NET platform. ZK (a web application framework written in Java) and KnockoutJS (a JavaScript library) use model–view–binder.

Components of MVVM Pattern

Model

> *Model* refers either to a domain model, which represents real state content (an object-oriented approach), or to the data access layer, which represents content (a data-centric approach).

View

> As in the MVC and MVP patterns, the *view* is the structure, layout, and appearance of what a user sees on the screen. (UI).

View model

> The *view model* is an abstraction of the view exposing public properties and commands. Instead of the controller of the MVC pattern, or the presenter of the MVP pattern, MVVM has a *binder*. In the view model, the binder mediates communication between the view and the data binder. The view model has been described as a state of the data in the model.

Binder

> Declarative data- and command-binding are implicit in the MVVM pattern. In the Microsoft solution stack, the binder is a markup language called XAML. The

binder frees the developer from being obliged to write boiler-plate logic to synchronize the view model and view. When implemented outside of the Microsoft stack the presence of a declarative databinding technology is a key enabler of the pattern.

Rationale

MVVM was designed to make use of data binding functions in WPF (Windows Presentation Foundation) to better facilitate the separation of view layer development from the rest of the pattern, by removing virtually all GUI code ("code-behind") from the view layer. Instead of requiring user experience (UX) developers to write GUI code, they can use the framework markup language (e.g., XAML) and create data bindings to the view model, which is written and maintained by application developers. The separation of roles allows interactive designers to focus on UX needs rather than programming of business logic. The layers of an application can thus be developed in multiple work streams for higher productivity. Even when a single developer works on the entire code base a proper separation of the view from the model is more productive as user interface typically changes frequently and late in the development cycle based on end-user feedback.

The MVVM pattern attempts to gain both advantages of separation of functional development provided by MVC, while leveraging the advantages of data bindings and the framework by binding data as close to the pure application model as possible. It uses the binder, view model, and any business layers' data-checking features to validate incoming data. The result is the model and framework drive as much of the operations as possible, eliminating or minimizing application logic which directly manipulates the view (e.g., code-behind).

Criticism

A criticism of the pattern comes from MVVM creator John Gossman himself, who points out overhead in implementing MVVM is "overkill" for simple UI operations. He states for larger applications, generalizing the ViewModel becomes more difficult. Moreover, he illustrates data binding in very large applications can result in considerable memory consumption.

Model–View–Controller

Model–view–controller (MVC) is a software design pattern for implementing user interfaces on computers. It divides a given software application into three interconnected parts, so as to separate internal representations of information from the ways that information is presented to or accepted from the user.

Traditionally used for desktop graphical user interfaces (GUIs), this architecture has become popular for designing web applications and even mobile, desktop and other clients.

Description

As with other software architectures, MVC expresses the "core of the solution" to a problem while allowing it to be adapted for each system. Particular MVC architectures can vary significantly from the traditional description here.

Components

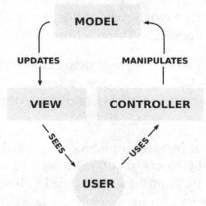

A typical collaboration of the MVC components.

The central component of MVC, the *model*, captures the behavior of the application in terms of its problem domain, independent of the user interface.

- The *model* directly manages the data, logic, and rules of the application.

- A *view* can be any output representation of information, such as a chart or a diagram. Multiple views of the same information are possible, such as a bar chart for management and a tabular view for accountants.

- The third part, the *controller*, accepts input and converts it to commands for the model or view.

Interactions

In addition to dividing the application into three kinds of components, the model–view–controller design defines the interactions between them.

- A *model* stores data that is retrieved according to commands from the controller and displayed in the view.

- A *view* generates new output to the user based on changes in the model.

- A *controller* can send commands to the model to update the model's state (e.g., editing a document). It can also send commands to its associated view to change the view's presentation of the model (e.g., by scrolling through a document).

History

One of the seminal insights in the early development of graphical user interfaces, MVC became one of the first approaches to describe and implement software constructs in terms of their responsibilities.

Trygve Reenskaug introduced MVC into Smalltalk-76 while visiting the Xerox Palo Alto Research Center (PARC) in the 1970s. In the 1980s, Jim Althoff and others implemented a version of MVC for the Smalltalk-80 class library.

The MVC pattern has subsequently evolved, giving rise to variants such as hierarchical model–view–controller (HMVC), model–view–adapter (MVA), model–view–presenter (MVP), model–view–viewmodel (MVVM), and others that adapted MVC to different contexts.

The use of the MVC pattern in web applications exploded in popularity after the introduction of Apple's WebObjects in 1996, which was originally written in Objective-C (that borrowed heavily from Smalltalk) and helped enforce MVC principles. Later, the MVC pattern became popular with Java developers when WebObjects was ported to Java. Later frameworks for Java, such as Spring (released in 2002), continued the strong bond between Java and MVC. The introduction of the frameworks Rails (December 2005, for Ruby) and Django (July 2005, for Python), both of which had a strong emphasis on rapid deployment, increased MVC's popularity outside the traditional enterprise environment in which it has long been popular. MVC web frameworks now hold large market-shares relative to non-MVC web toolkits.

Use in Web Applications

Although originally developed for desktop computing, model–view–controller has been widely adopted as an architecture for World Wide Web applications in major programming languages. Several commercial and noncommercial web frameworks have been created that enforce the pattern. These software frameworks vary in their interpretations, mainly in the way that the MVC responsibilities are divided between the client and server.

Early web MVC frameworks took a thin client approach that placed almost the entire model, view and controller logic on the server. This is still reflected in popular frameworks such as Ruby on Rails, Django, ASP.NET MVC. In this approach, the client sends either hyperlink requests or form input to the controller and then receives a complete and updated web page (or other document) from the view; the model exists entirely on the server. As client technologies have matured, frameworks such as AngularJS, EmberJS, JavaScriptMVC and Backbone have been created that allow the MVC components to execute partly on the client.

Multitier Architecture

In software engineering, multitier architecture (often referred to as *n*-tier architecture) or multilayered architecture is a client–server architecture in which presentation, application processing, and data management functions are physically separated. The most widespread use of multitier architecture is the three-tier architecture.

N-tier application architecture provides a model by which developers can create flexible and reusable applications. By segregating an application into tiers, developers acquire the option of modifying or adding a specific layer, instead of reworking the entire application. A three-tier architecture is typically composed of a *presentation* tier, a *domain logic* tier, and a *data storage* tier.

While the concepts of layer and tier are often used interchangeably, one fairly common point of view is that there is indeed a difference. This view holds that a *layer* is a logical structuring mechanism for the elements that make up the software solution, while a *tier* is a physical structuring mechanism for the system infrastructure. For example, a three-layer solution could easily be deployed on a single tier, such as a personal workstation.

Common Layers

In a logical multilayered architecture for an information system with an object-oriented design, the following four are the most common:

- Presentation layer (a.k.a. UI layer, view layer, presentation tier in multitier architecture)

- Application layer (a.k.a. service layer or GRASP Controller Layer)

- Business layer (a.k.a. business logic layer (BLL), domain layer)

- Data access layer (a.k.a. persistence layer, logging, networking, and other services which are required to support a particular business layer)

The book *Domain Driven Design* describes some common uses for the above four layers, although its primary focus is the domain layer.

If the application architecture has no explicit distinction between the business layer and the presentation layer (i.e., the presentation layer is considered part of the business layer), then a traditional client-server (two-tier) model has been implemented.

The more usual convention is that the application layer (or service layer) is considered a sublayer of the business layer, typically encapsulating the API definition surfacing the supported business functionality. The application/business layers can, in fact, be further subdivided to emphasize additional sublayers of distinct responsibility. For example, if the Model View Presenter pattern is used, the presenter sublayer might be used as an additional layer between the user interface layer and the business/application layer (as represented by the model sublayer).

Some also identify a separate layer called the business infrastructure layer (BI), located between the business layer(s) and the infrastructure layer(s). It's also sometimes called the "low-level business layer" or the "business services layer". This layer is very general and can be used in several application tiers (e.g. a CurrencyConverter).

The infrastructure layer can be partitioned into different levels (high-level or low-level technical services). Developers often focus on the persistence (data access) capabilities of the infrastructure layer and therefore only talk about the persistence layer or the data access layer (instead of an infrastructure layer or technical services layer). In other words, the other kind of technical services are not always explicitly thought of as part of any particular layer.

A layer is on top of another, because it depends on it. Every layer can exist without the layers above it, and requires the layers below it to function. Another common view is that layers do not always strictly depend on only on the adjacent layer on below. For example, in a relaxed layered system (as opposed to a strict layered system) a layer can also depend on all the layers below it.

Three-tier Architecture

Three-tier architecture is a client–server software architecture pattern in which the user interface (presentation), functional process logic ("business rules"), computer data storage and data access are developed and maintained as independent modules, most often on separate platforms. It was developed by John J. Donovan in Open Environment Corporation (OEC), a tools company he founded in Cambridge, Massachusetts.

Apart from the usual advantages of modular software with well-defined interfaces, the three-tier architecture is intended to allow any of the three tiers to be upgraded or replaced independently in response to changes in requirements or technology. For example, a change of operating system in the *presentation tier* would only affect the user interface code.

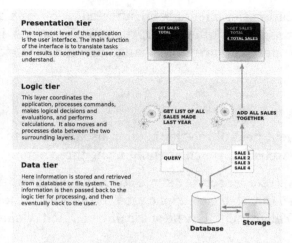

Presentation tier

The top-most level of the application is the user interface. The main function of the interface is to translate tasks and results to something the user can understand.

Logic tier

This layer coordinates the application, processes commands, makes logical decisions and evaluations, and performs calculations. It also moves and processes data between the two surrounding layers.

Data tier

Here information is stored and retrieved from a database or file system. The information is then passed back to the logic tier for processing, and then eventually back to the user.

Overview of a three-tier application.

Typically, the user interface runs on a desktop PC or workstation and uses a standard graphical user interface, functional process logic that may consist of one or more separate modules running on a workstation or application server, and an RDBMS on a database server or mainframe that contains the computer data storage logic. The middle tier may be multitiered itself (in which case the overall architecture is called an "*n*-tier architecture").

Three-tier architecture:

Presentation tier

> This is the topmost level of the application. The presentation tier displays information related to such services as browsing merchandise, purchasing and shopping cart contents. It communicates with other tiers by which it puts out the results to the browser/client tier and all other tiers in the network. In simple terms, it is a layer which users can access directly (such as a web page, or an operating system's GUI).

Application tier (business logic, logic tier, or middle tier)

> The logical tier is pulled out from the presentation tier and, as its own layer, it controls an application's functionality by performing detailed processing.

Data tier

> The data tier includes the data persistence mechanisms (database servers, file shares, etc.) and the data access layer that encapsulates the persistence mechanisms and exposes the data. The data access layer should provide an API to the application tier that exposes methods of managing the stored data without exposing or creating dependencies on the data storage mechanisms. Avoiding dependencies on the storage mechanisms allows for updates or changes with-

out the application tier clients being affected by or even aware of the change. As with the separation of any tier, there are costs for implementation and often costs to performance in exchange for improved scalability and maintainability.

Web Development Usage

In the web development field, three-tier is often used to refer to websites, commonly electronic commerce websites, which are built using three tiers:

1. A front-end web server serving static content, and potentially some cached dynamic content. In web based application, Front End is the content rendered by the browser. The content may be static or generated dynamically.

2. A middle dynamic content processing and generation level application server (e.g., ASP.NET, Ruby on Rails, Django (web framework), Laravel, Spring Framework, CodeIgniter, Symfony, Flask (web framework))

3. A back-end database or data store, comprising both data sets and the database management system software that manages and provides access to the data.

Other Considerations

Data transfer between tiers is part of the architecture. Protocols involved may include one or more of SNMP, CORBA, Java RMI, .NET Remoting, Windows Communication Foundation, sockets, UDP, web services or other standard or proprietary protocols. Often middleware is used to connect the separate tiers. Separate tiers often (but not necessarily) run on separate physical servers, and each tier may itself run on a cluster.

Traceability

The end-to-end traceability of data flows through n-tier systems is a challenging task which becomes more important when systems increase in complexity. The Application Response Measurement defines concepts and APIs for measuring performance and correlating transactions between tiers. Generally, the term "tiers" is used to describe physical distribution of components of a system on separate servers, computers, or networks (processing nodes). A three-tier architecture then will have three processing nodes. The term "layers" refer to a logical grouping of components which may or may not be physically located on one processing node.

Blackboard (Design Pattern)

In software engineering, the blackboard pattern is a behavioral design pattern that provides a computational framework for the design and implementation of systems that used to integrate large and diverse specialized modules, and implement complex, non deterministic control strategies.

This pattern has been identified by the members of the HEARSAY-II project and first applied for speech recognition.

Structure

The blackboard model defines three main components:

- blackboard - a structured global memory containing objects from the solution space

- knowledge sources - highly specialized modules with their own representation

- control component - selects, configures and execute knowledge sources.

Implementation

First step is to design the solution space (i.e. various solutions) that leads to the definition of blackboard structure. Then, knowledge source are to be identified. These two activities are very related.

The next step is to specify the control component that is generally in the form of a complex scheduler that makes use of a set of domain-specific heuristics to rate the relevance of executable knowledge sources.

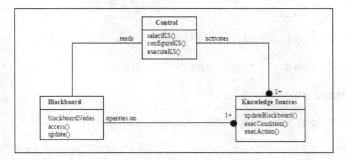

System Structure

Known Uses

Some usage-domains are:

- speech recognition

- vehicle identification and tracking

- identification of the structure of protein molecules

- sonar signals interpretation.

Consequences

The blackboard pattern provides effective solutions for designing and implementing complex systems where heterogeneous modules have to be dynamically combined to solve a problem. This provides properties such as:

- reusability

- changeability

- robustness.

Blackboard pattern allows multiple processes to work closer together on separate threads, polling, and reacting, if it is needed.

Example

Sample radar defense system is provided as an example (in CSharp).

Code for MainWindow.xaml:

```
<ListBox ItemsSource="{Binding blackboard.CurrentObjects}" ItemsPanel="{DynamicResource ItemsPanelTemplate1}" ItemContainerStyle="{DynamicResource ItemContainerStyle}" ItemTemplate="{DynamicResource ItemTemplate}" Margin="20,20,20,10" Foreground="#FFDE6C6C" >

    <ListBox.Resources>

        <ItemsPanelTemplate x:Key="ItemsPanelTemplate1">

            <Canvas IsItemsHost="True"/>

        </ItemsPanelTemplate>

 Code for item container for positioning

<Style x:Key="ItemContainerStyle" TargetType="{x:Type ListBoxItem}">

    <Setter Property="Background" Value="Transparent"/>

    <Setter Property="HorizontalContentAlignment" Value="{Binding HorizontalContentAlignment, RelativeSource={RelativeSource AncestorType={x:Type ItemsControl}}}"/>

    <Setter Property="VerticalContentAlignment" Value="{Binding VerticalContentAlignment, RelativeSource={RelativeSource AncestorType={x:Type ItemsControl}}}"/>
```

```
<Setter Property="Canvas.Left" Value="{Binding X}"/>

<Setter Property="Canvas.Top" Value="{Binding Y}"/>

<Setter Property="Template">

    <Setter.Value>

        <ControlTemplate TargetType="{x:Type ListBoxItem}">

            <Border x:Name="Bd" BorderBrush="{TemplateBinding
BorderBrush}"  BorderThickness="{TemplateBinding  BorderThick-
ness}" Background="{TemplateBinding Background}" Padding="{Tem-
plateBinding Padding}" SnapsToDevicePixels="true">

                <ContentPresenter HorizontalAlignment="{-
TemplateBinding HorizontalContentAlignment}" SnapsToDevicePix-
els="{TemplateBinding  SnapsToDevicePixels}"  VerticalAlign-
ment="{TemplateBinding VerticalContentAlignment}"/>

            </Border>

        </ControlTemplate>

    </Setter.Value>

</Setter>

</Style>
```

Code for Item (ItemTemplate defines the object, an Image and TextBoxes):

```
<DataTemplate x:Key="ItemTemplate">

    <Border>

        <Border.Style>

            <Style TargetType="{x:Type Border}">

                <Style.Triggers>

                    <DataTrigger Binding="{Binding IsThreat}"
Value="true">

                        <Setter Property="Background" Value="Red"/>
                    </DataTrigger>

                    <DataTrigger Binding="{Binding IsThreat}"
Value="false">
```

```xml
                              <Setter Property="Background" Val-
ue="Green"/>
                     </DataTrigger>
                 </Style.Triggers>
             </Style>
        </Border.Style>
        <Grid Margin="3">
            <Image Height="48" Source="{Binding Image}" />
          <StackPanel Margin="0,0,0,-30" VerticalAlignment="Bot-
tom" >
                <TextBlock Text="{Binding Type}"/>
                <TextBlock Text="{Binding Name}"/>
            </StackPanel>
                <TextBlock HorizontalAlignment="Right" Text-
Wrapping="Wrap" Text="{Binding DistanceFromDestruction}" Ver-
ticalAlignment="Bottom"    Width="Auto"    Visibility="{Binding
IsThreat, Converter={StaticResource BooleanToVisibilityConvert-
er}}"/>
        </Grid>
    </Border>
</DataTemplate>
```

Code behind the Blackboard component in MVVM ViewModel implementation:

```csharp
public Blackboard blackboard { get; set; }
Controller controller;


public MainWindow()
{
    InitializeComponent();

    DataContext = this;
```

```
    blackboard = new Blackboard();

    controller = new Controller(blackboard);
}
```

Code behind the Controller:

```
private void Button_Click(object sender, System.Windows.RoutedE-
ventArgs e)

{

    controller.AddSignalProcessor();

}
```

Code for the base class IObject:

```
public interface IObject

{

    ObjectType Type { get; set; }

    string Name { get; set; }

    WriteableBitmap Image { get; set; }

    bool? IsThreat { get; set; }

    ProcessingStage Stage { get; set; }

    int X { get; set; }

    int Y { get; set; }


    IObject Clone();

}
```

Code in the radar module:

```
AllObjects = new List<IObject>

{
```

```
    new BirdObject(ObjectType.Bird, "", new WriteableBitmap(new
System.Windows.Media.Imaging.BitmapImage(new     Uri(@"pack://ap-
plication:,,,/Media/Bird.bmp",     UriKind.Absolute))),     false,
false),

    new PlaneObject(ObjectType.Plane, "", new WriteableBitmap(new
System.Windows.Media.Imaging.BitmapImage(new     Uri(@"pack://ap-
plication:,,,/Media/Plane.bmp",     UriKind.Absolute))),     false,
false),

    new RocketObject(ObjectType.Rocket, "", new WriteableBitmap(new
System.Windows.Media.Imaging.BitmapImage(new     Uri(@"pack://ap-
plication:,,,/Media/Rocket.bmp",     UriKind.Absolute))),     false,
false),

};
```

Code to handle incoming object:

```
public IncomingObject(IObject obj)

    : base(ObjectType.Unknown, null, null, true, null)

{

    actualObject = obj;

    ProcessedPixels = new  bool[16, 16];


    //Paint the image as all red to start with

     Image = new  WriteableBitmap(48, 48, 72, 72, PixelFormats.
Bgr32, null);

    int[] ary = new  int[(48*48)];

    for (var x = 0; x < 48; x++)

        for (var y = 0; y < 48; y++)

            ary[48*y + x] = 255*256*256;

    Image.WritePixels(new Int32Rect(0, 0, 48, 48), ary, 4*48, 0);

}
```

Code for knowledge source interface:

```
public interface IKnowledgeSource
{
    bool IsEnabled { get; }
    void Configure(Blackboard board);
    void ExecuteAction();


    KnowledgeSourceType KSType { get; }
    KnowledgeSourcePriority Priority { get; }
    void Stop();
}
```

implementation for signal processor:

```
public override bool IsEnabled
{
    get
    {
        for (var ix = 0; ix < blackboard.CurrentObjects.Count();
ix++)
            if (blackboard.CurrentObjects[ix].Stage < Process-
ingStage.Analysed)
                return true;


        return false;
    }
}


public override void ExecuteAction()
{
    for (var ix = 0; ix < blackboard.CurrentObjects.Count();
```

```
ix++)
        if (blackboard.CurrentObjects[ix].Stage < Processing-
Stage.Analysed)
            ProcessAnotherBit(blackboard.CurrentObjects[ix]);
}


void ProcessAnotherBit(IObject obj)
{
    int GRANULARITY = 16;
    int blockWidth = obj.Image.PixelWidth/GRANULARITY;
```

code segments for copying between writablebitmaps:

```
int stride = obj.Image.PixelWidth*obj.Image.Format.BitsPerPix-
el/8;
int byteSize = stride*obj.Image.PixelHeight*obj.Image.Format.
BitsPerPixel/8;
var ary = new byte[byteSize];
obj.Image.CopyPixels(ary, stride, 0);


var unk = obj as IncomingObject;
unk.GetActualObject().Image.CopyPixels(aryOrig, stride, 0);


for (var iy = 0; iy < blockWidth; iy++)
{
    for (var ix = 0; ix < blockWidth; ix++)
        for (var b = 0; b < 4; b++)
        {
            ary[curix] = aryOrig[curix];
            curix++;
```

```
        }

    curix = curix + stride - (blockWidth*4);

}


obj.Image.WritePixels(new Int32Rect(0, 0, obj.Image.PixelWidth,
obj.Image.PixelHeight), ary, stride, 0);


Code for comparing pixel in image recognition:
for (var ix = 0; ix < blockWidth; ix++)
{
    var argb1 = (ary[curix + 1]*256*256) + (ary[curix + 2]*256)
+ ary[curix + 3];
    var argb2 = (aryKnown[curix + 1]*256*256) + (aryKnown[curix
+ 2]*256) + aryKnown[curix + 3];
    if (argb1 != 255*256*256 && argb1 != argb2)
    {
        nomatch = true;
        break;
    }
    curix += 4;
}


if (matches.Count() == 1)
{
    obj.Type = matches.Type;
    obj.Name = matches.Name;
    obj.IsThreat = matches.IsThreat;


    obj.Image = new  WriteableBitmap(matches.Image); //Create
new image instance
```

```
    if (obj.Type != ObjectType.Plane)

        obj.Stage = ProcessingStage.Identified;

    else

        obj.Stage = ProcessingStage.Analysed;

}
```

Code for plane identification:

```
for (var ix = 0; ix < blackboard.CurrentObjects.Count(); ix++)

{

    var obj = blackboard.CurrentObjects[ix];

    if (obj.Stage == ProcessingStage.Analysed && obj.Type == Ob-
jectType.Plane)

        {

            var unk = obj as IncomingObject;

            var actual = unk.GetActualObject();

            obj.Name = actual.Name;

            obj.IsThreat = actual.IsThreat;

            obj.Stage = ProcessingStage.Identified;

        }

}
```

Code for the war machine:

```
public override void ExecuteAction()

{

    for (var ix = 0; ix < blackboard.CurrentObjects.Count();
ix++)

    {

        var obj = blackboard.CurrentObjects[ix] as IncomingOb-
```

```
ject;

        if (obj.IsThreat != null && obj.IsThreat.Value && (obj.
Stage != ProcessingStage.Actioned))

        {

            if (obj.MoveHitsTarget())

                DestroyTarget(obj);

        }

    }

}


private void DestroyTarget(IncomingObject obj)
{
    int stride = obj.Image.PixelWidth*obj.Image.Format.BitsPer-
Pixel/8;

     int byteSize = stride*obj.Image.PixelHeight*obj.Image.For-
mat.BitsPerPixel/8;

    var ary = new byte[byteSize];

    obj.Image.CopyPixels(ary, stride, 0);


    DrawCross(stride, ary);


     obj.Image.WritePixels(new Int32Rect(0, 0, obj.Image.Pixel-
Width, obj.Image.PixelHeight), ary, stride, 0);

    obj.Stage = ProcessingStage.Actioned;

}


private static void DrawCross(int stride, byte[] ary)
{
    for (var y = 1; y < 47; y++)

    {
```

```
    var line1Pos = (y*stride) + (y*4);

    var line2Pos = (y*stride) + (stride - 4) - (y*4);

    for (var a = -1; a < 2; a++)

    {

        ary[line1Pos + 4 + (a*4)] = ary[line2Pos + 4 + (a*4)]
= 255;

        ary[line1Pos + 5 + (a*4)] = ary[line2Pos + 5 + (a*4)]
= 0;

        ary[line1Pos + 6 + (a*4)] = ary[line2Pos + 6 + (a*4)]
= 0;

        ary[line1Pos + 7 + (a*4)] = ary[line2Pos + 7 + (a*4)]
= 0;

    }

  }

}
```

References

- Thomas Erl, Benjamin Carlyle, Cesare Pautasso, Raj Balasubramanian (2013). "5.1". In Thomas Erl. SOA with REST. Prentice Hall. ISBN 978-0-13-701251-0.

- Richardson, Leonard; Amundsen, Mike (2013), RESTful Web APIs, O'Reilly Media, ISBN 978-1-449-35806-8, retrieved 15 September 2015

- Michael Bell (2008). "Introduction to Service-Oriented Modeling". Service-Oriented Modeling: Service Analysis, Design, and Architecture. Wiley & Sons. p. 3. ISBN 978-0-470-14111-3.

- Michael Bell (2010). SOA Modeling Patterns for Service-Oriented Discovery and Analysis. Wiley & Sons. p. 390. ISBN 978-0-470-48197-4.

- Lübke, Daniel and van Lessen, Tammo (2016). "Modeling Test Cases in BPMN for Behavior-Driven Development". IEEE Software. 33 (5): 15–21. doi:10.1109/MS.2016.117.

- Olaf Zimmermann, Cesare Pautasso, Gregor Hohpe, Bobby Woolf (2016). "A Decade of Enterprise Integration Patterns". IEEE Software. 33 (1): 13–19. doi:10.1109/MS.2016.11.

- "Web Services Architecture". World Wide Web Consortium. 11 February 2004. 3.1.3 Relationship to the World Wide Web and REST Architectures. Retrieved 29 September 2016.

- "Fielding discusses the development of the REST style". Tech.groups.yahoo.com. Archived from the original on November 11, 2009. Retrieved 2014-09-14.

- "The Advantages of a Shared Nothing Architecture for Truly Non-Disruptive Upgrades". solidfire.com. 2014-09-17. Retrieved 2015-04-21.

- Microsoft Windows Communication Foundation team (2012). "Principles of Service Oriented Design". msdn.microsoft.com. Retrieved September 3, 2012.

- Blankenhorn, Dana (February 27, 2006). "Shared nothing coming to open source". ZDNet. Retrieved June 21, 2012.

- Wildermuth, Shawn. "Windows Presentation Foundation Data Binding: Part 1". Microsoft. Retrieved 24 March 2012.

- K. Julisch et al., Compliance by Design – Bridging the Chasm between Auditors and IT Architects. Computers & Security, Elsevier. Volume 30, Issue 6-7, Sep.-Oct. 2011.

- Fox C, Evans M, Pearson M, Prescott T (2011). "Towards hierarchical blackboard mapping on a whiskered robot" (PDF). Robotics and Autonomous Systems. 60 (11): 1356–66.

## 5

Software Design Patterns

A software design pattern is a solution that is used for a problem that usually happens in software design. Design patterns are practices that programmers use for solving problems when they are designing a system or an application. Façade pattern, active record pattern, flyweight pattern, builder pattern, composite pattern and specification pattern are some of the patterns discussed in the following chapter.

Software Design Pattern

In software engineering, a software design pattern is a general reusable solution to a commonly occurring problem within a given context in software design. It is not a finished design that can be transformed directly into source or machine code. It is a description or template for how to solve a problem that can be used in many different situations. Design patterns are formalized best practices that the programmer can use to solve common problems when designing an application or system.

Object-oriented design patterns typically show relationships and interactions between classes or objects, without specifying the final application classes or objects that are involved. Patterns that imply mutable state may be unsuited for functional programming languages, some patterns can be rendered unnecessary in languages that have built-in support for solving the problem they are trying to solve, and object-oriented patterns are not necessarily suitable for non-object-oriented languages.

Design patterns may be viewed as a structured approach to computer programming intermediate between the levels of a programming paradigm and a concrete algorithm.

Types

Design patterns reside in the domain of modules and interconnections. At a higher level there are architectural patterns which are larger in scope, usually describing an overall pattern followed by an entire system.

There are many types of design patterns, for instance

Algorithm strategy patterns

> Addressing concerns related to high-level strategies describing how to exploit application characteristics on a computing platform.

Computational design patterns

> Addressing concerns related to key computation identification.

Execution patterns

> Which address issues related to lower-level support of application execution, including strategies for executing streams of tasks and for the definition of building blocks to support task synchronization.

Implementation strategy patterns

> Addressing concerns related to implementing source code to support

> 1. program organization, and

> 2. the common data structures specific to parallel programming.

Structural design patterns

> Addressing concerns related to global structures of applications being developed.

History

Patterns originated as an architectural concept by Christopher Alexander (1977/79). In 1987, Kent Beck and Ward Cunningham began experimenting with the idea of applying patterns to programming – specifically pattern languages – and presented their results at the OOPSLA conference that year. In the following years, Beck, Cunningham and others followed up on this work.

Design patterns gained popularity in computer science after the book *Design Patterns: Elements of Reusable Object-Oriented Software* was published in 1994 by the so-called "Gang of Four" (Gamma et al.), which is frequently abbreviated as "GoF". That same year, the first Pattern Languages of Programming Conference was held and the following year, the Portland Pattern Repository was set up for documentation of design patterns. The scope of the term remains a matter of dispute. Notable books in the design pattern genre include:

- Gamma, Erich; Helm, Richard; Johnson, Ralph; Vlissides, John (1995). Design Patterns: Elements of Reusable Object-Oriented Software. Addison-Wesley. ISBN 0-201-63361-2.

- Brinch Hansen, Per (1995). Studies in Computational Science: Parallel Programming Paradigms. Prentice Hall. ISBN 0-13-439324-4.

- Buschmann, Frank; Meunier, Regine; Rohnert, Hans; Sommerlad, Peter (1996). Pattern-Oriented Software Architecture, Volume 1: A System of Patterns. John

Wiley & Sons. ISBN 0-471-95869-7.

- Schmidt, Douglas C.; Stal, Michael; Rohnert, Hans; Buschmann, Frank (2000). Pattern-Oriented Software Architecture, Volume 2: Patterns for Concurrent and Networked Objects. John Wiley & Sons. ISBN 0-471-60695-2.

- Fowler, Martin (2002). Patterns of Enterprise Application Architecture. Addison-Wesley. ISBN 978-0-321-12742-6.

- Hohpe, Gregor; Woolf, Bobby (2003). Enterprise Integration Patterns: Designing, Building, and Deploying Messaging Solutions. Addison-Wesley. ISBN 0-321-20068-3.

- Freeman, Eric T; Robson, Elisabeth; Bates, Bert; Sierra, Kathy (2004). Head First Design Patterns. O'Reilly Media. ISBN 0-596-00712-4.

Although design patterns have been applied practically for a long time, formalization of the concept of design patterns languished for several years.

Practice

Design patterns can speed up the development process by providing tested, proven development paradigms. Effective software design requires considering issues that may not become visible until later in the implementation. Reusing design patterns helps to prevent subtle issues that can cause major problems, and it also improves code readability for coders and architects who are familiar with the patterns.

In order to achieve flexibility, design patterns usually introduce additional levels of indirection, which in some cases may complicate the resulting designs and hurt application performance.

By definition, a pattern must be programmed anew into each application that uses it. Since some authors see this as a step backward from software reuse as provided by components, researchers have worked to turn patterns into components. Meyer and Arnout were able to provide full or partial componentization of two-thirds of the patterns they attempted.

Software design techniques are difficult to apply to a broader range of problems. Design patterns provide general solutions, documented in a format that does not require specifics tied to a particular problem.

Structure

Design patterns are composed of several sections. Of particular interest are the Structure, Participants, and Collaboration sections. These sections describe a *design motif*: a prototypical *micro-architecture* that developers copy and adapt to their particular designs to solve the recurrent problem described by the design pattern. A micro-architecture is a set of program constituents (e.g., classes, methods...) and their relationships. Developers use the design pattern by introducing in their designs this prototypical micro-architecture, which means that micro-architectures in their designs will have structure and organization similar to the chosen design motif.

Domain-specific Patterns

Efforts have also been made to codify design patterns in particular domains, including use of existing design patterns as well as domain specific design patterns. Examples include user interface design patterns, information visualization, secure design, "secure usability", Web design and business model design.

The annual Pattern Languages of Programming Conference proceedings include many examples of domain-specific patterns.

Classification and List

Design patterns were originally grouped into the categories: creational patterns, structural patterns, and behavioral patterns, and described using the concepts of delegation, aggregation, and consultation. For further background on object-oriented design, see coupling and cohesion, inheritance, interface, and polymorphism. Another classification has also introduced the notion of architectural design pattern that may be applied at the architecture level of the software such as the Model–View–Controller pattern.

Creational Patterns

Name	Description	In Design Patterns	In Code Complete	Other
Abstract factory	Provide an interface for creating families of related or dependent objects without specifying their concrete classes.	Yes	Yes	N/A
Builder	Separate the construction of a complex object from its representation, allowing the same construction process to create various representations.	Yes	No	N/A
Factory method	Define an interface for creating a single object, but let subclasses decide which class to instantiate. Factory Method lets a class defer instantiation to subclasses (dependency injection).	Yes	Yes	N/A

Lazy initialization	Tactic of delaying the creation of an object, the calculation of a value, or some other expensive process until the first time it is needed. This pattern appears in the GoF catalog as "virtual proxy", an implementation strategy for the Proxy pattern.	Yes	No	PoEAA
Multiton	Ensure a class has only named instances, and provide a global point of access to them.	No	No	N/A
Object pool	Avoid expensive acquisition and release of resources by recycling objects that are no longer in use. Can be considered a generalisation of connection pool and thread pool patterns.	No	No	N/A
Prototype	Specify the kinds of objects to create using a prototypical instance, and create new objects from the 'skeleton' of an existing object, thus boosting performance and keeping memory footprints to a minimum.	Yes	No	N/A
Resource acquisition is initialization (RAII)	Ensure that resources are properly released by tying them to the lifespan of suitable objects.	No	No	N/A
Singleton	Ensure a class has only one instance, and provide a global point of access to it.	Yes	Yes	N/A

Structural Patterns

Name	Description	In Design Patterns	In Code Complete	Other
Adapter or Wrapper or Translator	Convert the interface of a class into another interface clients expect. An adapter lets classes work together that could not otherwise because of incompatible interfaces. The enterprise integration pattern equivalent is the translator.	Yes	Yes	N/A
Bridge	Decouple an abstraction from its implementation allowing the two to vary independently.	Yes	Yes	N/A
Composite	Compose objects into tree structures to represent part-whole hierarchies. Composite lets clients treat individual objects and compositions of objects uniformly.	Yes	Yes	N/A
Decorator	Attach additional responsibilities to an object dynamically keeping the same interface. Decorators provide a flexible alternative to subclassing for extending functionality.	Yes	Yes	N/A

Extension object	Adding functionality to a hierarchy without changing the hierarchy.	No	No	Agile Software Development, Principles, Patterns, and Practices
Facade	Provide a unified interface to a set of interfaces in a subsystem. Facade defines a higher-level interface that makes the subsystem easier to use.	Yes	Yes	N/A
Flyweight	Use sharing to support large numbers of similar objects efficiently.	Yes	No	N/A
Front controller	The pattern relates to the design of Web applications. It provides a centralized entry point for handling requests.	No	Yes	N/A
Marker	Empty interface to associate metadata with a class.	No	No	Effective Java
Module	Group several related elements, such as classes, singletons, methods, globally used, into a single conceptual entity.	No	No	N/A
Proxy	Provide a surrogate or placeholder for another object to control access to it.	Yes	No	N/A
Twin	Twin allows modeling of multiple inheritance in programming languages that do not support this feature.	No	No	N/A

Behavioral Patterns

Name	Description	In Design Patterns	In Code Complete	Other
Blackboard	Artificial intelligence pattern for combining disparate sources of data	No	No	N/A
Chain of responsibility	Avoid coupling the sender of a request to its receiver by giving more than one object a chance to handle the request. Chain the receiving objects and pass the request along the chain until an object handles it.	Yes	No	N/A
Command	Encapsulate a request as an object, thereby allowing for the parameterization of clients with different requests, and the queuing or logging of requests. It also allows for the support of undoable operations.	Yes	No	N/A
Interpreter	Given a language, define a representation for its grammar along with an interpreter that uses the representation to interpret sentences in the language.	Yes	No	N/A

Iterator	Provide a way to access the elements of an aggregate object sequentially without exposing its underlying representation.	Yes	Yes	N/A
Mediator	Define an object that encapsulates how a set of objects interact. Mediator promotes loose coupling by keeping objects from referring to each other explicitly, and it allows their interaction to vary independently.	Yes	No	N/A
Memento	Without violating encapsulation, capture and externalize an object's internal state allowing the object to be restored to this state later.	Yes	No	N/A
Null object	Avoid null references by providing a default object.	No	No	N/A
Observer or Publish/subscribe	Define a one-to-many dependency between objects where a state change in one object results in all its dependents being notified and updated automatically.	Yes	Yes	N/A
Servant	Define common functionality for a group of classes.	No	No	N/A
Specification	Recombinable business logic in a Boolean fashion.	No	No	N/A
State	Allow an object to alter its behavior when its internal state changes. The object will appear to change its class.	Yes	No	N/A
Strategy	Define a family of algorithms, encapsulate each one, and make them interchangeable. Strategy lets the algorithm vary independently from clients that use it.	Yes	Yes	N/A
Template method	Define the skeleton of an algorithm in an operation, deferring some steps to subclasses. Template method lets subclasses redefine certain steps of an algorithm without changing the algorithm's structure.	Yes	Yes	N/A
Visitor	Represent an operation to be performed on the elements of an object structure. Visitor lets a new operation be defined without changing the classes of the elements on which it operates.	Yes	No	N/A

Concurrency Patterns

Name	Description	In POSA2	Other
Active Object	Decouples method execution from method invocation that reside in their own thread of control. The goal is to introduce concurrency, by using asynchronous method invocation and a scheduler for handling requests.	Yes	N/A
Balking	Only execute an action on an object when the object is in a particular state.	No	N/A

Binding properties	Combining multiple observers to force properties in different objects to be synchronized or coordinated in some way.	No	N/A
Blockchain	Decentralized way to store data and agree on ways of processing it in a Merkle tree, optionally using Digital signature for any individual contributions.	No	N/A
Double-checked locking	Reduce the overhead of acquiring a lock by first testing the locking criterion (the 'lock hint') in an unsafe manner; only if that succeeds does the actual locking logic proceed. Can be unsafe when implemented in some language/hardware combinations. It can therefore sometimes be considered an anti-pattern.	Yes	N/A
Event-based asynchronous	Addresses problems with the asynchronous pattern that occur in multithreaded programs.	No	N/A
Guarded suspension	Manages operations that require both a lock to be acquired and a precondition to be satisfied before the operation can be executed.	No	N/A
Join	Join-pattern provides a way to write concurrent, parallel and distributed programs by message passing. Compared to the use of threads and locks, this is a high-level programming model.	No	N/A
Lock	One thread puts a "lock" on a resource, preventing other threads from accessing or modifying it.	No	PoEAA
Messaging design pattern (MDP)	Allows the interchange of information (i.e. messages) between components and applications.	No	N/A
Monitor object	An object whose methods are subject to mutual exclusion, thus preventing multiple objects from erroneously trying to use it at the same time.	Yes	N/A
Reactor	A reactor object provides an asynchronous interface to resources that must be handled synchronously.	Yes	N/A
Read-write lock	Allows concurrent read access to an object, but requires exclusive access for write operations.	No	N/A
Scheduler	Explicitly control when threads may execute single-threaded code.	No	N/A
Thread pool	A number of threads are created to perform a number of tasks, which are usually organized in a queue. Typically, there are many more tasks than threads. Can be considered a special case of the object pool pattern.	No	N/A
Thread-specific storage	Static or "global" memory local to a thread.	Yes	N/A

Documentation

The documentation for a design pattern describes the context in which the pattern is used, the forces within the context that the pattern seeks to resolve, and the suggested solution. There is no single, standard format for documenting design patterns. Rather, a variety of different formats have been used by different pattern authors. However, according to Martin Fowler, certain pattern forms have become more well-known than others, and consequently become common starting points for new pattern-writing efforts. One example of a commonly used documentation format is the one used by Erich Gamma, Richard Helm, Ralph Johnson and John Vlissides (collectively known as the "Gang of Four", or GoF for short) in their book *Design Patterns*. It contains the following sections:

- Pattern Name and Classification: A descriptive and unique name that helps in identifying and referring to the pattern.

- Intent: A description of the goal behind the pattern and the reason for using it.

- Also Known As: Other names for the pattern.

- Motivation (Forces): A scenario consisting of a problem and a context in which this pattern can be used.

- Applicability: Situations in which this pattern is usable; the context for the pattern.

- Structure: A graphical representation of the pattern. Class diagrams and Interaction diagrams may be used for this purpose.

- Participants: A listing of the classes and objects used in the pattern and their roles in the design.

- Collaboration: A description of how classes and objects used in the pattern interact with each other.

- Consequences: A description of the results, side effects, and trade offs caused by using the pattern.

- Implementation: A description of an implementation of the pattern; the solution part of the pattern.

- Sample Code: An illustration of how the pattern can be used in a programming language.

- Known Uses: Examples of real usages of the pattern.

- Related Patterns: Other patterns that have some relationship with the pattern; discussion of the differences between the pattern and similar patterns.

Criticism

The concept of design patterns has been criticized in several ways.

The design patterns may just be a sign of some missing features of a given programming language (Java or C++ for instance). Peter Norvig demonstrates that 16 out of the 23 patterns in the *Design Patterns* book (which is primarily focused on C++) are simplified or eliminated (via direct language support) in Lisp or Dylan. Related observations were made by Hannemann and Kiczales who implemented several of the 23 design patterns using an aspect-oriented programming language (AspectJ) and showed that code-level dependencies were removed from the implementations of 17 of the 23 design patterns and that aspect-oriented programming could simplify the implementations of design patterns.

Moreover, inappropriate use of patterns may unnecessarily increase complexity.

Facade Pattern

The facade pattern (or façade pattern) is a software design pattern commonly used with object-oriented programming. The name is by analogy to an architectural facade.

A facade is an object that provides a simplified interface to a larger body of code, such as a class library. A facade can:

- make a software library easier to use, understand and test, since the facade has convenient methods for common tasks;

- make the library more readable, for the same reason;

- reduce dependencies of outside code on the inner workings of a library, since most code uses the facade, thus allowing more flexibility in developing the system;

- wrap a poorly designed collection of APIs with a single well-designed API.

The Facade design pattern is often used when a system is very complex or difficult to understand because the system has a large number of interdependent classes or its source code is unavailable. This pattern hides the complexities of the larger system and provides a simpler interface to the client. It typically involves a single wrapper class which contains a set of members required by client. These members access the system on behalf of the facade client and hide the implementation details.

Usage

A Facade is used when an easier or simpler interface to an underlying object is desired. Alternatively, an adapter can be used when the wrapper must respect a particular interface and must support polymorphic behavior. A decorator makes it possible to add or alter behavior of an interface at run-time.

Pattern	Intent
Adapter	Converts one interface to another so that it matches what the client is expecting
Decorator	Dynamically adds responsibility to the interface by wrapping the original code
Facade	Provides a simplified interface

The facade pattern is typically used when:

- a simple interface is required to access a complex system;

- the abstractions and implementations of a subsystem are tightly coupled;

- need an entry point to each level of layered software; or

- a system is very complex or difficult to understand.

Structure

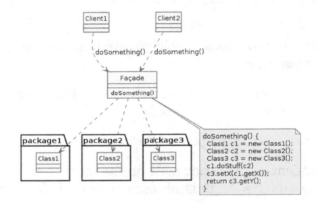

Facade

   The facade class abstracts Packages 1, 2, and 3 from the rest of the application.

Clients

   The objects are using the Facade Pattern to access resources from the Packages.

Example

This is an abstract example of how a client ("you") interacts with a facade (the "computer") to a complex system (internal computer parts, like CPU and HardDrive).

C#

Implementation

```
namespace Designpattern.Facade
```

```
{
    class SubsystemA
    {
        public string OperationA1()
        {
            return "Subsystem A, Method A1\n";
        }
        public string OperationA2()
        {
            return "Subsystem A, Method A2\n";
        }
    }

    class SubsystemB
    {
        public string OperationB1()
        {
            return "Subsystem B, Method B1\n";
        }

        public string OperationB2()
        {
            return "Subsystem B, Method B2\n";
        }
    }

    class SubsystemC
    {
```

```
    public string OperationC1()

    {

        return "Subsystem C, Method C1\n";

    }


    public string OperationC2()

    {

        return "Subsystem C, Method C2\n";

    }

}


public class Facade

{

    private readonly SubsystemA a = new SubsystemA();

    private readonly SubsystemB b = new SubsystemB();

    private readonly SubsystemC c = new SubsystemC();

    public void Operation1()

    {

        Console.WriteLine("Operation 1\n" +

            a.OperationA1() +

            b.OperationB1() +

            c.OperationC1());

    }

    public void Operation2()

    {

        Console.WriteLine("Operation 2\n" +

            a.OperationA2() +

            b.OperationB2() +
```

```
                        c.OperationC2());

        }

    }

}
```

Sample Code

```
namespace DesignPattern.Facade.Sample

{

    // The 'Subsystem ClassA' class

    class CarModel

    {

        public void SetModel()

        {

            Console.WriteLine(" CarModel - SetModel");

        }

    }


    /// <summary>

    /// The 'Subsystem ClassB' class

    /// </summary>

    class CarEngine

    {

        public void SetEngine()

        {

            Console.WriteLine(" CarEngine - SetEngine");

        }

    }


    // The 'Subsystem ClassC' class
```

```
class CarBody

{

    public void SetBody()

    {

        Console.WriteLine(" CarBody - SetBody");

    }

}


// The 'Subsystem ClassD' class
class CarAccessories

{

    public void SetAccessories()

    {

      Console.WriteLine(" CarAccessories - SetAccessories");

    }

}


// The 'Facade' class
public class CarFacade

{

    private readonly CarModel model;

    private readonly CarEngine engine;

    private readonly CarBody body;

    private readonly CarAccessories accessories;


    public CarFacade()

    {

        model = new CarModel();
```

```
        engine = new CarEngine();

        body = new CarBody();

        accessories = new CarAccessories();

    }


    public void CreateCompleteCar()

    {

    Console.WriteLine("******** Creating a Car **********");

        model.SetModel();

        engine.SetEngine();

        body.SetBody();

        accessories.SetAccessories();


        Console.WriteLine("******** Car creation is complet-
ed. **********");

    }

}


// Facade pattern demo

class Program

{

    static void Main(string[] args)

    {

        var facade = new CarFacade();


        facade.CreateCompleteCar();


        Console.ReadKey();

    }
```

```
        }
}
```

Java

```java
/* Complex parts */

class CPU {
    public void freeze() { ... }
    public void jump(long position) { ... }
    public void execute() { ... }
}


class Memory {
    public void load(long position, byte[] data) { ... }
}


class HardDrive {
    public byte[] read(long lba, int size) { ... }
}


/* Facade */

class ComputerFacade {
    private CPU processor;
    private Memory ram;
    private HardDrive hd;

    public ComputerFacade() {
        this.processor = new CPU();
```

```
        this.ram = new Memory();

        this.hd = new HardDrive();

    }


    public void start() {

        processor.freeze();

      ram.load(BOOT_ADDRESS, hd.read(BOOT_SECTOR, SECTOR_SIZE));

        processor.jump(BOOT_ADDRESS);

        processor.execute();

    }

}


/* Client */


class You {

    public static void main(String[] args) {

        ComputerFacade computer = new ComputerFacade();

        computer.start();

    }

}
```

Ruby

```ruby
# Complex Parts
class CPU
  def freeze; end
  def jump(position); end
  def execute; end
end
```

```ruby
class Memory
  def load(position, data); end
end


class HardDrive
  def read(lba, size); end
end


# Facade
class ComputerFacade

  def initialize
    @processor = CPU.new
    @ram = Memory.new
    @hd = HardDrive.new
  end

  def start
    @processor.freeze
    @ram.load(BOOT_ADDRESS, @hd.read(BOOT_SECTOR, SECTOR_SIZE))
    @processor.jump(BOOT_ADDRESS)
    @processor.execute
  end
end


# Client
computer_facade = ComputerFacade.new
computer_facade.start
```

Active Record Pattern

In software engineering, the active record pattern is an architectural pattern found in software that stores in-memory object data in relational databases. It was named by Martin Fowler in his 2003 book *Patterns of Enterprise Application Architecture*. The interface of an object conforming to this pattern would include functions such as Insert, Update, and Delete, plus properties that correspond more or less directly to the columns in the underlying database table.

The active record pattern is an approach to accessing data in a database. A database table or view is wrapped into a class. Thus, an object instance is tied to a single row in the table. After creation of an object, a new row is added to the table upon save. Any object loaded gets its information from the database. When an object is updated, the corresponding row in the table is also updated. The wrapper class implements accessor methods or properties for each column in the table or view.

This pattern is commonly used by object persistence tools and in object-relational mapping (ORM). Typically, foreign key relationships will be exposed as an object instance of the appropriate type via a property.

Implementations

Implementations of the concept can be found in various frameworks for many programming environments. For example, if in a database there is a table parts with columns name (string type) and price (number type), and the Active Record pattern is implemented in the class Part, the pseudo-code

```
part = new Part()

part.name = "Sample part"

part.price = 123.45

part.save()
```

will create a new row in the parts table with the given values, and is roughly equivalent to the SQL command

```
INSERT INTO parts (name, price) VALUES ('Sample part', 123.45);
```

Conversely, the class can be used to query the database:

```
b = Part.find_first("name", "gearbox")
```

This will find a new Part object based on the first matching row from the parts table whose name column has the value "gearbox". The SQL command used might be similar to the following, depending on the SQL implementation details of the database:

```
SELECT * FROM parts WHERE name = 'gearbox' LIMIT 1; -- MySQL or
PostgreSQL
```

ColdFusion

ColdFusion has an open source implementation of the active record pattern.

The ColdFusion on Wheels framework has an implementation of the active record pattern. It is open source and has the added advantage of requiring no complex configuration.

PHP

PHP ActiveRecord is one open-source library designed to fulfill the active record pattern.

Several open-source PHP frameworks also bundle their own ORM implementing the active record pattern. Most implementations support relationships, behaviors, validation, serialization and support for multiple data sources.

- Boiler, an MVC framework for PHP, contains a set of tools for auto-generation of active record models. The project, designed for data-centered projects, aims to automate as much of the development process as possible, using Apache Ant. Although a new addition to Open Source market, the project is already in use in many live applications, both commercially and open. The framework currently only supports MySQL though the developers have reported some commercial work in Postgres.

- Cygnite PHP Framework's default database layer implements Active Record pattern which closely resemble with Ruby on Rails.

- Laravel contains an ORM called 'Eloquent' which implements the active record pattern, closely resembling that of Ruby on Rails

- CakePHP's ORM implements the active record pattern, but as of version 2.x queries return arrays of data, with levels of related data as required. Version 3.0 uses objects.

- Lithium's ORM implements active record.

- Symfony's default database layer and ORM "Doctrine" does not implement active record but rather a data mapper approach.

- CodeIgniter has a query builder it calls "ActiveRecord", but which does not implement the Active Record pattern. Instead, it implements what the user guide refers to as a modified version of the pattern. The Active Record functionality in CodeIgniter can be achieved by using either CodeIgniter DataMapper library or CodeIgniter Gas ORM library.

- Yii's ORM also implements the active record pattern.

- Propel also implements the active record pattern.

- Paris is A lightweight Active Record implementation for PHP5, built on top of Idiorm.

Ruby

The Ruby library ActiveRecord implements ORM. It creates a persistable domain model from business objects and database tables, where logic and data are presented as a unified package. ActiveRecord adds inheritance and associations to the pattern above, solving two substantial limitations of that pattern. A set of macros acts as a domain language for the latter, and the Single Table Inheritance pattern is integrated for the former; thus, ActiveRecord increases the functionality of the active record pattern approach to database interaction. ActiveRecord is the default 'model' component of the model-view-controller web-application framework Ruby on Rails, and is also a standalone ORM package for other Ruby applications. In both forms, it was conceived of by David Heinemeier Hansson, and has been improved upon by a number of contributors.

Other, less popular ORMs have been released since ActiveRecord first took the stage. For example, DataMapper and Sequel show major improvements over the original ActiveRecord framework. As a response to their release and adoption by the Rails community, Ruby on Rails v3.0 is independent of an ORM system, so Rails users can easily plug in DataMapper or Sequel to use as their ORM of choice.

Java

The Java language implements the Active Record pattern via the ActiveJDBC library. ActiveJDBC is an implementation of Active Record design pattern inspired by Ruby on Rails ActiveRecord. ActiveJDBC is lightweight, fast, small and does not require any configuration.

ActiveJPA and jOOQ (for Java Object Oriented Querying) implements the Active record pattern, combining active records with source code generation and a querying DSL similar to SQL allowing for retrieving active records using complex SQL statements.

The Play framework is a Java web framework which implements the Active Record pattern, using ideas from Ruby on Rails.

JActiveRecord is yet another library providing easy ORM mapping for Java, inspired by Ruby on Rails ActiveRecord but more focused on Java's type-safety.

Dart

The Dart language implements the Active Record pattern via the Dartabase Migration and Dartabase Model packages

Dartabase Migration Serverside Database Object Models for simple data manipulation currently supporting MySQL/PGSQL inspired by Ruby on Rails Migration

Dartabase Model Serverside Database migration for simple version controlled database structure manipulation currently supporting MySQL/PGSQL inspired by Ruby on Rails Model now console and GUI (build in Polymer 1.0)

Other Languages

There are several open source implementations of the Active Record pattern in other languages, including JavaScript (e.g., ActiveJS's Active Record), Perl (DBIx::Class), ActionScript, Python, Haxe (SPOD), C#, Objective-C and Scala.

Criticism

Testability

Due to the coupling of database interaction and application logic when using the active record pattern, unit testing an active record object without a database becomes difficult. The negative effects on testability in the active record pattern can be minimized by using mocking or dependency injection frameworks to substitute the real data tier with a simulated one.

Single Responsibility Principle and Separation of Concerns

Another critique of the active record pattern is that, also due to the strong coupling of database interaction and application logic, an active record object does not follow the single responsibility principle and separation of concerns as opposed to multitier architecture which properly addresses these practices. Because of this, the active record pattern is best and most often employed in simple applications that are all forms-over-data with CRUD functionality, or only as one part of an architecture. Typically that part is data access and why several ORMs implement the active record pattern.

Flyweight Pattern

In computer programming, flyweight is a software design pattern. A flyweight is an object that minimizes memory use by sharing as much data as possible with other similar objects; it is a way to use objects in large numbers when a simple repeated representation would use an unacceptable amount of memory. Often some parts of the object state can be shared, and it is common practice to hold them in external data structures and pass them to the flyweight objects temporarily when they are used.

A classic example usage of the flyweight pattern is the data structures for graphical representation of characters in a word processor. It might be desirable to have, for each character in a document, a glyph object containing its font outline, font metrics, and other formatting data, but this would amount to hundreds or thousands of bytes for each character. Instead, for every character there might be a reference to a flyweight glyph object shared by every instance of the same character in the document; only the position of each character (in the document and/or the page) would need to be stored internally.

Another example is string interning.

In other contexts the idea of sharing identical data structures is called hash consing.

History

According to the textbook *Design Patterns: Elements of Reusable Object-Oriented Software*, the flyweight pattern was first coined and extensively explored by Paul Calder and Mark Linton in 1990 to efficiently handle glyph information in a WYSIWYG document editor, although similar techniques were already used in other systems, e.g., an application framework by Weinand et al. (1988).

Immutability and Equality

To enable safe sharing, between clients and threads, Flyweight objects must be immutable. Flyweight objects are by definition value objects. The identity of the object instance is of no consequence therefore two Flyweight instances of the same value are considered equal.

Example in C# (note Equals and GetHashCode overrides as well as == and != operator overloads):

```
public class CoffeeFlavour {

    private readonly string _flavour;


    public CoffeeFlavour(string flavour) {

        _flavour = flavour;

    }


    public string Flavour {

        get { return _flavour; }

    }
```

```
    public override bool Equals(object obj) {
        if (ReferenceEquals(null, obj)) return false;
        return obj is CoffeeFlavour && Equals((CoffeeFlavour)
obj);
    }


    public bool Equals(CoffeeFlavour other) {
        return string.Equals(_flavour, other._flavour);
    }


    public override int GetHashCode() {
        return (_flavour != null ? _flavour.GetHashCode() : 0);
    }


    public static bool operator ==(CoffeeFlavour a, CoffeeFla-
vour b) {
        return Equals(a, b);
    }


    public static bool operator !=(CoffeeFlavour a, CoffeeFla-
vour b) {
        return !Equals(a, b);
    }
}
```

Concurrency

Special consideration must be made in scenarios where Flyweight objects are created on multiple threads. If the list of values is finite and known in advance the Flyweights can be instantiated ahead of time and retrieved from a container on multiple threads with no contention. If Flyweights are instantiated on multiple threads there are two options:

1. Make Flyweight instantiation single threaded thus introducing contention and ensuring one instance per value.

2. Allow concurrent threads to create multiple Flyweight instances thus eliminating contention and allowing multiple instances per value. This option is only viable if the equality criterion is met.

Example in C#

```csharp
using System.Collections.Concurrent;

using System.Collections.Generic;

using System.Threading;


public interface ICoffeeFlavourFactory {

    CoffeeFlavour GetFlavour(string flavour);

}


public class ReducedMemoryFootprint : ICoffeeFlavourFactory {

    private readonly object _cacheLock = new object();

    private readonly IDictionary<string, CoffeeFlavour> _cache =
new Dictionary<string, CoffeeFlavour>();


    public CoffeeFlavour GetFlavour(string flavour) {

        if (_cache.ContainsKey(flavour)) return _cache[flavour];

        var coffeeFlavour = new CoffeeFlavour(flavour);

            ThreadPool.QueueUserWorkItem(AddFlavourToCache, cof-
feeFlavour);

        return coffeeFlavour;

    }


    private void AddFlavourToCache(object state) {

        var coffeeFlavour = (CoffeeFlavour)state;

        if (!_cache.ContainsKey(coffeeFlavour.Flavour)) {
```

```
        lock (_cacheLock) {
                if (!_cache.ContainsKey(coffeeFlavour.Flavour))
_cache.Add(coffeeFlavour.Flavour, coffeeFlavour);
            }
        }
    }
}


public class MinimumMemoryFootprint : ICoffeeFlavourFactory {
    private readonly ConcurrentDictionary<string, CoffeeFlavour>
_cache = new ConcurrentDictionary<string, CoffeeFlavour>();


    public CoffeeFlavour GetFlavour(string flavour) {
        return _cache.GetOrAdd(flavour, flv => new CoffeeFlavour(-
flv));
    }
}
```

Simple Implementation

Flyweight allows you to share bulky data that are common to each object. In other words, if you think that same data is repeating for every object, you can use this pattern to point to the single object and hence can easily save space. Here the FlyweightPointer creates a static member Company, which is used for every object of MyObject.

```
// Defines Flyweight object that repeats itself.

public class FlyWeight
{
    public string CompanyName { get; set; }
    public string CompanyLocation { get; set; }
    public string CompanyWebSite { get; set; }
    //Bulky Data
    public byte[] CompanyLogo { get; set; }
```

```
}


public static class FlyWeightPointer

{

    public static readonly FlyWeight Company = new FlyWeight

    {

        CompanyName = "Abc",

        CompanyLocation = "XYZ",

        CompanyWebSite = "www.abc.com"

        // Load CompanyLogo here

    };

}


public class MyObject

{

    public string Name { get; set; }

    public string Company

    {

        get

        {

            return FlyWeightPointer.Company.CompanyName;

        }

    }

}
```

Example in Java

```java
import java.util.List;

import java.util.Map;

import java.util.Vector;
```

```java
import java.util.concurrent.ConcurrentHashMap;


// Instances of CoffeeFlavour will be the Flyweights
class CoffeeFlavour {
  private final String name;


  CoffeeFlavour(final String newFlavor) {
    this.name = newFlavor;
  }


  @Override
  public String toString() {
    return name;
  }
}


// Menu acts as a factory and cache for CoffeeFlavour flyweight
objects
class Menu {
   private Map<String, CoffeeFlavour> flavours = new Concurren-
tHashMap<String, CoffeeFlavour>();


  CoffeeFlavour lookup(final String flavorName) {
    if (!flavours.containsKey(flavorName))
      flavours.put(flavorName, new CoffeeFlavour(flavorName));
    return flavours.get(flavorName);
  }


  int totalCoffeeFlavoursMade() {
```

```
      return flavours.size();
   }
}


// Order is the context of the CoffeeFlavour flyweight.
class Order {
   private final int tableNumber;
   private final CoffeeFlavour flavour;

   Order(final int tableNumber, final CoffeeFlavour flavor) {
      this.tableNumber = tableNumber;
      this.flavour = flavor;
   }

   void serve() {
      System.out.println("Serving " + flavour + " to table " + table-
Number);
   }
}


public class CoffeeShop {
   private final List<Order> orders = new Vector<Order>();
   private final Menu menu = new Menu();

   void takeOrder(final String flavourName, final int table) {
      CoffeeFlavour flavour = menu.lookup(flavourName);
      Order order = new Order(table, flavour);
      orders.add(order);
   }
```

```
void service() {

  for (Order order : orders)

    order.serve();

}


String report() {

  return "\ntotal CoffeeFlavour objects made: "

      + menu.totalCoffeeFlavoursMade();

}


public static void main(final String[] args) {

  CoffeeShop shop = new CoffeeShop();


  shop.takeOrder("Cappuccino", 2);

  shop.takeOrder("Frappe", 1);

  shop.takeOrder("Espresso", 1);

  shop.takeOrder("Frappe", 897);

  shop.takeOrder("Cappuccino", 97);

  shop.takeOrder("Frappe", 3);

  shop.takeOrder("Espresso", 3);

  shop.takeOrder("Cappuccino", 3);

  shop.takeOrder("Espresso", 96);

  shop.takeOrder("Frappe", 552);

  shop.takeOrder("Cappuccino", 121);

  shop.takeOrder("Espresso", 121);


  shop.service();
```

```
        System.out.println(shop.report());
    }
}
```

Example in Scala

```scala
/*
https://gist.github.com/pkinsky/111aee2f129c03ff1d0d
run as a script using `scala flyweight.scala`
expected output:
  Serving CoffeeFlavour(Espresso) to table 121
  Serving CoffeeFlavour(Cappuccino) to table 121
  Serving CoffeeFlavour(Frappe) to table 552
  Serving CoffeeFlavour(Espresso) to table 96
  Serving CoffeeFlavour(Cappuccino) to table 3
  Serving CoffeeFlavour(Espresso) to table 3
  Serving CoffeeFlavour(Frappe) to table 3
  Serving CoffeeFlavour(Cappuccino) to table 97
  Serving CoffeeFlavour(Frappe) to table 897
  Serving CoffeeFlavour(Espresso) to table 1
  Serving CoffeeFlavour(Frappe) to table 1
  Serving CoffeeFlavour(Cappuccino) to table 2
  total CoffeeFlavour objects made: 3
*/


class CoffeeFlavour(val name: String){
    override def toString = s"CoffeeFlavour($name)"
}


object CoffeeFlavour {
```

```scala
import scala.collection.mutable.Map
private val cache = Map.empty[String, CoffeeFlavour]


def apply(name: String): CoffeeFlavour =
  cache.getOrElseUpdate(name, new CoffeeFlavour(name))


def totalCoffeeFlavoursMade = cache.size
}



case class Order(tableNumber: Int, flavour: CoffeeFlavour){

  def serve: Unit =
    println(s"Serving $flavour to table $tableNumber")
}


object CoffeeShop {
  var orders = List.empty[Order]

  def takeOrder(flavourName: String, table: Int) {
    val flavour = CoffeeFlavour(flavourName)
    val order = Order(table, flavour)
    orders = order :: orders
  }


  def service: Unit = orders.foreach(_.serve)


  def report =
```

```
        s"total CoffeeFlavour objects made: ${CoffeeFlavour.total-
CoffeeFlavoursMade}"

}



CoffeeShop.takeOrder("Cappuccino", 2)

CoffeeShop.takeOrder("Frappe", 1)

CoffeeShop.takeOrder("Espresso", 1)

CoffeeShop.takeOrder("Frappe", 897)

CoffeeShop.takeOrder("Cappuccino", 97)

CoffeeShop.takeOrder("Frappe", 3)

CoffeeShop.takeOrder("Espresso", 3)

CoffeeShop.takeOrder("Cappuccino", 3)

CoffeeShop.takeOrder("Espresso", 96)

CoffeeShop.takeOrder("Frappe", 552)

CoffeeShop.takeOrder("Cappuccino", 121)

CoffeeShop.takeOrder("Espresso", 121)



CoffeeShop.service

println(CoffeeShop.report)
```

Example in Ruby

```ruby
# Flyweight Object
class Lamp
  attr_reader :color
  #attr_reader makes color attribute available outside
  #of the class by calling .color on a Lamp instance

  def initialize(color)
```

```ruby
    @color = color
  end
end


class TreeBranch
  def initialize(branch_number)
    @branch_number = branch_number
  end


  def hang(lamp)
    puts "Hang #{lamp.color} lamp on branch #{@branch_number}"
  end
end


# Flyweight Factory
class LampFactory
  def initialize
    @lamps = {}
  end


  def find_lamp(color)
    if @lamps.has_key?(color)
      # if the lamp already exists, reference it instead of cre-
ating a new one
      lamp = @lamps[color]
    else
      lamp = Lamp.new(color)
      @lamps[color] = lamp
    end
```

```ruby
      lamp
    end


    def total_number_of_lamps_made
      @lamps.size
    end
  end


  class ChristmasTree
    def initialize
      @lamp_factory = LampFactory.new
      @lamps_hung = 0


      dress_up_the_tree
    end


    def hang_lamp(color, branch_number)
      TreeBranch.new(branch_number).hang(@lamp_factory.find_lamp(-
  color))
      @lamps_hung += 1
    end


    def dress_up_the_tree
      hang_lamp('red', 1)
      hang_lamp('blue', 1)
      hang_lamp('yellow', 1)
      hang_lamp('red', 2)
      hang_lamp('blue', 2)
      hang_lamp('yellow', 2)
```

```
    hang_lamp('red', 3)

    hang_lamp('blue', 3)

    hang_lamp('yellow', 3)

    hang_lamp('red', 4)

    hang_lamp('blue', 4)

    hang_lamp('yellow', 4)

    hang_lamp('red', 5)

    hang_lamp('blue', 5)

    hang_lamp('yellow', 5)

    hang_lamp('red', 6)

    hang_lamp('blue', 6)

    hang_lamp('yellow', 6)

    hang_lamp('red', 7)

    hang_lamp('blue', 7)

    hang_lamp('yellow', 7)

    puts "Made #{@lamp_factory.total_number_of_lamps_made} total
lamps"

    puts "Hung #{@lamps_hung} total lamps"

  end

end
```

Example in Python

By default, instances of Python's new-style classes have a dictionary to store instance data. When there are many instances, the total space consumed by the many dictionaries can be large. Accordingly, new-style classes support a __slots__ class variable to save space. It works by suppressing the instance dictionary and instead making more compact objects with fixed pointers to predefined attributes. This forgoes the ability to easily add new attributes, but saves the space overhead of a sparse hash table for each instance.

```
class Part(object):
```

```
    __slots__ = ['part_number', 'part_name', 'unit_cost']


    def __init__(self, part_number, part_name, unit_cost):
        self.part_number = part_number
        self.part_name = part_name
        self.unit_cost = unit_cost


    def total_cost(self, quantity):
        return self.unit_cost * quantity


assembly = [(30, Part('XL123', 'xwidget', 1.25)),
            (20, Part('CQ456', 'jcog', 3.75)),
            (12, Part('MT789', 'cgear', 2.50))]


print(sum(part.total_cost(quantity) for quantity, part in assem-
bly))
```

Example in Swift

```swift
import Foundation


// Instances of CoffeeFlavour will be the Flyweights
struct CoffeeFlavor : CustomStringConvertible {
    var flavor: String
    var description: String { return flavor }
}


// Menu acts as a factory and cache for CoffeeFlavour flyweight
objects
struct Menu {
    private var flavors = [String: CoffeeFlavor]()
```

```
    mutating func lookup(flavor: String) -> CoffeeFlavor {
        if let f = flavors[flavor] { return f }
        else {
            let cFlavor = CoffeeFlavor(flavor: flavor)
            flavors[flavor] = cFlavor
            return cFlavor
        }
    }
}


struct CoffeeShop {
    private var orders = [Int: CoffeeFlavor]()
    private var menu = Menu()

    mutating func takeOrder(flavor flavor: String, table: Int) {
        orders[table] = menu.lookup(flavor)
    }

    func serve() {
        for (table, flavor) in orders {
            print("Serving \(flavor) to table \(table)")
        }
    }
}


let coffeeShop = CoffeeShop()
coffeeShop.takeOrder(flavor: "Cappuccino", table: 1)
```

```
coffeeShop.takeOrder(flavor: "Frappe", table: 3);

coffeeShop.takeOrder(flavor: "Espresso", table: 2);

coffeeShop.takeOrder(flavor: "Frappe", table: 15);

coffeeShop.takeOrder(flavor: "Cappuccino", table: 10);

coffeeShop.takeOrder(flavor: "Frappe", table: 8);

coffeeShop.takeOrder(flavor: "Espresso", table: 7);

coffeeShop.takeOrder(flavor: "Cappuccino", table: 4);

coffeeShop.takeOrder(flavor: "Espresso", table: 9);

coffeeShop.takeOrder(flavor: "Frappe", table: 12);

coffeeShop.takeOrder(flavor: "Cappuccino", table: 13);

coffeeShop.takeOrder(flavor: "Espresso", table: 5);

coffeeShop.serve()
```

Bridge Pattern

The bridge pattern is a design pattern used in software engineering that is meant to *"decouple an abstraction from its implementation so that the two can vary independently"*, introduced by the Gang of Four (GoF). The *bridge* uses encapsulation, aggregation, and can use inheritance to separate responsibilities into different classes.

When a class varies often, the features of object-oriented programming become very useful because changes to a program's code can be made easily with minimal prior knowledge about the program. The bridge pattern is useful when both the class and what it does vary often. The class itself can be thought of as the *abstraction* and what the class can do as the *implementation*. The bridge pattern can also be thought of as two layers of abstraction.

When there is only one fixed implementation, this pattern is known as the Pimpl idiom in the C++ world.

The bridge pattern is often confused with the adapter pattern. In fact, the bridge pattern is often implemented using the class adapter pattern, e.g. in the Java code below.

Variant: The implementation can be decoupled even more by deferring the presence of the implementation to the point where the abstraction is utilized.

Structure

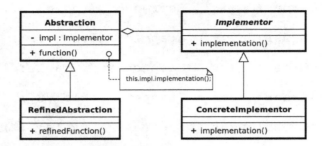

Abstraction (abstract class)

    defines the abstract interface

    maintains the Implementor reference.

RefinedAbstraction (normal class)

    extends the interface defined by Abstraction

Implementor (interface)

    defines the interface for implementation classes

ConcreteImplementor (normal class)

    implements the Implementor interface

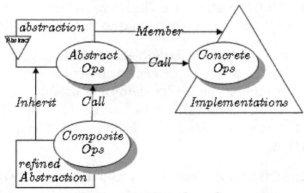

Bridge in LePUS3 (legend)

Example

C#

Bridge pattern compose objects in tree structure. It decouples abstraction from implementation. Here abstraction represents the client from which the objects will be called.

An example to implement in C# is given below

```csharp
// Helps in providing truly decoupled architecture
public interface IBridge
{
    void Function1();
    void Function2();
}


public class Bridge1 : IBridge
{
    public void Function1()
    {
        throw new NotImplementedException();
    }

    public void Function2()
    {
        throw new NotImplementedException();
    }
}


public class Bridge2 : IBridge
{
    public void Function1()
    {
        throw new NotImplementedException();
    }
```

```csharp
    public void Function2()
    {
        throw new NotImplementedException();
    }
}


public interface IAbstractBridge
{
    void CallMethod1();
    void CallMethod2();
}


public class AbstractBridge : IAbstractBridge
{
    public IBridge bridge;

    public AbstractBridge(IBridge bridge)
    {
        this.bridge = bridge;
    }

    public void CallMethod1()
    {
        this.bridge.Function1();
    }

    public void CallMethod2()
    {
```

```
        this.bridge.Function2();

    }

}
```

As you can see the Bridge classes are the Implementation, which uses the same interface oriented architecture to create objects. On the other hand, the abstraction takes an object of the implementation phase and runs its method. Thus makes it completely decoupled with one another.

Java

The following Java (SE 6) program illustrates a 'shape'.

```
/** "Implementor" */

interface DrawingAPI {

    public void drawCircle(final double x, final double y, final
double radius);

}


/** "ConcreteImplementor"  1/2 */

class DrawingAPI1 implements DrawingAPI {

    public void drawCircle(final double x, final double y, final
double radius) {

        System.out.printf("API1.circle at %f:%f radius %f\n", x,
y, radius);

    }

}


/** "ConcreteImplementor" 2/2 */

class DrawingAPI2 implements DrawingAPI {

    public void drawCircle(final double x, final double y, final
double radius) {

        System.out.printf("API2.circle at %f:%f radius %f\n", x,
y, radius);

    }
```

```
}


/** "Abstraction" */
abstract class Shape {
    protected DrawingAPI drawingAPI;


    protected Shape(final DrawingAPI drawingAPI){
        this.drawingAPI = drawingAPI;

    }


    public abstract void draw();                            //
low-level
        public abstract void resizeByPercentage(final double pct);
// high-level
}


/** "Refined Abstraction" */
class CircleShape extends Shape {
    private double x, y, radius;
    public CircleShape(final double x, final double y, final double
radius, final DrawingAPI drawingAPI) {
        super(drawingAPI);
        this.x = x;  this.y = y;  this.radius = radius;

    }


    // low-level i.e. Implementation specific
    public void draw() {
        drawingAPI.drawCircle(x, y, radius);
    }
```

```java
    // high-level i.e. Abstraction specific
    public void resizeByPercentage(final double pct) {
        radius *= (1.0 + pct/100.0);
    }
}


/** "Client" */
class BridgePattern {
    public static void main(final String[] args) {
        Shape[] shapes = new Shape[] {
            new CircleShape(1, 2, 3, new DrawingAPI1()),
            new CircleShape(5, 7, 11, new DrawingAPI2())
        };

        for (Shape shape : shapes) {
            shape.resizeByPercentage(2.5);
            shape.draw();
        }
    }
}
```

It will output:

```
API1.circle at 1.000000:2.000000 radius 3.075000
API2.circle at 5.000000:7.000000 radius 11.275000
```

PHP

```php
interface DrawingAPI {
    function drawCircle($x, $y, $radius);
}
```

```
class DrawingAPI1 implements DrawingAPI {
    public function drawCircle($x, $y, $radius) {
        echo "API1.circle at $x:$y radius $radius.\n";
    }
}


class DrawingAPI2 implements DrawingAPI {
    public function drawCircle($x, $y, $radius) {
        echo "API2.circle at $x:$y radius $radius.\n";
    }
}


abstract class Shape {
    protected $drawingAPI;

    public abstract function draw();
    public abstract function resizeByPercentage($pct);

    protected function __construct(DrawingAPI $drawingAPI) {
        $this->drawingAPI = $drawingAPI;
    }
}


class CircleShape extends Shape {
    private $x;
    private $y;
    private $radius;
```

```php
        public function __construct($x, $y, $radius, DrawingAPI
$drawingAPI) {

        parent::__construct($drawingAPI);

        $this->x = $x;

        $this->y = $y;

        $this->radius = $radius;

    }


    public function draw() {

            $this->drawingAPI->drawCircle($this->x,  $this->y,
$this->radius);

    }


    public function resizeByPercentage($pct) {

        $this->radius *= $pct;

    }

}


class Tester {
    public static function main()  {
        $shapes = array(
            new CircleShape(1, 3, 7,  new DrawingAPI1()),
            new CircleShape(5, 7, 11, new DrawingAPI2()),
        );


        foreach ($shapes as $shape) {
            $shape->resizeByPercentage(2.5);
            $shape->draw();

        }
```

```
      }
}


Tester::main();
```

Output:

```
API1.circle at 1:3 radius 17.5
API2.circle at 5:7 radius 27.5
```

Scala

```
trait DrawingAPI {
  def drawCircle(x: Double, y: Double, radius: Double)
}


class DrawingAPI1 extends DrawingAPI {
  def drawCircle(x: Double, y: Double, radius: Double) = print-
ln(s"API #1 $x $y $radius")
}


class DrawingAPI2 extends DrawingAPI {
  def drawCircle(x: Double, y: Double, radius: Double) = print-
ln(s"API #2 $x $y $radius")
}


abstract class Shape(drawingAPI: DrawingAPI) {
  def draw()
  def resizePercentage(pct: Double)
}


class CircleShape(x: Double, y: Double, var radius: Double, draw-
ingAPI: DrawingAPI)
```

```
    extends Shape (drawingAPI: DrawingAPI) {

  def draw() = drawingAPI.drawCircle(x, y, radius)

  def resizePercentage(pct: Double) { radius *= pct }
}


object BridgePattern {
  def main(args: Array[String]) {
    Seq (
      new CircleShape(1, 3, 5, new DrawingAPI1),
      new CircleShape(4, 5, 6, new DrawingAPI2)
    ) foreach { x =>
       x.resizePercentage(3)
       x.draw()
    }
  }
}
```

Builder Pattern

The builder pattern is an object creation software design pattern. Unlike the abstract factory pattern and the factory method pattern whose intention is to enable polymorphism, the intention of the builder pattern is to find a solution to the telescoping constructor anti-pattern. The telescoping constructor anti-pattern occurs when the increase of object constructor parameter combination leads to an exponential list of constructors. Instead of using numerous constructors, the builder pattern uses another object, a builder, that receives each initialization parameter step by step and then returns the resulting constructed object at once.

The builder pattern has another benefit. It can be used for objects that contain flat data (html code, SQL query, X.509 certificate...), that is to say, data that can't be easily edited. This type of data can't be edited step by step and must be edited at once.

Builder often builds a Composite. Often, designs start out using Factory Method (less complicated, more customizable, subclasses proliferate) and evolve toward Abstract Factory, Prototype, or Builder (more flexible, more complex) as the designer discovers where more flexibility is needed. Sometimes creational patterns are complementary: Builder can use one of the other patterns to implement which components are built. Builders are good candidates for a fluent interface.

Definition

The intent of the Builder design pattern is to separate the construction of a complex object from its representation. By doing so the same construction process can create different representations.

Advantages

- Allows you to vary a product's internal representation.
- Encapsulates code for construction and representation.
- Provides control over steps of construction process.

Disadvantages

- Requires creating a separate ConcreteBuilder for each different type of Product.

Structure

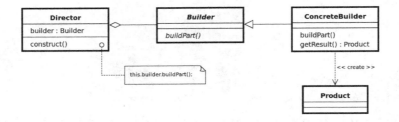

Builder

> Abstract interface for creating objects (product).

ConcreteBuilder

> Provides implementation for Builder. It is an object able to construct other objects. Constructs and assembles parts to build the objects.

Pseudocode

We have a Car class. The problem is that a car has many options. The combination of each option would lead to a huge list of constructors for this class. So we will create a builder class, CarBuilder. We will send to the CarBuilder each car option step by step and then construct the final car with the right options:

```
class Car is

    Can have GPS, trip computer and various numbers of seats.

    Can be a city car, a sports car, or a cabriolet.


class CarBuilder is

  method getResult() is

      output:  a Car with the right options

    Construct and return the car.


  method setSeats(number) is

      input:  the number of seats the car may have.

    Tell the builder the number of seats.


  method setCityCar() is

    Make the builder remember that the car is a city car.


  method setCabriolet() is

    Make the builder remember that the car is a cabriolet.


  method setSportsCar() is

    Make the builder remember that the car is a sports car.


  method setTripComputer() is

    Make the builder remember that the car has a trip computer.
```

```
method unsetTripComputer() is
```

Make the builder remember that the car does not have a trip computer.

```
method setGPS() is
```

Make the builder remember that the car has a global positioning system.

```
method unsetGPS() is
```

Make the builder remember that the car does not have a global positioning system.

```
Construct a CarBuilder called carBuilder

carBuilder.setSeats(2)

carBuilder.setSportsCar()

carBuilder.setTripComputer()

carBuilder.unsetGPS()

car := carBuilder.getResult()
```

Of course one could dispense with Builder and just do this:

```
car = new Car();

car.seats = 2;

car.type = CarType.SportsCar;

car.setTripComputer();

car.unsetGPS();

car.isValid();
```

So this indicates that the Builder pattern is more than just a means to limit constructor proliferation. It removes what could be a complex building process from being the responsibility of the user of the object that is built. It also allows for inserting new implementations of how an object is built without disturbing the client code.

Examples

C#

```csharp
//Represents a product created by the builder
public class Car
{
    public Car()
    {
    }

    public int Wheels { get; set; }

    public string Colour { get; set; }
}


//The builder abstraction
public interface ICarBuilder
{
    // Adding NotNull attribute to prevent null input argument
    void SetColour([NotNull]string colour);

    // Adding NotNull attribute to prevent null input argument
    void SetWheels([NotNull]int count);

    Car GetResult();
}


//Concrete builder implementation
public class CarBuilder : ICarBuilder
```

```csharp
{
    private Car _car;

    public CarBuilder()
    {
        this._car = new Car();
    }

    public void SetColour(string colour)
    {
        this._car.Colour = colour;
    }

    public void SetWheels(int count)
    {
        this._car.Wheels = count;
    }

    public Car GetResult()
    {
        return this._car;
    }
}


//The director
public class CarBuildDirector
{
    public Car Construct()
```

```
    {

        CarBuilder builder = new CarBuilder();


        builder.SetColour("Red");

        builder.SetWheels(4);


        return builder.GetResult();

    }

}
```

The Director assembles a car instance in the example above, delegating the construction to a separate builder object.

C++

```
////// Product declarations and inline impl. (possibly Product.h) //////

class Product{

        public:

                // use this class to construct Product

                class Builder;



        private:

                // variables in need of initialization to make
valid object

                const int i;

                const float f;

                const char c;



                // Only one simple constructor - rest is handled
by Builder

                Product( const int i, const float f, const char c )
: i(i), f(f), c(c) {}
```

```cpp
    public:

            // Product specific functionality
            void print();
            void doSomething();
            void doSomethingElse();
};



class Product::Builder{
        private:
                // variables needed for construction of object of
Product class
                int i;
                float f;
                char c;


        public:
                // default values for variables
                static const int defaultI = 1;
                static const float defaultF = 3.1415f;
                static const char defaultC = 'a';


                // create Builder with default values assigned
                // (in C++11 they can be simply assigned above on
declaration instead)
                Builder() : i( defaultI ), f( defaultF ), c( de-
faultC ){}
```

```
                    // sets custom values for Product creation

                    // returns Builder for shorthand inline usage (same
way as cout <<)

                    Builder& setI( const int i ){ this->i = i; return
*this; }

                    Builder& setF( const float f ){ this->f = f; return
*this; }

                    Builder& setC( const char c ){ this->c = c; return
*this; }


                    // prepare specific frequently desired Product

                    // returns Builder for shorthand inline usage (same
way as cout <<)

                    Builder& setProductP(){

                        this->i = 42;

                        this->f = -1.0f/12.0f;

                        this->c = '@';


                        return *this;

                    }


                    // produce desired Product

                    Product build(){

                        // here optionaly check variable consisten-
cy

                        // and also if Product is buildable from
given information

                        return Product( this->i, this->f, this->c
);

                    }
```

```cpp
};
///// Product implementation (possibly Product.cpp) /////
#include <iostream>

void Product::print(){
        using namespace std;

        cout << "Product internals dump:" << endl;
        cout << "i: " << this->i << endl;
        cout << "f: " << this->f << endl;
        cout << "c: " << this->c << endl;
}


void Product::doSomething(){}
void Product::doSomethingElse(){}
////////////////////// Usage of Builder (replaces Director from
diagram)
int main(){
        // simple usage
        Product  p1  =  Product::Builder().setI(2).setF(0.5f).
setC('x').build();

        p1.print(); // test p1

        // advanced usage
        Product::Builder b;
        b.setProductP();
        Product p2 = b.build(); // get Product P object
        b.setC('!'); // customize Product P
        Product p3 = b.build();
```

```java
        p2.print(); // test p2
        p3.print(); // test p3
}
```

Java

```java
/**
 * Represents the product created by the builder.
 */
class Car {
    private int wheels;
    private String color;

    public Car() {
    }

    @Override
    public String toString() {
        return "Car [wheels=" + wheels + ", color=" + color + "]";
    }

    public int getWheels() {
        return wheels;
    }

    public void setWheels(int wheels) {
        this.wheels = wheels;
    }

    public String getColor() {
```

```
            return color;

        }


        public void setColor(String color) {

            this.color = color;

        }

    }


    /**

     * The builder abstraction.

     */

    interface CarBuilder {

        void setWheels(int wheels);


        void setColor(String color);


        Car getResult();

    }


    class CarBuilderImpl implements CarBuilder {

        private Car car;


        public CarBuilderImpl() {

            car = new Car();

        }


        @Override

        public void setWheels(int wheels) {
```

```java
        car.setWheels(wheels);
    }


    @Override
    public void setColor(String color) {
        car.setColor(color);
    }


    @Override
    public Car getResult() {
        return car;
    }

}

public class CarBuildDirector {
    private CarBuilder builder;


    public CarBuildDirector(CarBuilder builder) {
        this.builder = builder;
    }


    public Car construct() {
        builder.setWheels(4);
        builder.setColor("Red");
        return builder.getResult();
    }


    public static void main(String[] args) {
```

```java
        CarBuilder builder = new CarBuilderImpl();

         CarBuildDirector carBuildDirector = new CarBuildDirec-
tor(builder);

        System.out.println(carBuildDirector.construct());

    }

}
```

PHP

```php
abstract class GetterSetter
{
    public function __get($name)
    {
        $method = sprintf('get%s', ucfirst($name));

        if (!method_exists($this, $method)) {
            throw new Exception();
        }

        return $this->$method();
    }

    public function __set($name, $v)
    {
        $method = sprintf('set%s', ucfirst($name));

        if (!method_exists($this, $method)) {
            throw new Exception();
        }
```

```
            $this->$method($v);

    }

}


//Represents a product created by the builder
class Car extends GetterSetter
{
    private $wheels;
    private $colour;


    function __construct()
    {

    }


    public function setWheels($wheels)
    {
        $this->wheels = $wheels;
    }


    public function getWheels()
    {
        return $this->wheels;
    }


    public function setColour($colour)
```

```php
    {
        $this->colour = $colour;
    }


    public function getColour()
    {
        return $this->colour;
    }
}


//The builder abstraction
interface ICarBuilder
{
    public function SetColour($colour);
    public function SetWheels($count);
    public function GetResult();
}


//Concrete builder implementation
class CarBuilder implements ICarBuilder
{
    private $_car;

    function __construct()
    {
        $this->_car = new Car();
```

```php
    }

    public function SetColour($colour)
    {
        $this->_car->Colour = $colour;
    }

    public function SetWheels($count)
    {
        $this->_car->Wheels = $count;
    }

    public function GetResult()
    {
        return $this->_car;
    }
}

//The director
class CarBuildDirector
{
    public $builder;

    function __construct($color = "White", $wheels = 4)
    {
        $this->builder = new CarBuilder();
```

```
        $this->builder->SetColour($color);

        $this->builder->SetWheels($wheels);

    }


    public function GetResult()

    {

        return $this->builder->GetResult();

    }

}
```

Composite Pattern

In software engineering, the composite pattern is a partitioning design pattern. The composite pattern describes that a group of objects is to be treated in the same way as a single instance of an object. The intent of a composite is to "compose" objects into tree structures to represent part-whole hierarchies. Implementing the composite pattern lets clients treat individual objects and compositions uniformly.

Motivation

When dealing with Tree-structured data, programmers often have to discriminate between a leaf-node and a branch. This makes code more complex, and therefore, error prone. The solution is an interface that allows treating complex and primitive objects uniformly. In object-oriented programming, a composite is an object designed as a composition of one-or-more similar objects, all exhibiting similar functionality. This is known as a "has-a" relationship between objects. The key concept is that you can manipulate a single instance of the object just as you would manipulate a group of them. The operations you can perform on all the composite objects often have a least common denominator relationship. For example, if defining a system to portray grouped shapes on a screen, it would be useful to define resizing a group of shapes to have the same effect (in some sense) as resizing a single shape.

When to use

Composite should be used when clients ignore the difference between compositions of objects and individual objects. If programmers find that they are using multiple objects in the same way, and often have nearly identical code to handle each of them, then composite is a good choice; it is less complex in this situation to treat primitives and composites as homogeneous.

Structure

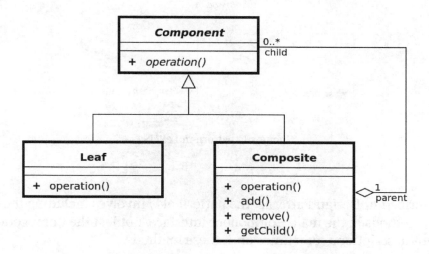

Composite pattern in UML.

Component

- is the abstraction for all components, including composite ones

- declares the interface for objects in the composition

- (optional) defines an interface for accessing a component's parent in the recursive structure, and implements it if that's appropriate

Leaf

- represents leaf objects in the composition

- implements all Component methods

Composite

- represents a composite Component (component having children)

- implements methods to manipulate children

- implements all Component methods, generally by delegating them to its children

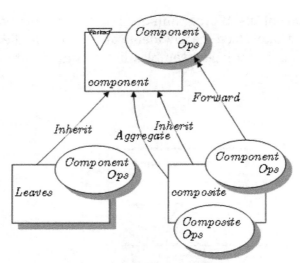

Composite pattern in LePUS3.

Variation

As it is described in Design Patterns, the pattern also involves including the child-manipulation methods in the main Component interface, not just the Composite subclass. More recent descriptions sometimes omit these methods.

Example

The following example, written in Java, implements a graphic class, which can be either an ellipse or a composition of several graphics. Every graphic can be printed. In Backus-Naur form,

        Graphic ::= ellipse | GraphicList

        GraphicList ::= empty | Graphic GraphicList

It could be extended to implement several other shapes (rectangle, etc.) and methods (translate, etc.).

Java

```
/** "Component" */

interface Graphic {


    //Prints the graphic.

    public void print();

}
```

```java
/** "Composite" */
import java.util.List;
import java.util.ArrayList;
class CompositeGraphic implements Graphic {

    //Collection of child graphics.
    private List<Graphic> childGraphics = new ArrayList<Graphic>();

    //Prints the graphic.
    public void print() {
        for (Graphic graphic : childGraphics) {
            graphic.print();
        }
    }

    //Adds the graphic to the composition.
    public void add(Graphic graphic) {
        childGraphics.add(graphic);
    }

    //Removes the graphic from the composition.
    public void remove(Graphic graphic) {
        childGraphics.remove(graphic);
    }
}

/** "Leaf" */
```

```java
class Ellipse implements Graphic {

    //Prints the graphic.
    public void print() {
        System.out.println("Ellipse");
    }
}


/** Client */
public class Program {

    public static void main(String[] args) {
        //Initialize four ellipses
        Ellipse ellipse1 = new Ellipse();
        Ellipse ellipse2 = new Ellipse();
        Ellipse ellipse3 = new Ellipse();
        Ellipse ellipse4 = new Ellipse();


        //Initialize three composite graphics
        CompositeGraphic graphic = new CompositeGraphic();
        CompositeGraphic graphic1 = new CompositeGraphic();
        CompositeGraphic graphic2 = new CompositeGraphic();


        //Composes the graphics
        graphic1.add(ellipse1);
        graphic1.add(ellipse2);
        graphic1.add(ellipse3);
```

```
    graphic2.add(ellipse4);

    graphic.add(graphic1);

    graphic.add(graphic2);


    //Prints the complete graphic (four times the string
"Ellipse").

    graphic.print();
  }

}
```

C#

The following example, written in C#.

```
namespace CompositePattern
{
    using System;
    using System.Collections.Generic;
    using System.Linq;
    //Client
    class Program
    {
        static void Main(string[] args)
        {
            // initialize variables
            var compositeGraphic = new CompositeGraphic();
            var compositeGraphic1 = new CompositeGraphic();
            var compositeGraphic2 = new CompositeGraphic();

            //Add 1 Graphic to compositeGraphic1
```

```
        compositeGraphic1.Add(new Ellipse());

        //Add 2 Graphic to compositeGraphic2
        compositeGraphic2.AddRange(new Ellipse(),
            new Ellipse());

        /*Add 1 Graphic, compositeGraphic1, and
            compositeGraphic2 to compositeGraphic */
        compositeGraphic.AddRange(new Ellipse(),
            compositeGraphic1,
            compositeGraphic2);

        /*Prints the complete graphic
        (four times the string "Ellipse").*/
        compositeGraphic.Print();
        Console.ReadLine();
    }
}
//Component
public interface IGraphic
{
    void Print();
}
//Leaf
public class Ellipse : IGraphic
{
    //Prints the graphic
    public void Print()
```

```
        {
            Console.WriteLine("Ellipse");
        }
    }
//Composite
public class CompositeGraphic : IGraphic
{
    //Collection of Graphics.
    private readonly List<IGraphic> graphics;

    //Constructor
    public CompositeGraphic()
    {
        //initialize generic Collection(Composition)
        graphics = new List<IGraphic>();
    }
    //Adds the graphic to the composition
    public void Add(IGraphic graphic)
    {
        graphics.Add(graphic);
    }
    //Adds multiple graphics to the composition
    public void AddRange(params IGraphic[] graphic)
    {
        graphics.AddRange(graphic);
    }
    //Removes the graphic from the composition
    public void Delete(IGraphic graphic)
```

```
        {
            graphics.Remove(graphic);
        }
        //Prints the graphic.
        public void Print()
        {
            foreach (var childGraphic in graphics)
            {
                childGraphic.Print();
            }
        }
    }
}
//////Ad
```

Simple Example

```
/// Treats elements as composition of one or more elements, so
that components can be separated
/// between one another
public interface IComposite
{
    void CompositeMethod();
}


public class LeafComposite :IComposite
{
    public void CompositeMethod()
    {
        //To Do something
```

```
        }
    }


/// Elements from IComposite can be separated from others
public class NormalComposite : IComposite
{
    public void CompositeMethod()
    {
        //To Do Something
    }


    public void DoSomethingMore()
    {
        //Do Something more.
    }
}
```

Strategy Pattern

In computer programming, the strategy pattern (also known as the policy pattern) is a behavioural software design pattern that enables an algorithm's behavior to be selected at runtime. The strategy pattern

- defines a family of algorithms,

- encapsulates each algorithm, and

- makes the algorithms interchangeable within that family.

Strategy lets the algorithm vary independently from clients that use it. Strategy is one of the patterns included in the influential book *Design Patterns* by Gamma et al. that popularized the concept of using patterns to describe software design.

For instance, a class that performs validation on incoming data may use a strategy pattern to select a validation algorithm based on the type of data, the source of the data, user choice, or other discriminating factors. These factors are not known for each case until run-time, and may require radically different validation to be performed. The validation strategies, encapsulated separately from the validating object, may be used by other validating objects in different areas of the system (or even different systems) without code duplication.

The essential requirement in the programming language is the ability to store a reference to some code in a data structure and retrieve it. This can be achieved by mechanisms such as the native function pointer, the first-class function, classes or class instances in object-oriented programming languages, or accessing the language implementation's internal storage of code via reflection.

Structure

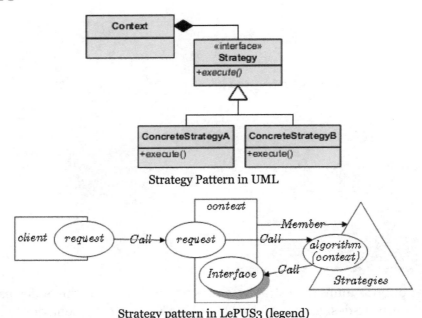

Strategy Pattern in UML

Strategy pattern in LePUS3 (legend)

Example

C#

The following example is in C#.

```
1 using System;
2
3 public class Program
4 {
```

```
5      public static void Main()

6      {

7              CalculateClient client = new CalculateClient();

8

9              client.SetCalculate(new Minus());

10             Console.WriteLine("Minus: " + client.Calculate(7,
1));

11

12             client.SetCalculate(new Plus());

13             Console.WriteLine("Plus: " + client.Calculate(7,
1));

14     }

15 }

16

17 //The interface for the strategies

18 public interface ICalculate

19 {

20    int Calculate(int value1, int value2);

21 }

22

23 //strategies

24 //Strategy 1: Minus

25 public class Minus : ICalculate

26 {

27     public int Calculate(int value1, int value2)

28     {

29          return value1 - value2;

30     }

31 }
```

```
32
33 //Strategy 2: Plus
34 public class Plus : ICalculate
35 {
36     public int Calculate(int value1, int value2)
37     {
38          return value1 + value2;
39     }
40 }
41
42 //The client
43 public class CalculateClient
44 {
45     private ICalculate strategy;
46
47     //Executes the strategy
48     public int Calculate(int value1, int value2)
49     {
50          return strategy.Calculate(value1, value2);
51     }
52
53     //Change the strategy
54     public void SetCalculate(ICalculate strategy){
55          this.strategy = strategy;
56     }
57 }
```

Java

The following example is in Java.

```java
import java.util.ArrayList;

import java.util.List;


public class StrategyPatternWiki {


    public static void main(final String[] arguments) {

        Customer firstCustomer = new Customer(new NormalStrate-
gy());


        // Normal billing

        firstCustomer.add(1.0, 1);


        // Start Happy Hour

        firstCustomer.setStrategy(new HappyHourStrategy());

        firstCustomer.add(1.0, 2);


        // New Customer

        Customer secondCustomer = new Customer(new HappyHour-
Strategy());

        secondCustomer.add(0.8, 1);

        // The Customer pays

        firstCustomer.printBill();


        // End Happy Hour

        secondCustomer.setStrategy(new NormalStrategy());

        secondCustomer.add(1.3, 2);

        secondCustomer.add(2.5, 1);

        secondCustomer.printBill();

    }
```

```java
}


class Customer {

    private List<Double> drinks;
    private BillingStrategy strategy;

    public Customer(final BillingStrategy strategy) {
        this.drinks = new ArrayList<Double>();
        this.strategy = strategy;
    }


    public void add(final double price, final int quantity) {
        drinks.add(strategy.getActPrice(price*quantity));
    }


    // Payment of bill
    public void printBill() {
        double sum = 0;
        for (Double i : drinks) {
            sum += i;
        }
        System.out.println("Total due: " + sum);
        drinks.clear();
    }


    // Set Strategy
    public void setStrategy(final BillingStrategy strategy) {
```

```java
            this.strategy = strategy;
    }


}


interface BillingStrategy {
    public double getActPrice(final double rawPrice);
}


// Normal billing strategy (unchanged price)
class NormalStrategy implements BillingStrategy {

    @Override
    public double getActPrice(final double rawPrice) {
        return rawPrice;
    }

}


// Strategy for Happy hour (50% discount)
class HappyHourStrategy implements BillingStrategy {

    @Override
    public double getActPrice(final double rawPrice) {
        return rawPrice*0.5;
    }

}
```

A much simpler example in "modern Java" (Java 8 and later), using lambdas, may be found here.

Strategy and Open/Closed Principle

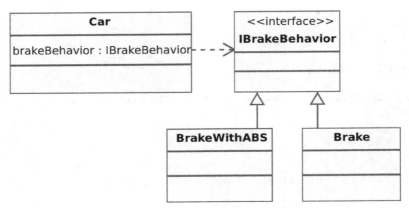

Accelerate and brake behaviors must be declared in each new car model.

According to the strategy pattern, the behaviors of a class should not be inherited. Instead they should be encapsulated using interfaces. As an example, consider a car class. Two possible functionalities for car are *brake* and *accelerate*.

Since accelerate and brake behaviors change frequently between models, a common approach is to implement these behaviors in subclasses. This approach has significant drawbacks: accelerate and brake behaviors must be declared in each new Car model. The work of managing these behaviors increases greatly as the number of models increases, and requires code to be duplicated across models. Additionally, it is not easy to determine the exact nature of the behavior for each model without investigating the code in each.

The strategy pattern uses composition instead of inheritance. In the strategy pattern, behaviors are defined as separate interfaces and specific classes that implement these interfaces. This allows better decoupling between the behavior and the class that uses the behavior. The behavior can be changed without breaking the classes that use it, and the classes can switch between behaviors by changing the specific implementation used without requiring any significant code changes. Behaviors can also be changed at run-time as well as at design-time. For instance, a car object's brake behavior can be changed from BrakeWithABS() to Brake() by changing the brakeBehavior member to:

```
brakeBehavior = new Brake();

/* Encapsulated family of Algorithms

 * Interface and its implementations

 */
```

```java
public interface IBrakeBehavior {
    public void brake();
}


public class BrakeWithABS implements IBrakeBehavior {
    public void brake() {
        System.out.println("Brake with ABS applied");
    }
}


public class Brake implements IBrakeBehavior {
    public void brake() {
        System.out.println("Simple Brake applied");
    }
}


/* Client that can use the algorithms above interchangeably */
public abstract class Car {
    protected IBrakeBehavior brakeBehavior;

    public void applyBrake() {
        brakeBehavior.brake();
    }

    public void setBrakeBehavior(final IBrakeBehavior brakeType) {
        this.brakeBehavior = brakeType;
    }
}
```

```java
/* Client 1 uses one algorithm (Brake) in the constructor */
public class Sedan extends Car {
    public Sedan() {
        this.brakeBehavior = new Brake();
    }
}


/* Client 2 uses another algorithm (BrakeWithABS) in the con-
structor */
public class SUV extends Car {
    public SUV() {
        this.brakeBehavior = new BrakeWithABS();
    }
}


/* Using the Car example */
public class CarExample {
    public static void main(final String[] arguments) {
        Car sedanCar = new Sedan();
        sedanCar.applyBrake();  // This will invoke class "Brake"


        Car suvCar = new SUV();
        suvCar.applyBrake();    // This will invoke class "Brake-
WithABS"


        // set brake behavior dynamically
        suvCar.setBrakeBehavior( new Brake() );
        suvCar.applyBrake();    // This will invoke class "Brake"
```

```
        }

}
```

This gives greater flexibility in design and is in harmony with the Open/closed principle (OCP) that states that classes should be open for extension but closed for modification.

Specification Pattern

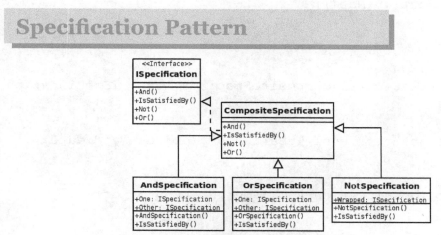

Specification Pattern in UML

In computer programming, the specification pattern is a particular software design pattern, whereby business rules can be recombined by chaining the business rules together using boolean logic. The pattern is frequently used in the context of domain-driven design.

A specification pattern outlines a business rule that is combinable with other business rules. In this pattern, a unit of business logic inherits its functionality from the abstract aggregate Composite Specification class. The Composite Specification class has one function called IsSatisfiedBy that returns a boolean value. After instantiation, the specification is "chained" with other specifications, making new specifications easily maintainable, yet highly customizable business logic. Furthermore, upon instantiation the business logic may, through method invocation or inversion of control, have its state altered in order to become a delegate of other classes such as a persistence repository.

Code Examples

C#

```csharp
public interface ISpecification
{
    bool IsSatisfiedBy(object candidate);
```

```
        ISpecification And(ISpecification other);

        ISpecification AndNot(ISpecification other);

        ISpecification Or(ISpecification other);

        ISpecification OrNot(ISpecification other);

        ISpecification Not();
    }


public abstract class CompositeSpecification : ISpecification
{
        public abstract bool IsSatisfiedBy(object candidate);


        public ISpecification And(ISpecification other)
        {
             return new AndSpecification(this, other);
        }


        public ISpecification AndNot(ISpecification other)
        {
             return new AndNotSpecification(this, other);
        }


        public ISpecification Or(ISpecification other)
        {
             return new OrSpecification(this, other);
        }


        public ISpecification OrNot(ISpecification other)
        {
```

```
            return new OrNotSpecification(this, other);

        }


        public ISpecification Not()

        {

            return new NotSpecification(this);

        }

    }


    public class AndSpecification : CompositeSpecification

    {

        private ISpecification leftCondition;

        private ISpecification rightCondition;


        public AndSpecification(ISpecification left, ISpecification
right)

        {

            leftCondition = left;

            rightCondition = right;

        }


        public override bool IsSatisfiedBy(object candidate)

        {

            return leftCondition.IsSatisfiedBy(candidate) && right-
Condition.IsSatisfiedBy(candidate);

        }

    }


    public class AndNotSpecification : CompositeSpecification
```

```
    {

        private ISpecification leftCondition;

        private ISpecification rightCondition;


        public AndNotSpecification(ISpecification left, ISpecifi-
cation right)

            {

                leftCondition = left;

                rightCondition = right;

            }


        public override bool IsSatisfiedBy(object candidate)

            {

                return leftCondition.IsSatisfiedBy(candidate) && right-
Condition.IsSatisfiedBy(candidate) != true;

            }

        }


    public class OrSpecification : CompositeSpecification

        {

        private ISpecification leftCondition;

        private ISpecification rightCondition;


        public OrSpecification(ISpecification left, ISpecification
right)

            {

                leftCondition = left;

                rightCondition = right;

            }
```

```
    public override bool IsSatisfiedBy(object candidate)

    {

        return leftCondition.IsSatisfiedBy(candidate) || right-
Condition.IsSatisfiedBy(candidate);

    }

}


public class OrNotSpecification : CompositeSpecification

{

    private ISpecification leftCondition;

    private ISpecification rightCondition;


    public OrNotSpecification(ISpecification left, ISpecifica-
tion right)

    {

        leftCondition = left;

        rightCondition = right;

    }


    public override bool IsSatisfiedBy(object candidate)

    {

        return leftCondition.IsSatisfiedBy(candidate) || right-
Condition.IsSatisfiedBy(candidate) != true;

    }

}


public class NotSpecification : CompositeSpecification

{
```

```
    private ISpecification Wrapped;


    public NotSpecification(ISpecification x)
    {
        Wrapped = x;
    }


    public override bool IsSatisfiedBy(object candidate)
    {
        return !Wrapped.IsSatisfiedBy(candidate);
    }

}
```

C# 3.0, Simplified with Generics and Extension Methods

```
public interface ISpecification<T>
{
    bool IsSatisfiedBy(T entity);
    ISpecification<T> And(ISpecification<T> other);
    ISpecification<T> AndNot(ISpecification<T> other);
    ISpecification<T> Or(ISpecification<T> other);
    ISpecification<T> OrNot(ISpecification<T> other);
    ISpecification<T> Not();
}


public abstract class LinqSpecification<T> : CompositeSpeci-
fication<T>
{
    public abstract Expression<Func<T, bool>> AsExpression();
```

```csharp
        public override bool IsSatisfiedBy(T entity)

        {

            Func<T, bool> predicate = AsExpression().Compile();

            return predicate(entity);

        }

    }


    public abstract class CompositeSpecification<T> : ISpecifica-
tion<T>

    {

        public abstract bool IsSatisfiedBy(T entity);


        public ISpecification<T> And(ISpecification<T> other)

        {

            return new AndSpecification<T>(this, other);

        }


        public ISpecification<T> AndNot(ISpecification<T> other)

        {

            return new AndNotSpecification<T>(this, other);

        }


        public ISpecification<T> Or(ISpecification<T> other)

        {

            return new OrSpecification<T>(this, other);

        }


        public ISpecification<T> OrNot(ISpecification<T> other)

        {
```

```
                return new OrNotSpecification<T>(this, other);

        }


        public ISpecification<T> Not()

        {

                return new NotSpecification<T>(this);

        }


    }


    public class AndSpecification<T> : CompositeSpecification<T>

    {

        private readonly ISpecification<T> left;

        private readonly ISpecification<T> right;


         public AndSpecification(ISpecification<T> left, ISpecifi-
cation<T> right)

        {

            this.left = left;

            this.right = right;

        }


        public override bool IsSatisfiedBy(T candidate)

        {

            return left.IsSatisfiedBy(candidate) && right.IsSat-
isfiedBy(candidate);

        }

    }
```

```
public class AndNotSpecification<T> : CompositeSpecification<T>

   {

       private readonly ISpecification<T> left;

       private readonly ISpecification<T> right;


       public AndNotSpecification(ISpecification<T> left, ISpec-
ification<T> right)

       {

           this.left = left;

           this.right = right;

       }


       public override bool IsSatisfiedBy(T candidate)

       {

               return left.IsSatisfiedBy(candidate) && right.IsSat-
isfiedBy(candidate) != true;

       }

   }


   public class OrSpecification<T> : CompositeSpecification<T>

   {

       private readonly ISpecification<T> left;

       private readonly ISpecification<T> right;


       public OrSpecification(ISpecification<T> left, ISpecifica-
tion<T> right)

       {

           this.left = left;

           this.right = right;
```

```
        }


        public override bool IsSatisfiedBy(T candidate)

        {
                return left.IsSatisfiedBy(candidate) || right.IsSat-
isfiedBy(candidate);

        }

    }

    public class OrNotSpecification<T> : CompositeSpecification<T>

    {

        private readonly ISpecification<T> left;

        private readonly ISpecification<T> right;


        public OrNotSpecification(ISpecification<T> left, ISpeci-
fication<T> right)

        {

            this.left = left;

            this.right = right;

        }


        public override bool IsSatisfiedBy(T candidate)

        {
                return left.IsSatisfiedBy(candidate) || right.IsSat-
isfiedBy(candidate) != true;

        }

    }


    public class NotSpecification<T> : CompositeSpecification<T>

    {
```

```
        private readonly ISpecification<T> other;


        public NotSpecification(ISpecification<T> other)
        {
            this.other = other;
        }


        public override bool IsSatisfiedBy(T candidate)
        {
            return !other.IsSatisfiedBy(candidate);
        }

    }
```

Example of use

In the following example, we are retrieving invoices and sending them to a collection agency if

1. they are overdue,

2. notices have been sent, and

3. they are not already with the collection agency.

This example is meant to show the end result of how the logic is 'chained' together.

This usage example assumes a previously defined OverdueSpecification class that is satisfied when an invoice's due date is 30 days or older, a NoticeSentSpecification class that is satisfied when three notices have been sent to the customer, and an InCollectionSpecification class that is satisfied when an invoice has already been sent to the collection agency. The implementation of these classes isn't important here.

Using these three specifications, we created a new specification called SendToCollection which will be satisfied when an invoice is overdue, when notices have been sent to the customer, and are not already with the collection agency.

```
var OverDue = new OverDueSpecification();

var NoticeSent = new NoticeSentSpecification();

var InCollection = new InCollectionSpecification();
```

```
// example of specification pattern logic chaining
var SendToCollection = OverDue.And(NoticeSent).And(InCollection.
Not());


var InvoiceCollection = Service.GetInvoices();


foreach (var currentInvoice in InvoiceCollection) {
    if (SendToCollection.IsSatisfiedBy(currentInvoice))  {
        currentInvoice.SendToCollection();
    }
}
```

Criticisms

The Specification Pattern could be considered a software Anti-Pattern:

- Cargo Cult Programming - There lacks a well-defined purpose for this pattern, and there's no guide when to implement it or not.

- Inner-platform effect - And function which directly replicate && in C#. Also, Not and potentially more.

- Spaghetti/Lasagna Code - Separate classes for each part of the specification fragments what could be a cohesive object. In the example above, OverDue is an extra layer between the Logic for SendToCollection and the OverDueSpecification implementation.

Most natural programming languages can accommodate domain-driven design with the core Object Oriented concepts.

Alternative example, without the Specification Pattern:

```
var InvoiceCollection = Service.GetInvoices();
foreach (Invoice invoice in InvoiceCollection) {
    invoice.SendToCollectionIfNecessary();
}
```

```
// Invoice methods:
public void SendToCollectionIfNecessary()
{
    if (ShouldSendToCollection())
    {
        SendToCollection();
    }
}


private bool ShouldSendToCollection()
{
    return currentInvoice.OverDue
        && currentInvoice.NoticeSent
        && !currentInvoice.InCollection;
}
```

This alternative uses foundation concepts of Get-Only Properties, Condition-Logic, and Functions. The key alternative here is Get-Only Properties, which are well-named to maintain the Domain-Driven language, and enable the continued use of the natural && operator, instead of the Specification Pattern's And() function. Furthermore, the creation of a well-named function SendToCollectionIfNecessary is potentially more useful and descriptive, than the previous example (which could also be contained in such a function, except not directly on the object apparently).

References

- McConnell, Steve (June 2004). "Design in Construction". Code Complete (2nd ed.). Microsoft Press. p. 104. ISBN 978-0-7356-1967-8. Table 5.1 Popular Design Patterns

- Fowler, Martin (2002). Patterns of Enterprise Application Architecture. Addison-Wesley. ISBN 978-0-321-12742-6.

- C. Martin, Robert (2002). "28. Extension object". Agile Software Development, Principles, Patterns, and Practices. p. 408. ISBN 978-0135974445.

- Bloch, Joshua (2008). "Item 37: Use marker interfaces to define types". Effective Java (Second edition). Addison-Wesley. p. 179. ISBN 978-0-321-35668-0.

- Schmidt, Douglas C.; Stal, Michael; Rohnert, Hans; Buschmann, Frank (2000). Pattern-Oriented

Software Architecture, Volume 2: Patterns for Concurrent and Networked Objects. John Wiley & Sons. ISBN 0-471-60695-2.

- Nagel, Christian; Evjen, Bill; Glynn, Jay; Watson, Karli; Skinner, Morgan (2008). "Event-based Asynchronous Pattern". Professional C# 2008. Wiley. pp. 570–571. ISBN 0-470-19137-6.

- Gamma, Erich; Richard Helm; Ralph Johnson; John Vlissides (1995). Design Patterns: Elements of Reusable Object-Oriented Software. Addison-Wesley. pp. 205–206. ISBN 0-201-63361-2.

- Gamma, Erich; Richard Helm; Ralph Johnson; John M. Vlissides (1995). Design Patterns: Elements of Reusable Object-Oriented Software. Addison-Wesley. p. 395. ISBN 0-201-63361-2.

- Eric Freeman, Elisabeth Freeman, Kathy Sierra and Bert Bates, Head First Design Patterns, First Edition, Chapter 1, Page 24, O'Reilly Media, Inc, 2004. ISBN 978-0-596-00712-6

- "Category:Computational Thinking Patterns - Scalable Game Design wiki". sgd.cs.colorado.edu. Retrieved 2015-12-26.

- "Introduction to Software Engineering/Architecture/Design Patterns - Wikibooks, open books for an open world". en.wikibooks.org. Retrieved 2015-12-26.

- "Design Patterns: Dependency injection". Retrieved 2011-04-13. The use of a factory class is one common way to implement DI.

## 6

Various Architecture Description Languages

Architecture description language is used in a number of disciplines such as systems engineering and enterprise modelling and engineering. The other architecture description languages used are Darwin, DUALLy, EAST-ADL, ERIL and Wright. This section helps the readers in understanding the different architecture description languages.

Architecture Description Language

Architecture description languages (ADLs) are used in several disciplines: system engineering, software engineering, and enterprise modelling and engineering.

The system engineering community uses an architecture description language as a language and/or a conceptual model to describe and represent system architectures.

The software engineering community uses an architecture description language as a computer language to create a description of a software architecture. In the case of a so-called technical architecture, the architecture must be communicated to software developers; a functional architecture is communicated to various stakeholders and users. Some ADLs that have been developed are: Acme (developed by CMU), AADL (standardized by the SAE), C2 (developed by UCI), SBC-ADL (developed by National Sun Yat-Sen University), Darwin (developed by Imperial College London), and Wright (developed by CMU).

The up-to-date list of currently existing architectural languages might be found at Up-to-date list of ADLs.

The ISO/IEC/IEEE 42010 document, *Systems and software engineering—Architecture description*, defines an architecture description language as "any form of expression for use in architecture descriptions" and specifies minimum requirements on ADLs.

The enterprise modelling and engineering community have also developed architecture description languages catered for at the enterprise level. Examples include ArchiMate (now a standard of The Open Group), DEMO, ABACUS (developed by the University of Technology, Sydney). These languages do not necessarily refer to software components, etc. Most of them, however, refer to an application architecture as the architecture that is communicated to the software engineers.

Most of the writing below refers primarily to the perspective from the software engineering community.

Introduction

A standard notation (ADL) for representing architectures helps promote mutual communication, the embodiment of early design decisions, and the creation of a transferable abstraction of a system. Architectures in the past were largely represented by box-and-line drawing annotated with such things as the nature of the component, properties, semantics of connections, and overall system behavior. ADLs result from a linguistic approach to the formal representation of architectures, and as such they address its shortcomings. Also important, sophisticated ADLs allow for early analysis and feasibility testing of architectural design decisions.

History

ADLs have been classified into three broad categories: box-and-line informal drawings, formal architecture description language, and UML-based notations. Box-and-line have been for a long time the most predominant means for describing SAs. While providing useful documentation, the level of informality limited the usefulness of the architecture description. A more rigorous way for describing SAs was required. Quoting Allen and Garlan (1997), "while these [box-and-line] descriptions may provide useful documentation, the current level of informality limits their usefulness. Since it is generally imprecise what is meant by such architectural descriptions, it may be impossible to analyze an architecture for consistency or determine non-trivial properties of it. Moreover, there is no way to check that a system implementation is faithful to its architectural design." A similar conclusion is drawn in Perry and Wolf (1992), which reports that: "Aside from providing clear and precise documentation, the primary purpose of specifications is to provide automated analysis of the documents and to expose various kinds of problems that would otherwise go undetected."

Since then, a thread of research on formal languages for SA description has been carried out. Tens of formal ADLs have been proposed, each characterized by different conceptual architectural elements, different syntax or semantics, focusing on a specific operational domain, or only suitable for different analysis techniques. For example, domain-specific ADLs have been presented to deal with embedded and real-time systems (such as AADL, EAST-ADL, and EADL), control-loop applications (DiaSpec), product line architectures (Koala), and dynamic systems (Π-ADL)). Analysis-specific ADLs have been proposed to deal with availability, reliability, security, resource consumption, data quality and real-time performance analysis (AADL, behavioral analysis (Fractal)), and trustworthiness analysis (TADL).

However, these efforts have not seen the desired adoption by industrial practice. Some reasons for this lack of industry adoption have been analyzed by Woods and Hilliard, Pandey, Clements, and others: formal ADLs have been rarely integrated in the software life-cycle, they are seldom supported by mature tools, scarcely documented, focusing on very specific needs, and leaving no space for extensions enabling the addition of new features.

As a way to overcome some of those limitations, UML has been indicated as a possible successor of existing ADLs. Many proposals have been presented to use or extend the UML to more properly model software architectures.

In fact, as highlighted in a recent study conducted with practitioners, whilst practitioners are generally satisfied with the design capabilities provided by the languages they use, they are dissatisfied with the architectural language analysis features and their abilities to define extra-functional properties; architectural languages used in practice mostly originate from industrial development instead of from academic research; more formality and better usability are required of an architectural language.

Characteristics

There is a large variety in ADLs developed by either academic or industrial groups. Many languages were not intended to be an ADL, but they turn out to be suitable for representing and analyzing an architecture. In principle ADLs differ from requirements languages, because ADLs are rooted in the solution space, whereas requirements describe problem spaces. They differ from programming languages, because ADLs do not bind architectural abstractions to specific point solutions. Modeling languages represent behaviors, where ADLs focus on representation of components. However, there are domain specific modeling languages (DSMLs) that focus on representation of components.

Minimal Requirements

The language must:

- Be suitable for communicating an architecture to all interested parties

- Support the tasks of architecture creation, refinement and validation

- Provide a basis for further implementation, so it must be able to add information to the ADL specification to enable the final system specification to be derived from the ADL

- Provide the ability to represent most of the common architectural styles

- Support analytical capabilities or provide quick generating prototype implementations

ADLs have in common:

- Graphical syntax with often a textual form and a formally defined syntax and semantics

- Features for modeling distributed systems

- Little support for capturing design information, except through general purpose annotation mechanisms

- Ability to represent hierarchical levels of detail including the creation of substructures by instantiating templates

ADLs differ in their ability to:

- Handle real-time constructs, such as deadlines and task priorities, at the architectural level

- Support the specification of different architectural styles. Few handle object oriented class inheritance or dynamic architectures

- Support the analysis of the architecture

- Handle different instantiations of the same architecture, in relation to product line architectures

Positive Elements of ADL

- ADLs are a formal way of representing architecture

- ADLs are intended to be both human and machine readable

- ADLs support describing a system at a higher level than previously possible

- ADLs permit analysis and assessment of architectures, for completeness, consistency, ambiguity, and performance

- ADLs can support automatic generation of software systems

Negative Elements of ADL

- There is no universal agreement on what ADLs should represent, particularly as regards the behavior of the architecture

- Representations currently in use are relatively difficult to parse and are not supported by commercial tools

- Most ADLs tend to be very vertically optimized toward a particular kind of analysis

Common Concepts of Architecture

The ADL community generally agrees that Software Architecture is a set of components and the connections among them. But there are different kind of architectures like:

Object Connection Architecture

- Configuration consists of the interfaces and connections of an object-oriented system
- Interfaces specify the features that must be provided by modules conforming to an interface
- Connections represented by interfaces together with call graph
- Conformance usually enforced by the programming language
  - Decomposition — associating interfaces with unique modules
  - Interface conformance — static checking of syntactic rules
  - Communication integrity — visibility between modules

Interface Connection Architecture

- Expands the role of interfaces and connections
  - Interfaces specify both "required" and "provided" features
  - Connections are defined between "required" features and "provided" features
- Consists of interfaces, connections and constraints
  - Constraints restrict behavior of interfaces and connections in an architecture
  - Constraints in an architecture map to requirements for a system

Most ADLs implement an interface connection architecture.

Architecture vs. Design

What is the difference between architecture and design?

Architecture, in the context of software systems, is roughly divided into categories, primarily software architecture, network architecture, and systems architecture. Within each of these categories, there is a tangible but fuzzy distinction between architecture and design. To draw this distinction as universally and clearly as possible, it is best to consider design as a noun rather than as a verb, so that the comparison is between two nouns.

Design is the abstraction and specification of patterns and organs of functionality that have been or will be implemented. Architecture is a degree higher in both abstraction and granularity. Consequentially, architecture is also more topological in nature than design, in that it specifies where major components meet and how they relate to one another. Architecture focuses on the partitioning of major regions of functionality into high level components, where they will physically or virtually reside, what off-the-shelf components may be employed effectively, in general what interfaces each component will expose, what protocols will be employed between them, and what practices and high level patterns may best meet extensibility, maintainability, reliability, durability, scalability, and other non-functional objectives. Design is a detailing of these choices and a more concrete clarification of how functional requirements will be met through the delegation of pieces of that functionality to more granular components and how these smaller components will be organized within the larger ones.

Oftentimes, a portion of architecture is done during the conceptualization of an application, system, or network and may appear in the non-functional sections of requirement documentation. Canonically, design is not specified in requirements, but is rather driven by them.

The process of defining an architecture may involve heuristics, acquired by the architect or architectural team through experience within the domain. As with design, architecture often evolves through a series of iterations, and just as the wisdom of a high level design is often tested when low level design and implementation occurs, the wisdom of an architecture is tested during the specification of a high level design. In both cases, if the wisdom of the specification is called into question during detailing, another iteration of either architecture or design, as the case may be, may become necessary.

In summary, the primary differences between architecture and design are ones of granularity and abstraction, and (consequentially) chronology. (Architecture generally precedes design, although overlap and circular iteration is a common reality.)

Examples

Below the list gives the candidates for being the best ADL to date.

For an up-to-date list of currently existing architectural languages, please refer Up-to-date list of ADLs.

- Primary candidates
    - ABACUS (UTS)
    - ACME / ADML (CMU/USC)
    - ADML (No longer in development)

- ByADL (Build Your ADL) - University of L'Aquila
- LePUS3 and Class-Z (University of Essex)
- Rapide (Stanford)
- Wright (CMU)
- Unicon (CMU)
- Secondary candidates
  - Aesop (CMU)
  - MetaH (Honeywell)
  - AADL (SAE) - Architecture Analysis & Design Language
  - C2 SADL (UCI)
  - SADL (SRI) - System Architecture Description Language
- Others (unclassified)
  - Lileanna - Library Interconnect Language Extended with Annotated Ada
  - Dually: Providing Architectural Languages and Tools Interoperability through Model Transformation Technologies
  - ArchC SystemC-like, focus on instruction sets & memory models.
  - AO-ADL
  - ArchiMate An example of an ADL for enterprise architecture
  - DAOP-ADL
  - DEMO Another example of an enterprise architecture ADL
  - DiaSpec an approach and tool to generate a distributed framework from a software architecture
  - SSEP
  - Unicon
  - xADL

Approaches to Architecture

Approaches to Architecture

- Academic Approach

- focus on analytic evaluation of architectural models

- individual models

- rigorous modeling notations

- powerful analysis techniques

- depth over breadth

- special-purpose solutions

- Industrial Approach

  - focus on wide range of development issues

  - families of models

  - practicality over rigor

  - architecture as the big picture in development

  - breadth over depth

  - general-purpose solutions

Architecture Analysis & Design Language

The Architecture Analysis & Design Language (AADL) is an architecture description language standardized by SAE. AADL was first developed in the field of avionics, and was known formerly as the Avionics Architecture Description Language.

The Architecture Analysis & Design Language is derived from MetaH, an architecture description language made by the Advanced Technology Center of Honeywell. AADL is used to model the software and hardware architecture of an embedded, real-time system. Due to its emphasis on the embedded domain, AADL contains constructs for modeling both software and hardware components (with the hardware components named "execution platform" components within the standard). This architecture model can then be used either as a design documentation, for analyses (such as schedulability and flow control) or for code generation (of the software portion), like UML.

AADL Eco-system

AADL is defined by a core language that defines a single notation for both system and software aspects. Having a single model ease the analysis tools by having only one single representation of the system. The language specifies system-specific characteristics using properties.

The language can be extended with the following methods:

- user-defined properties: user can extend the set of applicable properties and add their own to specify their own requirements

- language annexes: the core language is enhanced by annex languages that enrich the architecture description. For now, the following annexes have been defined.

  - Behavior annex: add components behavior with state machines

  - Error-model annex: specifies fault and propagation concerns

  - ARINC653 annex: defines modelling patterns for modelling avionics system

  - Data-Model annex: describes the modelling of specific data constraint with AADL

AADL Tools

AADL is supported by a wide range of tools:

- OSATE that includes a modeling platform, a graphical viewer and a constraint query languages

- Ocarina, an AADL toolchain for generating code from models

- TASTE toolchain supported by the European Space Agency

Related Projects

AADL has been used for the following research projects:

- AVSI/SAVI: an initiative that leverages AADL (among other languages) to perform virtual integration of aerospace and defense systems

- META: a DARPA project for improving software engineering methods

- PARSEC: a French initiative to validate and implement avionics systems from architecture models

- TASTE: a platform for designing safety-critical systems from models

Darwin (ADL)

Darwin is an architecture description language (ADL). It can be used in a software engineering context to describe the organisation of a piece of software in terms of components, their interfaces and the bindings between components.

Darwin encourages a component- or object-based approach to program structuring in which the unit of structure (the component) hides its behaviour behind a well-defined interface. Programs are constructed by creating instances of component types and binding their interfaces together. Darwin considers such compositions also to be types and hence encourages hierarchical composition. The general form of a Darwin program is therefore the tree in which the root and all intermediate nodes are composite components; the leaves are primitive components encapsulating behavioural as opposed to structural aspects.

DUALLy

DUALLy is an MDE framework to create interoperability among Architecture Description Languages (ADLs). It is developed at the Computer Science Department of the University of L'Aquila. DUALLy enables the transformation of a model conforming to a specific architecture description language into corresponding models conforming to other architecture description languages.

ISO/IEC/IEEE 42010 Standard

As highlighted in the official ISO/IEC/IEEE 42010 website, "the use of multiple views for design can get very complicated. Their consistency is a potential problem whenever multiple models and views are used. Sometimes, consistency rules or procedures are defined as a part of viewpoints. In other cases, organizations have practices they use to check and enforce consistency".

The solution provided by the ISO/IEC/IEEE 42010 standard consists in using correspondences and correspondence rules to define the various relationships that may exist within an architecture description. Under this perspective, DUALLy can be seen as an approach in which special kinds of correspondence rules can keep in a consistent state architecture models belonging to different views. Those special correspondence rules are defined between ADLs and have the additional feature of being proactive; that is, when an inconsistency is detected between different architectural models, the DUALLy interoperability engine actively transforms the models in order to restore consistency.

Interoperability

Supporting ADLs interoperability and change propagation is intrinsically complex.

Furthermore, the lack of automation does not allow the easy addition of new description languages, and does not guarantee change propagation to multiple models in a finite number of steps. In general, changes occurring in an architecture model have a strong impact on all the other related architecture models (each of them possibly conforming to different architecture description languages). In order to keep models in a consistent state, changes need to be propagated from the updated model to all the others. When dealing with multiple architecture description languages, propagating changes may be a complex task; such a task is inevitable and requires to be managed by a dedicated approach.

In DUALLy, the interoperability among various architecture description languages is ensured via model transformation techniques. Instead of creating a point-to-point relationship among all languages, DUALLY defines the transformations among architecture description languages by passing through Ao, which is a core set of architectural concepts defined as generally as possible (to potentially represent and support any kind of architectural representation) and extensible (in order to add domain specificities). In other words, Ao acts as a bridge among the different architectural languages to be related together. The star architecture of DUALLy enables an agile and easy integration of architecture description languages. The DUALLy transformation system is made of a series of model-to-model transformations that enable information migration among architecture models. These model-to-model transformations are constructed automatically by executing higher-order transformations (i.e., transformations taking other transformations as input or producing other transformations as output).

While DUALLy transforms a model into any other by passing first through an Ao model, model changes are propagated accordingly first to the Ao model and successively forwarded to any other architectural model (it has to be noted that the obtained result is independent from the order followed in the forwarding). Under the assumption that concurrent modifications to different models cannot apply, the DUALLY architecture ensures the convergence of the change propagation process, that is, it ensures by construction that a modification of a model within the network is propagated to all the other models in a finite number of steps.

EAST-ADL

EAST-ADL is an Architecture Description Language (ADL) for automotive embedded systems, developed in several European research projects. It is designed to complement AUTOSAR with descriptions at higher level of abstractions. Aspects covered by EAST-ADL include vehicle features, functions, requirements, variability, software components, hardware components and communication. Currently, it is maintained by the EAST-ADL Association in cooperation with the European FP7 MAENAD project.

Overview

EAST-ADL is a domain-specific language using meta-modeling constructs such as classes, attributes, and relationships. It is based on concepts from UML, SysML and AADL, but adapted for automotive needs and compliance with AUTOSAR. There is an EAST-ADL UML2 profile which is used in UML2 tools for user modeling. The EAST-ADL definition also serves as the specification for implementation in domain-specific tools.

EAST-ADL contains several abstraction levels. The software- and electronics-based functionality of the vehicle are described at different levels of abstraction. The proposed abstraction levels and the contained elements provide a separation of concerns and an implicit style for using the modeling elements. The embedded system is complete on each abstraction level, and parts of the model are linked with various traceability relations. This makes it possible to trace an entity from feature down to components in hardware and software.

EAST-ADL is defined with the development of safety-related embedded control systems as a benchmark. The EAST-ADL scope comprises support for the main phases of software development, from early analysis via functional design to the implementation and back to integration and validation on vehicle level. The main role of EAST-ADL is that of providing an integrated system model. On this basis, several concerns are addressed:

- Documentation, in terms of an integrated system model.

- Communication between engineers, by providing predefined views as well as related information.

- Analysis, through the description of system structure and properties.

Behavioural models for simulation or code generation are supported as references from EAST-ADL functions to external models, such as a subsystem in MATLAB/Simulink.

Organisation of EAST-ADL Meta-Model

The EAST-ADL meta-model is organized according to 4 abstraction levels:

- Vehicle level contains modeling elements to represent intended functionality in a solution-independent way

- Analysis level represents the abstract functional decomposition of the vehicle with the principal internal and external interfaces.

- Design level has the detailed functional definition, a hardware architecture and allocations of functions to hardware.

- Implementation level relies on AUTOSAR elements and does not have EAST-ADL-specific constructs for the core structure.

For all abstraction levels, relevant extension elements for requirements, behavior, variability and dependability are associated to the core structure.

Relation between EAST-ADL and AUTOSAR

Instead of providing modeling entities for the lowest abstraction level, i.e. implementation level, EAST-ADL uses unmodified AUTOSAR entities for this purpose and provides means to link EAST-ADL elements on higher abstraction levels to AUTOSAR elements. Thus, EAST-ADL and AUTOSAR in concert provide means for efficient development and management of the complexity of automotive embedded systems from early analysis right down to implementation. Concepts from model-based development and component-based development reinforce one another. An early, high-level representation of the system can evolve seamlessly into the detailed specifications of the AUTOSAR language. In addition, the EAST-ADL incorporates the following system development concerns:

- Modeling of requirements and verification/validation information,

- Feature modeling and support for software system product lines,

- Modeling of variability of the system design,

- Structural and behavioral modeling of functions and hardware entities in the context of distributed systems,

- Environment, i.e., plant model and adjacent systems, and

- Non-functional operational properties such as a definition of function timing and failure modes, supporting system level analysis.

The EAST-ADL metamodel is specified according to the same rules as the AUTOSAR metamodel, which means that the two sets of elements can co-exist in the same model. The dependency is unidirectional from EAST-ADL to AUTOSAR, such that AUTOSAR is independent of EAST-ADL. However, relevant EAST-ADL elements can reference AUTOSAR elements to provide EAST-ADL support for requirements, variability, safety, etc. to the AUTOSAR domain.

A model may thus be defined where AUTOSAR elements represent the software architecture and EAST-ADL elements extend the AUTOSAR model with orthogonal aspects and represents abstract system information through e.g. function and feature models. Such model can be defined in UML, by applying both an EAST-ADL profile and an AUTOSAR profile, or in a domain specific tool based on a merged AUTOSAR and EAST-ADL metamodel.

History and Specification of EAST-ADL

The EAST-ADL language has been defined in several steps within European research projects:

Project name	Time	Bud-get	EAST-ADL Ver-sion	Support by research departments of follow-ing vehicle manufac-turers(OEMs)
EAST-EEA	1.7.2001 - 30.6.2004	40 M€	EAST-ADL Ver-sion 1.0	BMW, Daimler, Fiat, PSA (Peugeot/Citro-en), Renault, Volvo, Valeo
ATESST	1.1.2006 - 31.3. 2008	3.9 M€	EAST-ADL Ver-sion 2.0	Daimler, Volvo Group, VW/Carmeq
ATESST2	1.7.2008 - 30.6. 2010	3.8 M€	EAST-ADL Ver-sion 2.1	Fiat, Volvo Group, Volvo Cars, VW/Car-meq
MAENAD	1.9.2010 - 31.8. 2013	4.0 M€	V2.1.12	Fiat, Volvo Group

EAST-ADL is governed by the EAST-ADL Association, founded in September 2011. The EAST-ADL UML2 profile is represented in the EAST-ADL annex to the OMG MARTE profile.

Discussion

While interest from automotive companies in EAST-ADL is increasing over the past years, EAST-ADL is still to be seen as a research effort (as of 2012). The practical acceptance of EAST-ADL in the automotive industry is still very low, even though EAST-ADL addresses many important aspects of vehicle development. EAST-ADL is used as a reference model in other research projects, e.g. CESAR and TIMMO-2-USE

Modeling Tools and File Format

EAST-ADL tool support is still limited, although a UML profile is available and domain specific tools such as MentorGraphics VSA, MetaCase MetaEdit+ and Systemite SystemWeaver have been tailored for EAST-ADL in the context of research projects and with customers. Papyrus UML, extended within the ATESST project as a concept demonstrator has EAST-ADL support, and MagicDraw, can also provide EAST-ADL palettes, diagrams, etc. In the case of UML, developers also need to have knowledge of UML (classes, stereotypes, arrow types, ..) for modeling with EAST-ADL. Many automotive engineers, in particular mechanical engineers, hardware developers, process experts) do not have this knowledge and prefer other approaches. EATOP is an upcoming initiative to make an Eclipse-based implementation of the EAST-ADL meta-model.

An XML-based exchange format, EAXML, allows tools to exchange EAST-ADL models. The EAXML schema is autogenerated from the EAST-ADL metamodel according to the same principles as the AUTOSAR ARXML schema. Currently, the exchange format is supported by the EAST-ADL prototype of Mentor Graphics VSA, MetaEdit+ and SystemWeaver. For UML tooling, it is possible to exchange models using XMI, subject to the XMI compatibility between tools.

Similar Approaches

- Unified Modeling Language (UML)
- Systems Modeling Language (SysML)
- Architecture analysis and design language (AADL)
- AUTOSAR
- SystemDesk

ERIL

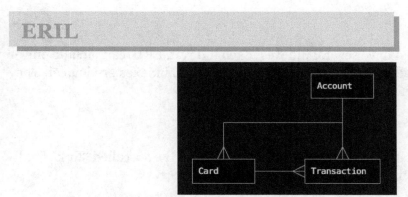

An example ERIL diagram with 3 classes and 3 one-to-many relationships.

ERIL (Entity-Relationship and Inheritance Language) is a visual language for representing the data structure of a computer system. As its name suggests, ERIL is based on entity-relationship diagrams and class diagrams. ERIL combines the relational and object-oriented approaches to data modeling.

Overview

ERIL can be seen as a set of guidelines aimed at improving the readability of structure diagrams. These guidelines were borrowed from DRAKON, a variant of flowcharts created within the Russian space program. ERIL itself was developed by Stepan Mitkin.

The ERIL guidelines for drawing diagrams:

- Lines must be straight, either strictly vertical or horizontal.
- Vertical lines mean ownership (composition).
- Horizontal lines mean peer relationships (aggregation).
- Line intersections are not allowed.
- It is not recommended to fit the whole data model on a single diagram. Draw many simple diagrams instead.
- The same class (table) can appear several times on the same diagram.
- Use the following standard symbols to indicate the type of the relationship.
  - One-to-one: a simple line.
  - One-to-many, two-way: a line with a "paw".
  - One-to-many, one-way: an arrow.
  - Many-to-many: a line with two "paws".
- Do not lump together inheritance and data relationships.

Indexes

A class (table) in ERIL can have several indexes. Each index in ERIL can include one or more fields, similar to indexes in relational databases. ERIL indexes are logical. They can optionally be implemented by real data structures.

Links

Links between classes (tables) in ERIL are implemented by the so-called "link" fields. Link fields can be of different types according to the link type:

- reference;
- collection of references.

Example: there is a one-to-many link between *Documents* and *Lines*. One *Document* can have many *Lines*. Then the *Document.Lines* field is a collection of references to the lines that belong to the document. *Line.Document* is a reference to the document that contains the line.

Link fields are also logical. They may or may not be implemented physically in the system.

Usage

ERIL is supposed to model any kind of data regardless of the storage. The same ERIL diagram can represent data stored in a relational database, in a NoSQL database, XML file or in the memory.

ERIL diagrams serve two purposes. The primary purpose is to explain the data structure of an existing or future system or component. The secondary purpose is to automatically generate source code from the model. Code that can be generated includes specialized collection classes, hash and comparison functions, data retrieval and modification procedures, SQL data-definition code, etc. Code generated from ERIL diagrams can ensure referential and uniqueness data integrity. Serialization code of different kinds can also be automatically generated. In some ways ERIL can be compared to object-relational mapping frameworks.

Wright (ADL)

In software architecture, Wright is an architecture description language developed at Carnegie Mellon University. Wright formalizes a software architecture in terms of concepts such as *components*, *connectors*, *roles*, and *ports*. The dynamic behavior of different ports of an individual component is described using the Communicating Sequential Processes (CSP) process algebra. The roles that different components interacting through a connector can take are also described using CSP. Due to the formal nature of the behavior descriptions, automatic checks of port/role compatibility, and overall system consistency can be performed.

Wright was principally developed by Robert Allen and David Garlan.

Unified Modeling Language

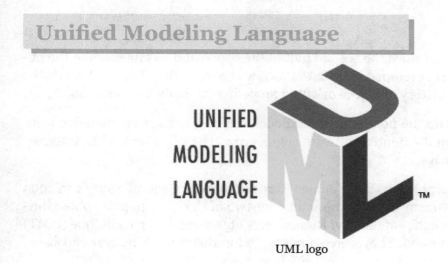

UML logo

The Unified Modeling Language (UML) is a general-purpose, developmental, modeling language in the field of software engineering, that is intended to provide a standard way to visualize the design of a system.

UML was originally motivated by the desire to standardize the disparate notational systems and approaches to software design developed by Grady Booch, Ivar Jacobson and James Rumbaugh at Rational Software in 1994–1995, with further development led by them through 1996.

In 1997 UML was adopted as a standard by the Object Management Group (OMG), and has been managed by this organization ever since. In 2005 UML was also published by the International Organization for Standardization (ISO) as an approved ISO standard. Since then it has been periodically revised to cover the latest revision of UML.

History

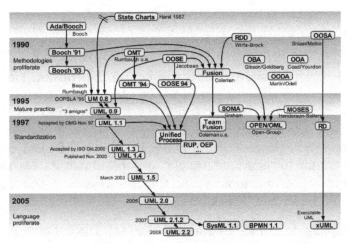

History of object-oriented methods and notation

Before UML 1.x

UML has been evolving since the second half of the 1990s and has its roots in the object-oriented methods developed in the late 1980s and early 1990s. The timeline shows the highlights of the history of object-oriented modeling methods and notation.

It is originally based on the notations of the Booch method, the object-modeling technique (OMT) and object-oriented software engineering (OOSE), which it has integrated into a single language.

Rational Software Corporation hired James Rumbaugh from General Electric in 1994 and after that the company became the source for two of the most popular object-oriented modeling approaches of the day: Rumbaugh's object-modeling technique (OMT) and Grady Booch's method. They were soon assisted in their efforts by Ivar Jacobson, the creator of the object-oriented software engineering (OOSE) method, who joined them at Rational in 1995.

UML 1.x

Under the technical leadership of those three (Rumbaugh, Jacobson and Booch), a consortium called the UML Partners was organized in 1996 to complete the *Unified Modeling Language (UML)* specification, and propose it to the Object Management Group (OMG) for standardisation. The partnership also contained additional interested parties (for example HP, DEC, IBM and Microsoft). The UML Partners' UML 1.0 draft was proposed to the OMG in January 1997 by the consortium. During the same month the UML Partners formed a group, designed to define the exact meaning of language constructs, chaired by Cris Kobryn and administered by Ed Eykholt, to finalize the specification and integrate it with other standardization efforts. The result of this work, UML 1.1, was submitted to the OMG in August 1997 and adopted by the OMG in November 1997.

After the first release a task force was formed to improve the language, which released several minor revisions, 1.3, 1.4, and 1.5.

The standards it produced (as well as the original standard) have been noted as being ambiguous and inconsistent.

UML 2.x

UML 2.0 major revision replaced version 1.5 in 2005, which was developed with an enlarged consortium to improve the language further to reflect new experience on usage of its features.

Although UML 2.1 was never released as a formal specification, versions 2.1.1 and 2.1.2 appeared in 2007, followed by UML 2.2 in February 2009. UML 2.3 was formally released in May 2010. UML 2.4.1 was formally released in August 2011. UML 2.5 was released in October 2012 as an "In process" version and was officially released in June 2015.

There are four parts to the UML 2.x specification:

1. The Superstructure that defines the notation and semantics for diagrams and their model elements

2. The Infrastructure that defines the core metamodel on which the Superstructure is based

3. The Object Constraint Language (OCL) for defining rules for model elements

4. The UML Diagram Interchange that defines how UML 2 diagram layouts are exchanged

The current versions of these standards follow: UML Superstructure version 2.4.1, UML Infrastructure version 2.4.1, OCL version 2.3.1, and UML Diagram Interchange version 1.0. It continues to be updated and improved by the revision task force, who resolve any issues with the language.

Design

UML offers a way to visualize a system's architectural blueprints in a diagram, including elements such as:

- any activities (jobs);
- individual components of the system;
    - and how they can interact with other software components;
- how the system will run;
- how entities interact with others (components and interfaces);
- external user interface.

Although originally intended for object-oriented design documentation, UML has been extended to a larger set of design documentation (as listed above), and been found useful in many contexts.

Software Development Methods

UML is not a development method by itself; however, it was designed to be compatible with the leading object-oriented software development methods of its time, for example OMT, Booch method, Objectory and especially RUP that it was originally intended to be used with when work began at Rational Software.

Modeling

It is important to distinguish between the UML model and the set of diagrams of a system. A diagram is a partial graphic representation of a system's model. The set of diagrams need not completely cover the model and deleting a diagram does not change the model. The model may also contain documentation that drives the model elements and diagrams (such as written use cases).

UML diagrams represent two different views of a system model:

- Static (or *structural*) view: emphasizes the static structure of the system using objects, attributes, operations and relationships. It includes class diagrams and composite structure diagrams.
- Dynamic (or *behavioral*) view: emphasizes the dynamic behavior of the system

by showing collaborations among objects and changes to the internal states of objects. This view includes sequence diagrams, activity diagrams and state machine diagrams.

UML models can be exchanged among UML tools by using the XML Metadata Interchange (XMI) format.

Diagrams

UML 2 has many types of diagrams, which are divided into two categories. Some types represent *structural* information, and the rest represent general types of *behavior*, including a few that represent different aspects of *interactions*. These diagrams can be categorized hierarchically as shown in the following class diagram:

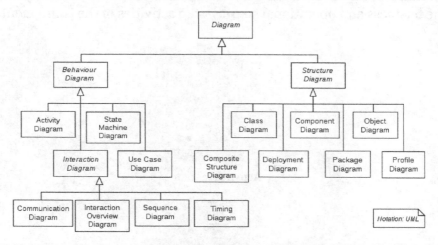

These diagrams may all contain comments or notes explaining usage, constraint, or intent.

Structure Diagrams

Structure diagrams emphasize the things that must be present in the system being modeled. Since structure diagrams represent the structure, they are used extensively in documenting the software architecture of software systems. For example, the component diagram describes how a software system is split up into components and shows the dependencies among these components.

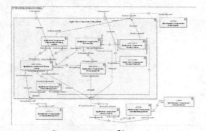

Component diagram

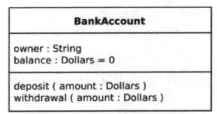

Class diagram

Behavior Diagrams

Behavior diagrams emphasize what must happen in the system being modeled. Since behavior diagrams illustrate the behavior of a system, they are used extensively to describe the functionality of software systems. As an example, the activity diagram describes the business and operational step-by-step activities of the components in a system.

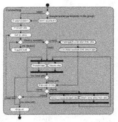

Activity diagram

Use case diagram

Interaction Diagrams

Interaction diagrams, a subset of behavior diagrams, emphasize the flow of control and data among the things in the system being modeled. For example, the sequence diagram shows how objects communicate with each other in terms of a sequence of messages.

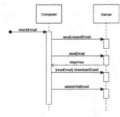

Sequence diagram

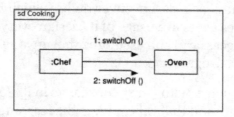

Communication diagram

Meta Modeling

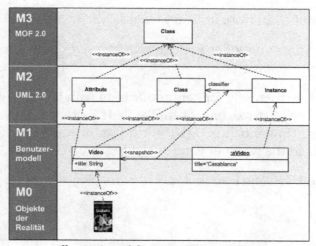

Illustration of the Meta-Object Facility

The Object Management Group (OMG) has developed a metamodeling architecture to define the UML, called the Meta-Object Facility. MOF is designed as a four-layered architecture, as shown in the image at right. It provides a meta-meta model at the top, called the M3 layer. This M3-model is the language used by Meta-Object Facility to build metamodels, called M2-models.

The most prominent example of a Layer 2 Meta-Object Facility model is the UML metamodel, which describes the UML itself. These M2-models describe elements of the M1-layer, and thus M1-models. These would be, for example, models written in UML. The last layer is the M0-layer or data layer. It is used to describe runtime instances of the system.

The meta-model can be extended using a mechanism called stereotyping. This has been criticised as being insufficient/untenable by Brian Henderson-Sellers and Cesar Gonzalez-Perez in "Uses and Abuses of the Stereotype Mechanism in UML 1.x and 2.0".

Adoption

UML has been found useful in many design contexts.

It has been treated, at times, as a design silver bullet, which has led to problems in its usage. Misuse of it includes excessive usage of it (design every little part of the system's code with it, which is unnecessary) and assuming that anyone can design anything with it (even those who haven't programmed).

It is seen to be a large language, with many constructs in it. Some (including Jacobson) feel that there are too many and that this hinders the learning (and therefore usage) of it.

Criticisms

Common criticisms of UML from industry include:

- not useful: "[does] not offer them advantages over their current, evolved practices and representations"

- too complex, particularly for communication with clients: "unnecessarily complex" and "The best reason not to use UML is that it is not 'readable' for all stakeholders. How much is UML worth if a business user (the customer) can not understand the result of your modelling effort?"

- need to keep UML and code in sync, as with documentation generally

Critique of UML 1.x

Cardinality notation

As with database Chen, Bachman, and ISO ER diagrams, class models are specified to use "look-across" cardinalities, even though several authors (Merise, Elmasri & Navathe amongst others) prefer same-side or "look-here" for roles and both minimum and maximum cardinalities. Recent researchers (Feinerer, Dullea et. alia) have shown that the "look-across" technique used by UML and ER diagrams is less effective and less coherent when applied to n-ary relationships of order strictly greater than 2.

Feinerer says: "Problems arise if we operate under the look-across semantics as used for UML associations. Hartmann investigates this situation and shows how and why different transformations fail.", and: "As we will see on the next few pages, the look-across interpretation introduces several difficulties which prevent the extension of simple mechanisms from binary to n-ary associations."

References

- Unified Modeling Language User Guide, The (2 ed.). Addison-Wesley. 2005. p. 496. ISBN 0321267974.
- John Hunt (2000). The Unified Process for Practitioners: Object-oriented Design, UML and

Java. Springer, 2000. ISBN 1-85233-275-1. p.5.door.

- Jon Holt Institution of Electrical Engineers (2004). UML for Systems Engineering: Watching the Wheels IET, 2004, ISBN 0-86341-354-4. p.58.

- "ISO/IEC 19501:2005 - Information technology - Open Distributed Processing - Unified Modeling Language (UML) Version 1.4.2". Iso.org. 2005-04-01. Retrieved 2015-05-07.

- "ISO/IEC 19505-1:2012 - Information technology - Object Management Group Unified Modeling Language (OMG UML) - Part 1: Infrastructure". Iso.org. 2012-04-20. Retrieved 2014-04-10.

- "OMG Unified Modeling Language (OMG UML), Superstructure. Version 2.4.1". Object Management Group. Retrieved 9 April 2014.

- "A Formal Treatment of UML Class Diagrams as an Efficient Method for Configuration Management 2007" (PDF). Retrieved 2011-09-22.

- "James Dullea, Il-Yeol Song, Ioanna Lamprou - An analysis of structural validity in entity-relationship modeling 2002" (PDF). Retrieved 2011-09-22.

- Li, J.; Pilkington, N. T.; Xie, F.; Liu, Q. (2010). "Embedded architecture description language". Journal of Systems and Software. 83 (2): 235. doi:10.1016/j.jss.2009.09.043.

- Pandey, R. K. (2010). "Architectural description languages (ADLs) vs UML". ACM SIGSOFT Software Engineering Notes. 35 (3): 1. doi:10.1145/1764810.1764828.

## 7

Component-based Software Engineering

Component-based software engineering is an important branch of software engineering. It is used to define and is also used in implementing independent components into a system. Component-based scalable logical architecture, composition over inheritance, common component architecture, component object model and distributed component object model are some of the topics discussed in the following chapter.

Component-based Software Engineering

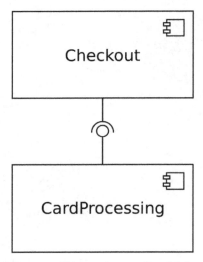

An example of two components expressed in UML 2.0. The checkout component, responsible for facilitating the customer's order, *requires* the card processing component to charge the customer's credit/debit card (functionality that the latter *provides*).

Component-based software engineering (CBSE), also known as component-based development (CBD), is a branch of software engineering that emphasizes the separation of concerns in respect of the wide-ranging functionality available throughout a given software system. It is a reuse-based approach to defining, implementing and composing loosely coupled independent components into systems. This practice aims to bring about an equally wide-ranging degree of benefits in both the short-term and the long-term for the software itself and for organizations that sponsor such software.

Software engineering practitioners regard components as part of the starting platform for service-orientation. Components play this role, for example, in web services, and more recently, in service-oriented architectures (SOA), whereby a component is converted by the web service into a *service* and subsequently inherits further characteristics beyond that of an ordinary component.

Components can produce or consume events and can be used for event-driven architectures (EDA).

Definition and Characteristics of Components

An individual software component is a software package, a web service, a web resource, or a module that encapsulates a set of related functions (or data).

All system processes are placed into separate components so that all of the data and functions inside each component are semantically related (just as with the contents of classes). Because of this principle, it is often said that components are *modular* and *cohesive*.

With regard to system-wide co-ordination, components communicate with each other via *interfaces*. When a component offers services to the rest of the system, it adopts a *provided* interface that specifies the services that other components can utilize, and how they can do so. This interface can be seen as a signature of the component - the client does not need to know about the inner workings of the component (implementation) in order to make use of it. This principle results in components referred to as *encapsulated*. The UML illustrations within this article represent provided interfaces by a lollipop-symbol attached to the outer edge of the component.

However, when a component needs to use another component in order to function, it adopts a *used* interface that specifies the services that it needs. In the UML illustrations in this article, *used interfaces* are represented by an open socket symbol attached to the outer edge of the component.

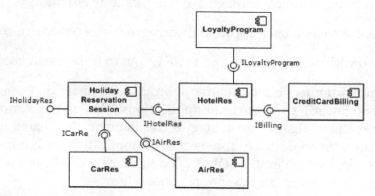

A simple example of several software components - pictured within a hypothetical holiday-reservation system represented in UML 2.0.

Another important attribute of components is that they are *substitutable*, so that a component can replace another (at design time or run-time), if the successor component meets the requirements of the initial component (expressed via the interfaces). Consequently, components can be replaced with either an updated version or an alternative without breaking the system in which the component operates.

As a rule of thumb for engineers substituting components, component B can immediately replace component A, if component B provides at least what component A provided and uses no more than what component A used.

Software components often take the form of objects (not classes) or collections of objects (from object-oriented programming), in some binary or textual form, adhering to some interface description language (IDL) so that the component may exist autonomously from other components in a computer. In other words, a component acts without changing its source code. Although, the behavior of the component's source code may change based on the application's extensibility, provided by its writer.

When a component is to be accessed or shared across execution contexts or network links, techniques such as serialization or marshalling are often employed to deliver the component to its destination.

Reusability is an important characteristic of a high-quality software component. Programmers should design and implement software components in such a way that many different programs can reuse them. Furthermore, component-based usability testing should be considered when software components directly interact with users.

It takes significant effort and awareness to write a software component that is effectively reusable. The component needs to be:

- fully documented
- thoroughly tested
    - robust - with comprehensive input-validity checking
    - able to pass back appropriate error messages or return codes
- designed with an awareness that it *will* be put to unforeseen uses

In the 1960s, programmers built scientific subroutine libraries that were reusable in a broad array of engineering and scientific applications. Though these subroutine libraries reused well-defined algorithms in an effective manner, they had a limited domain of application. Commercial sites routinely created application programs from reusable modules written in Assembler, COBOL, PL/1 and other second- and third-generation languages using both system and user application libraries.

As of 2010, modern reusable components encapsulate both data structures and the algorithms that are applied to the data structures. It builds on prior theories of software objects, software architectures, software frameworks and software design patterns, and the extensive theory of object-oriented programming and the object oriented design of all these. It claims that software components, like the idea of hardware components, used for example in telecommunications, can ultimately be made interchangeable and reliable. On the other hand, it is argued that it is a mistake to focus on independent components rather than the framework (without which they would not exist).

History

The idea that software should be componentized - built from prefabricated *components* - first became prominent with Douglas McIlroy's address at the NATO conference on software engineering in Garmisch, Germany, 1968, titled *Mass Produced Software Components*. The conference set out to counter the so-called software crisis. McIlroy's subsequent inclusion of pipes and filters into the Unix operating system was the first implementation of an infrastructure for this idea.

Brad Cox of Stepstone largely defined the modern concept of a software component. He called them *Software ICs* and set out to create an infrastructure and market for these components by inventing the Objective-C programming language. (He summarizes this view in his book *Object-Oriented Programming - An Evolutionary Approach* 1986.)

The software components are used in two different contexts and two kinds: (i) using components as parts to build a single executable, or (ii) each executable is treated as a component in a distributed environment, where components collaborate with each other using internet or intranet communication protocols for IPC (Inter Process Communications). The above belongs to former kind, while the below belongs to later kind.

IBM led the path with their System Object Model (SOM) in the early 1990s. As a reaction, Microsoft paved the way for actual deployment of component software with OLE and COM. As of 2010 many successful software component models exist.

Differences from Object-Oriented Programming

Proponents of object-oriented programming (OOP) maintain that software should be written according to a mental model of the actual or imagined objects it represents. OOP and the related disciplines of object-oriented analysis and object-oriented design focus on modeling real-world interactions and attempting to create "nouns" and "verbs" that can be used in more human-readable ways, ideally by end users as well as by programmers coding for those end users.

Component-based software engineering, by contrast, makes no such assumptions, and instead states that developers should construct software by gluing together prefabricated components - much like in the fields of electronics or mechanics. Some peers will even talk of modularizing systems as software components as a new programming paradigm. Example for possible paradigm: many experts feel adaptable to evolving needs is more important than reuse, since 80% of software engineering deals with maintaining or releasing new versions. So it is desirable to build complex system by assembling highly cohesive loosely coupled large components, where cost of re-designing each of such adoptable components (or replacing by a better component) must be minimized.

Some argue that earlier computer scientists made this distinction, with Donald Knuth's theory of "literate programming" optimistically assuming there was convergence between intuitive and formal models, and Edsger Dijkstra's theory in the article *The Cruelty of Really Teaching Computer Science*, which stated that programming was simply, and only, a branch of mathematics.

In both forms, this notion has led to many academic debates about the pros and cons of the two approaches and possible strategies for uniting the two. Some consider the different strategies not as competitors, but as descriptions of the same problem from different points of view.

One approach to creating component-based software using object-oriented programming is interface-based programming. However, interface-based programming does not inherently support distributed systems, and many computer systems are inherently distributed in the 21st century. Interface-based programming in the OOP sense may be extended to distributed systems with distributed component object models; however, many have argued in recent years that REST APIs or the actor model are more suitable approaches.

Architecture

A computer running several software components is often called an application server. This combination of application servers and software components is usually called distributed computing. Typical real-world application of this is in, e.g., financial applications or business software.

Models

A component model is a definition of standards for component implementation, documentation and deployment. Examples of component models are: Enterprise JavaBeans (EJB) model, Component Object Model (COM) model, .NET model and Common Object Request Broker Architecture (CORBA) component Model. The component model specifies how interfaces should be defined and the elements that should be included in an interface definition.

Technologies

- Business object technologies

- Newi
- Component-based software frameworks for specific domains
  - Advanced Component Framework
  - Earth System Modeling Framework (ESMF)
  - MASH IoT Platform for Asset Management
  - KOALA component model developed for software in consumer electronics
  - Software Communications Architecture (JTRS SCA)
- Component-oriented programming
  - Bundles as defined by the OSGi Service Platform
  - Component web platform for modular js, css, and other assets
  - Component Object Model (OCX/ActiveX/COM) and DCOM from Microsoft
  - TASCS - SciDAC Center for Technology for Advanced Scientific Component Software
  - Eiffel programming language
  - Enterprise JavaBeans from Sun Microsystems (now Oracle)
  - Flow-based programming
  - Fractal component model from ObjectWeb
  - MidCOM component framework for Midgard and PHP
  - Oberon, Component Pascal, and BlackBox Component Builder
  - rCOS method of component-based model driven design from UNU-IIST
  - SOFA component system from ObjectWeb
  - The System.ComponentModel namespace in Microsoft .NET
  - Unity developed by Unity Technologies
  - UNO from the OpenOffice.org office suite
  - VCL and CLX from Borland and similar free LCL library.

- XPCOM from Mozilla Foundation
- Compound document technologies
    - Active Documents in Oberon System and BlackBox Component Builder
    - KPart, the KDE compound document technology
    - Object linking and embedding (OLE)
    - OpenDoc
- Distributed computing software components
    - .NET Remoting from Microsoft
    - 9P distributed protocol developed for Plan 9, and used by Inferno and other systems.
    - CORBA and the CORBA Component Model from the Object Management Group
    - D-Bus from the freedesktop.org organization
    - DCOM and later versions of COM (and COM+) from Microsoft
    - DSOM and SOM from IBM (now scrapped)
    - ICE from ZeroC
    - Java EE from Sun
    - Kompics from SICS
    - Universal Network Objects (UNO) from OpenOffice.org
    - Web services
        - REST
    - Zope from Zope Corporation
    - AXCIOMA (the component framework for distributed, real-time, and embedded systems) by Remedy IT
    - COHORTE the cross-platform runtime for executing and managing robust and reliable distributed Service-oriented Component-based applications, by isandlaTech
- Generic programming emphasizes separation of algorithms from data representation

- Interface description languages (IDLs)

  - Open Service Interface Definitions (OSIDs)

  - Part of both COM and CORBA

  - Platform-Independent Component Modeling Language

  - SIDL - Scientific Interface Definition Language

    - Part of the Babel Scientific Programming Language Interoperability System (SIDL and Babel are core technologies of the CCA and the SciDAC TASCS Center.)

  - SOAP IDL from World Wide Web Consortium (W3C)

  - WDDX

  - XML-RPC, the predecessor of SOAP

- Inversion of Control (IoC) and Plain Old C++/Java Object (POCO/POJO) component frameworks

- Pipes and filters

  - Unix operating system

Component-based Scalable Logical Architecture

CSLA .NET is a software framework created by Rockford Lhotka that provides a standard way to create robust object oriented programs using business objects. Business objects are objects that abstract business entities in an object oriented program. Some examples of business entities include sales orders, employees, or invoices.

Although CSLA itself is free to download, the only documentation the creator provides are his books and videos, which are not free.

CSLA (*Component-based Scalable Logical Architecture*) was originally targeted toward Visual Basic 6 in the book *Visual Basic 6.0 Business Objects* by Lhotka. With the advent of Microsoft .NET, CSLA was completely rewritten from the ground up, with no code carried forward, and called CSLA .NET. This revision took advantage of Web Services and the object oriented languages that came with Microsoft .NET (in particular, Visual Basic.NET and C#).

CSLA .NET was expounded in *Expert C# Business Objects* and *Expert One-on-One Visual Basic .NET Business Objects* ISBN 1-59059-145-3, both written by Lhotka. Although CSLA and CSLA .NET were originally targeted toward Microsoft programming languages, most of the framework can be applied to most object oriented languages.

Current information about CSLA .NET is available through Lhotka's self-published *Using CSLA 4* ebook series.

Features of CSLA

Smart Data

A business object encapsulates all the data and behavior (business logic and rules) associated with the object it represents. For example, an OrderEdit object will contain the data and business rule implementations necessary for the application to correctly allow the user to edit order information.

Rules Engine

The CSLA .NET framework provides a rules engine that supports validation rules, business rules, and authorization rules. These rules are attached to object instances or properties, and are automatically invoked by CSLA .NET when necessary. Validation rules may be implemented using the CSLA .NET rule engine, or through the use of the DataAnnotations feature of Microsoft .NET.

Object Persistence

Data creation, retrieval, updates, and deletes (CRUD) are performed by clearly defined methods of the business object associated with the data testing. Data access logic is clearly separated from business logic, typically using a repository pattern or other mainstream object-oriented programming techniques.

Metastate Maintenance

CSLA .NET manages the *metastate* about each business object. For example, each business object tracks information about when it is new (it represents data that hasn't been saved yet) and when it is dirty (it needs to be saved to the database either because it is new or because its member data has been changed since it was last loaded). Business objects can also be marked for deletion so they can later be deleted (for example when a user has pressed a button confirming his or her intention to delete the rows.)

N-Level Undo

This feature makes it possible for an object or collection of objects to maintain a collection of states. This allows the object to easily revert to previous states. This can be useful when a user wants to undo previous edits multiple times in an application. The feature can also allow a user to redo multiple edits that were previously undone.

This feature can provide rich functionality for desktop application and web applications. One note of caution would be to consider the overhead for high transaction web based applications. n-Level undo capability will require storing the previous state of an application generally accessed by reflection. This is common practice in desktop applications where changes must be "Applied". In web based designs, the added storage may pose unnecessary overhead as changes are generally submitted in batch and do not require the same level of "undo" capability.

Business Rule Tracking

Allows objects to maintain collections of "broken rule" objects. Broken rules will exist for an object until it is in a valid state, meaning it is ready to be persisted to the database. *Broken-Rule* objects are usually associated with validation logic such as ensuring that no alphabetic characters are entered into a phone number field. For example, if an *Account* object has a *PhoneNumber* property, and that property is assigned a phone number with alphabetic characters, the *Account* object's *IsValid* property will become false (making it impossible to save to the database) and then a new *BrokenRule* object will be created and assigned to the Account's *Broken Rules* collection. The rule will disappear when the invalid phone number is corrected making the Account object capable of saving itself to the database.

Extended Features of CSLA

Simple UI Creation

Business objects created using CSLA .NET fully support data binding for all Microsoft .NET UI technologies, including Windows Runtime (WinRT), WPF, Web Forms, ASP. NET MVC, Windows Phone, Silverlight, and Windows Forms. Data-bound controls like DataGrids and ListBoxes can be bound to business objects instead of more generalized database objects like ADO.NET DataSets and DataTables.

Distributed Data Access

The CSLA .NET framework implements a concept called mobile objects or mobile agents to allow objects to move across network boundaries using WCF, Web Services, or other technologies. As a result, the data access enjoys location transparency, meaning that the logic may run on the client workstation or server depending on the application's configuration. It can also be configured to use manual database transactions or distributed two-phase commit transactions.

Data access logic is cleanly separated from business logic, and can be implemented using any data access technology available on the Microsoft .NET platform. Examples include ADO.NET Entity Framework, raw ADO.NET, nHibernate, etc.

Web Services Support

Business logic created with the CSLA .NET framework can easily be exposed as a web service to remote consumers. This can be done using server-side Microsoft .NET technologies such as Web API, WCF, and asmx web services.

Composition Over Inheritance

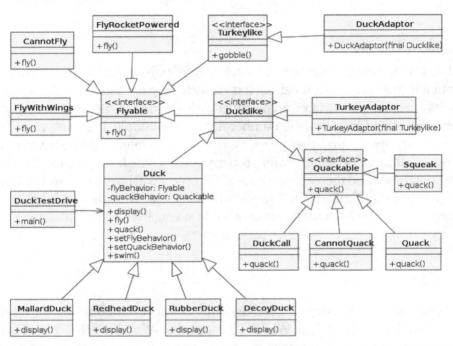

This diagram shows how the fly and sound behavior of an animal can be designed in a flexible way by using the composition over inheritance design principle.

Composition over inheritance (or composite reuse principle) in object-oriented programming is the principle that classes should achieve polymorphic behavior and code reuse by their composition (by containing instances of other classes that implement the desired functionality) rather than inheritance from a base or parent class. This is an often-stated principle of OOP, such as in the influential *Design Patterns:* "Favor 'object composition' over 'class inheritance'."

Basics

An implementation of composition over inheritance typically begins with the creation of various interfaces representing the behaviors that the system must exhibit. The use of interfaces allows this technique to support the Polymorphic behavior that is so valuable in object-oriented programming. Classes implementing the identified interfaces are built and added to business domain classes as needed. Thus, system behaviors are realized without inheritance. In fact, business domain classes may all be base classes without any inheritance at all. Alternative implementation of system behaviors is accomplished by providing another class that implements the desired behavior interface. Any business domain class that contains a reference to the interface can easily support any implementation of that interface and the choice can even be delayed until run time.

Example

Inheritance

An example in C++11 follows:

```
class GameObject

{

    public:

        virtual ~GameObject() {}

        virtual void update() {}

        virtual void draw() {}

        virtual void collide(Object objects[]) {}

};


class Visible : public GameObject

{

    public:

        virtual void draw() override { /* draw model at position
of this object */ };

    private:

        Model* model;

};


class Solid : public GameObject

{

    public:
```

```
        virtual void collide(GameObject objects[]) override { /*
check and react to collisions with objects */ };
};


class Movable : public GameObject
{
    public:
        virtual void update() override { /* update position */ };
};
```

Then, we have concrete classes:

- class Player - which is Solid, Movable and Visible

- class Cloud - which is Movable and Visible, but not Solid

- class Building - which is Solid and Visible, but not Movable

- class Trap - which is Solid, but neither Visible nor Movable

Note that multiple inheritance is dangerous if not implemented carefully, as it can lead to the diamond problem. One solution to avoid this is to create classes such as VisibleAndSolid, VisibleAndMovable, VisibleAndSolidAndMovable, etc. for every needed combination, though this leads to a large amount of repetitive code. Keep in mind that C++ solves the diamond problem of multiple inheritance by allowing virtual inheritance.

Composition and Interfaces

The following C# example demonstrates the principle of using composition and interfaces to achieve code reuse and polymorphism.

```
class Program {
    static void Main() {
        var player = new Player();
        player.Update();
        player.Collide();
        player.Draw();
    }
```

```
}


interface IVisible {

    void Draw();

}


class Invisible : IVisible {

    public void Draw() {

        Console.Write("I won't appear.");

    }

}


class Visible : IVisible {

    public void Draw() {

        Console.Write("I'm showing myself.");

    }

}


interface ICollidable {

    void Collide();

}


class Solid : ICollidable {

    public void Collide() {

        Console.Write("Bang!");

    }

}
```

```csharp
class NotSolid : ICollidable {

    public void Collide() {

        Console.Write("Splash!");

    }

}


interface IUpdatable {

    void Update();

}


class Movable : IUpdatable {

    public void Update() {

        Console.Write("Moving forward.");

    }

}


class NotMovable : IUpdatable {

    public void Update() {

        Console.Write("I'm staying put.");

    }

}


abstract class GameObject : IVisible, IUpdatable, ICollidable {

    private readonly IVisible _v;

    private readonly IUpdatable _u;

    private readonly ICollidable _c;


    public GameObject(IVisible visible, IUpdatable updatable,
ICollidable collidable) {
```

```
        _v = visible;

        _u = updatable;

        _c = collidable;

    }


    public void Update() {

        _u.Update();

    }


    public void Draw() {

        _v.Draw();

    }


    public void Collide() {

        _c.Collide();

    }
}

class Player : GameObject {

    public Player() : base(new Visible(), new Movable(), new
Solid()) { }
}


class Cloud : GameObject {

    public Cloud() : base(new Visible(), new Movable(), new Not-
Solid()) { }
}


class Building : GameObject {
```

```
    public Building() : base(new Visible(), new NotMovable(),
new Solid()) { }

}


class Trap : GameObject {

    public Trap() : base(new Invisible(), new NotMovable(), new
Solid()) { }

}
```

Benefits

To favor composition over inheritance is a design principle that gives the design higher flexibility. It is more natural to build business-domain classes out of various components than trying to find commonality between them and creating a family tree. For example, a gas pedal and a wheel share very few common traits, yet are both vital components in a car. What they can do and how they can be used to benefit the car is easily defined. Composition also provides a more stable business domain in the long term as it is less prone to the quirks of the family members. In other words, it is better to compose what an object can do (*HAS-A*) than extend what it is (*IS-A*).

Initial design is simplified by identifying system object behaviors in separate interfaces instead of creating a hierarchical relationship to distribute behaviors among business-domain classes via inheritance. This approach more easily accommodates future requirements changes that would otherwise require a complete restructuring of business-domain classes in the inheritance model. Additionally, it avoids problems often associated with relatively minor changes to an inheritance-based model that includes several generations of classes.

Eric S. Raymond, a Unix programmer and open-source software advocate, has noted that overuse of inheritance leads to thickly layered programs that destroy transparency. Favoring composition over inheritance can help preserve against such cases.

Some languages, notably Go, use type composition exclusively.

Drawbacks

One common drawback of using composition instead of inheritance is that methods being provided by individual components may have to be implemented in the derived type, even if they are only forwarding methods. In contrast, inheritance does not require all of the base class's methods to be re-implemented within the derived class. Rather, the derived class only need to implement (override) the methods having different behavior than the base class methods. This can require significantly less programming effort if the base class contains many methods providing default behavior and only a few of them need to be overridden within the derived class.

For example, in the code below, the variables and methods of the Employee base class are inherited by the HourlyEmployee and SalariedEmployee derived subclasses. Only the Pay() method needs to be implemented (specialized) by each derived subclass. The other methods are implemented by the base class itself, and are shared by all of its derived subclasses; they do not need to be re-implemented (overridden) or even mentioned in the subclass definitions.

```
// Base class

public abstract class Employee

{

    // Member variables

    protected string    m_name;

    protected int        m_id;

    protected decimal    m_payRate;

    protected int        m_hoursWorked;


    // Get/set the employee's name

    public string Name

    {

        get { return m_name; }

        set { m_name = value; }

    }


    // Get/set the employee's ID

    public int ID

    {

        get { return m_id; }

        set { m_id = value; }

    }
```

```
// Get/set the employee's pay rate
public decimal PayRate
{
    get { return m_payRate; }
    set { m_payRate = value; }
}


// Get hours worked in the current pay period
public int HoursWorked()
{
    return m_hoursWorked;
}


// Get pay for the current pay period
abstract public decimal Pay();
}


// Derived subclass
public HourlyEmployee: Employee
{
    // Get pay for the current pay period
    public decimal Pay()
    {
        // Time worked is in hours
        return m_hoursWorked * m_payRate;
    }
}
```

```
// Derived subclass
public SalariedEmployee: Employee
{
    // Get pay for the current pay period
    public decimal Pay()
    {
        // Pay rate is annual salary instead of hourly rate
        return m_hoursWorked * m_payRate/2087;
    }
}
```

This drawback can be avoided by using traits, mixins, or protocol extensions. Some languages, such as Perl 6, provide a handles keyword to facilitate method forwarding. In Java, Project Lombok lets you implement delegation using a single @Delegate annotation on the field instead of copying and maintaining names and types of all methods from the delegated field. In Swift, extensions can be used to define a default implementation of a protocol on the protocol itself, rather than within an individual type's implementation.

Empirical Studies of Composition and Inheritance

A 2013 study of 93 open source Java programs (of varying size) found that

While there is [no] huge opportunity to replace inheritance with composition (...), the opportunity is significant (median of 2% of uses [of inheritance] are only internal reuse, and a further 22% are only external or internal reuse). Our results suggest there is no need for concern regarding abuse of inheritance (at least in open-source Java software), but they do highlight the question regarding use of composition versus inheritance. If there are significant costs associated with using inheritance when composition could be used, then our results suggest there is some cause for concern.

— *Tempero et al., "What programmers do with inheritance in Java"*

Common Component Architecture

The Common Component Architecture was a standard for Component-based software engineering used in high-performance also known as scientific) computing. Features of the Common Component Architecture that distinguish it from commercial component standards Component Object Model, CORBA, Enterprise Java Beans include support for FORTRAN programmers, multi-dimensional data arrays, exotic hardware and operating systems, and a variety of network data transports not typically suited for wide area networks.

Common Component Architecture activity appears to have ceased, with no news on the webpage since 2006.

Common Object Request Broker Architecture

The Common Object Request Broker Architecture (CORBA) is a standard defined by the Object Management Group (OMG) designed to facilitate the communication of systems that are deployed on diverse platforms. CORBA enables collaboration between systems on different operating systems, programming languages, and computing hardware. CORBA uses an object-oriented model although the systems that use the CORBA do not have to be object-oriented. CORBA is an example of the distributed object paradigm.

Overview

CORBA enables communication between software written in different languages and running on different computers. Implementation details from specific operating systems, programming languages, and hardware platforms are all removed from the responsibility of developers who use CORBA. CORBA normalizes the method-call semantics between application objects residing either in the same address-space (application) or in remote address-spaces (same host, or remote host on a network). Version 1.0 was released in October 1991.

CORBA uses an interface definition language (IDL) to specify the interfaces that objects present to the outer world. CORBA then specifies a *mapping* from IDL to a specific implementation language like C++ or Java. Standard mappings exist for Ada, C, C++, C++11, COBOL, Java, Lisp, PL/I, Object Pascal, Python, Ruby and Smalltalk. Non-standard mappings exist for C#, Erlang, Perl, Tcl and Visual Basic implemented by object request brokers (ORBs) written for those languages.

The CORBA specification dictates there shall be an ORB through which an application would interact with other objects. This is how it is implemented in practice:

1.   The application simply initializes the ORB, and accesses an internal *Object Adapter*, which maintains things like reference counting, object (and reference) instantiation policies, and object lifetime policies.

2. The Object Adapter is used to register instances of the *generated code classes*. Generated code classes are the result of compiling the user IDL code, which translates the high-level interface definition into an OS- and language-specific class base for use by the user application. This step is necessary in order to enforce CORBA semantics and provide a clean user process for interfacing with the CORBA infrastructure.

Some IDL mappings are more difficult to use than others. For example, due to the nature of Java, the IDL-Java mapping is rather straightforward and makes usage of CORBA very simple in a Java application. This is also true of the IDL to Python mapping. The C++ mapping requires the programmer to learn datatypes that predate the C++ Standard Template Library (STL). By contrast, the C++11 mapping is easier to use, but requires heavy use of the STL. Since the C language is not object-oriented, the IDL to C mapping requires a C programmer to manually emulate object-oriented features.

In order to build a system that uses or implements a CORBA-based distributed object interface, a developer must either obtain or write the IDL code that defines the object-oriented interface to the logic the system will use or implement. Typically, an ORB implementation includes a tool called an IDL compiler that translates the IDL interface into the target language for use in that part of the system. A traditional compiler then compiles the generated code to create the linkable-object files for use in the application. This diagram illustrates how the generated code is used within the CORBA infrastructure:

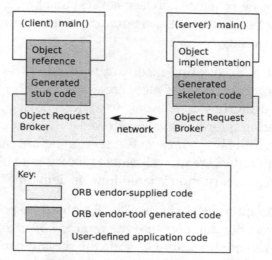

Illustration of the autogeneration of the infrastructure code from an interface defined using the CORBA IDL

This figure illustrates the high-level paradigm for remote interprocess communications using CORBA. The CORBA specification further addresses data typing, exceptions, network protocols, communication timeouts, etc. For example: Normally the server side has the Portable Object Adapter (POA) that redirects calls either to the local servants or (to balance the load) to the other servers. The CORBA specification (and thus this figure) leaves various aspects of distributed system to the application to define including object lifetimes (although reference counting semantics are available to applications), redundancy/fail-over, memory management, dynamic load balancing, and application-oriented models such as the separation between display/data/control semantics, etc.

In addition to providing users with a language and a platform-neutral remote procedure call (RPC) specification, CORBA defines commonly needed services such as transactions and security, events, time, and other domain-specific interface models.

Servants

A servant is the invocation target containing methods for handling the remote method invocations. In the newer CORBA versions, the remote object (on the server side) is split into the object *(that is exposed to remote invocations)* and servant *(to which the former part forwards the method calls)*. It can be one *servant* per remote *object*, or the same servant can support several (possibly all) objects, associated with the given Portable Object Adapter. The *servant* for each *object* can be set or found "once and forever" (servant activation) or dynamically chosen each time the method on that object is invoked (servant location). Both servant locator and servant activator can forward the calls to another server. In total, this system provides a very powerful means to balance the load, distributing requests between several machines. In the object-oriented languages, both remote *object* and its *servant* are objects from the viewpoint of the object-oriented programming.

Incarnation is the act of associating a servant with a CORBA object so that it may service requests. Incarnation provides a concrete servant form for the virtual CORBA object. Activation and deactivation refer only to CORBA objects, while the terms incarnation and etherealization refer to servants. However, the lifetimes of objects and servants are independent. You always incarnate a servant before calling activate_object(), but the reverse is also possible, create_reference() activates an object without incarnating a servant, and servant incarnation is later done on demand with a Servant Manager.

The *Portable Object Adapter* (POA) is the CORBA object responsible for splitting the server side remote invocation handler into the remote *object* and its *servant*. The object is exposed for the remote invocations, while the servant contains the methods that are actually handling the requests. The servant for each object can be chosen either statically (once) or dynamically (for each remote invocation), in both cases allowing the call forwarding to another server.

On the server side, the POAs form a tree-like structure, where each POA is responsible for one or more objects being served. The branches of this tree can be independently activated/deactivated, have the different code for the servant location or activation and the different request handling policies.

Features

The following describes some of the most significant ways that CORBA can be used to facilitate communication among distributed objects.

Objects by Reference

This reference is either acquired through a stringified Uniform Resource Locator (URL), NameService lookup (similar to Domain Name System (DNS)), or passed-in as a method parameter during a call.

Object references are lightweight objects matching the interface of the real object (remote or local). Method calls on the reference result in subsequent calls to the ORB and blocking on the thread while waiting for a reply, success or failure. The parameters, return data (if any), and exception data are marshaled internally by the ORB according to the local language and OS mapping.

Data by Value

The CORBA Interface Definition Language provides the language- and OS-neutral inter-object communication definition. CORBA Objects are passed by reference, while data (integers, doubles, structs, enums, etc.) are passed by value. The combination of Objects-by-reference and data-by-value provides the means to enforce strong data typing while compiling clients and servers, yet preserve the flexibility inherent in the CORBA problem-space.

Objects By Value (OBV)

Apart from remote objects, the CORBA and RMI-IIOP define the concept of the OBV and Valuetypes. The code inside the methods of Valuetype objects is executed locally by default. If the OBV has been received from the remote side, the needed code must be either *a priori* known for both sides or dynamically downloaded from the sender. To make this possible, the record, defining OBV, contains the Code Base that is a space-separated list of URLs whence this code should be downloaded. The OBV can also have the remote methods.

CORBA Component Model (CCM)

CORBA Component Model (CCM) is an addition to the family of CORBA definitions. It was introduced with CORBA 3 and it describes a standard application framework for CORBA components. Though not dependent on "language dependent Enterprise Java

Beans (EJB)", it is a more general form of EJB, providing four component types instead of the two that EJB defines. It provides an abstraction of entities that can provide and accept services through well-defined named interfaces called *ports*.

The CCM has a component container, where software components can be deployed. The container offers a set of services that the components can use. These services include (but are not limited to) notification, authentication, persistence and transaction processing. These are the most-used services any distributed system requires, and, by moving the implementation of these services from the software components to the component container, the complexity of the components is dramatically reduced.

Portable Interceptors

Portable interceptors are the "hooks", used by CORBA and RMI-IIOP to mediate the most important functions of the CORBA system. The CORBA standard defines the following types of interceptors:

1. IOR interceptors mediate the creation of the new references to the remote objects, presented by the current server.

2. Client interceptors usually mediate the remote method calls on the client (caller) side. If the object Servant exists on the same server where the method is invoked, they also mediate the local calls.

3. Server interceptors mediate the handling of the remote method calls on the server (handler) side.

The interceptors can attach the specific information to the messages being sent and IORs being created. This information can be later read by the corresponding interceptor on the remote side. Interceptors can also throw forwarding exceptions, redirecting request to another target.

General InterORB Protocol (GIOP)

The GIOP is an abstract protocol by which Object request brokers (ORBs) communicate. Standards associated with the protocol are maintained by the Object Management Group (OMG). The GIOP architecture provides several concrete protocols, including:

1. Internet InterORB Protocol (IIOP) – The Internet Inter-Orb Protocol is an implementation of the GIOP for use over the Internet, and provides a mapping between GIOP messages and the TCP/IP layer.

2. SSL InterORB Protocol (SSLIOP) – SSLIOP is IIOP over SSL, providing encryption and authentication.

3. HyperText InterORB Protocol (HTIOP) – HTIOP is IIOP over HTTP, providing transparent proxy bypassing.

4. Zipped IOP (ZIOP) – A zipped version of GIOP that reduces the bandwidth usage.

VMCID (Vendor Minor Codeset ID)

Each standard CORBA exception includes a minor code to designate the subcategory of the exception. Minor exception codes are of type unsigned long and consist of a 20-bit "Vendor Minor Codeset ID" (VMCID), which occupies the high order 20 bits, and the minor code proper which occupies the low order 12 bits.

Minor codes for the standard exceptions are prefaced by the VMCID assigned to OMG, defined as the unsigned long constant CORBA::OMGVMCID, which has the VMCID allocated to OMG occupying the high order 20 bits. The minor exception codes associated with the standard exceptions that are found in Table 3-13 on page 3-58 are or-ed with OMGVMCID to get the minor code value that is returned in the ex_body structure.

Within a vendor assigned space, the assignment of values to minor codes is left to the vendor. Vendors may request allocation of VMCIDs by sending email to tagrequest@omg.org.

The VMCID 0 and 0xfffff are reserved for experimental use. The VMCID OMGVMCID (Section 3.17.1, "Standard Exception Definitions," on page 3-52) and 1 through 0xf are reserved for OMG use.

The Common Object Request Broker: Architecture and Specification (CORBA 2.3)

Corba Location (CorbaLoc)

Corba Location (CorbaLoc) refers to a stringified object reference for a CORBA object that looks similar to a URL.

All CORBA products must support two OMG-defined URLs: "corbaloc:" and "corbaname:". The purpose of these is to provide a human readable and editable way to specify a location where an IOR can be obtained.

An example of corbaloc is shown below:

```
corbaloc::160.45.110.41:38693/StandardNS/NameServer-POA/_
root
```

A CORBA product may optionally support the "http:", "ftp:" and "file:" formats. The semantics of these is that they provide details of how to download a stringified IOR (or, recursively, download another URL that will eventually provide a stringified IOR). Some ORBs do deliver additional formats which are proprietary for that ORB.

Benefits

CORBA's benefits include language- and OS-independence, freedom from technology-linked implementations, strong data-typing, high level of tunability, and freedom from the details of distributed data transfers.

Language independence

CORBA was designed to free engineers from limitations of coupling their designs to a particular software language. Currently there are many languages supported by various CORBA providers, the most popular being Java and C++. There are also C++11, C-only, SmallTalk, Perl, Ada, Ruby, and Python implementations, just to mention a few.

OS-independence

CORBA's design is meant to be OS-independent. CORBA is available in Java (OS-independent), as well as natively for Linux/Unix, Windows, Solaris, OS X, OpenVMS, HPUX, Android, LynxOS, VxWorks, ThreadX, INTEGRITY, and others.

Freedom from technologies

One of the main implicit benefits is that CORBA provides a neutral playing field for engineers to be able to normalize the interfaces between various new and legacy systems. When integrating C, C++, Object Pascal, Java, Fortran, Python, and any other language or OS into a single cohesive system design model, CORBA provides the means to level the field and allow disparate teams to develop systems and unit tests that can later be joined together into a whole system. This does not rule out the need for basic system engineering decisions, such as threading, timing, object lifetime, etc. These issues are part of any system regardless of technology. CORBA allows system elements to be normalized into a single cohesive system model. For example, the design of a multitier architecture is made simple using Java Servlets in the web server and various CORBA servers containing the business logic and wrapping the database accesses. This allows the implementations of the business logic to change, while the interface changes would need to be handled as in any other technology. For example, a database wrapped by a server can have its database schema change for the sake of improved disk usage or performance (or even whole-scale database vendor change), without affecting the external interfaces. At the same time, C++ legacy code can talk to C/Fortran legacy code and Java database code, and can provide data to a web interface.

Data-typing

CORBA provides flexible data typing, for example an "ANY" datatype. COR-BA also enforces tightly coupled datatyping, reducing human errors. In a situation where Name-Value pairs are passed around, it is conceivable that a server provides a number where a string was expected. CORBA Interface Definition Language provides the mechanism to ensure that user-code conforms to method-names, return-, parameter-types, and exceptions.

High tunability

Many implementations (e.g. ORBexpress (Ada, C++, and Java implementation) and OmniORB (open source C++ and Python implementation)) have options for tuning the threading and connection management features. Not all ORB implementations provide the same features.

Freedom from data-transfer details

When handling low-level connection and threading, CORBA provides a high level of detail in error conditions. This is defined in the CORBA-defined standard exception set and the implementation-specific extended exception set. Through the exceptions, the application can determine if a call failed for reasons such as "Small problem, so try again", "The server is dead" or "The reference does not make sense." The general rule is: Not receiving an exception means that the method call completed successfully. This is a very powerful design feature.

Compression

CORBA marshals its data in a binary form and supports compression. IONA, Remedy IT, and Telefónica have worked on an extension to the CORBA standard that delivers compression. This extension is called ZIOP and this is now a formal OMG standard.

Problems and criticism

While CORBA delivered much in the way code was written and software constructed, it has been the subject of criticism.

Much of the criticism of CORBA stems from poor implementations of the standard and not deficiencies of the standard itself. Some of the failures of the standard itself were due to the process by which the CORBA specification was created and the compromises inherent in the politics and business of writing a common standard sourced by many competing implementors.

Initial implementation incompatibilities

The initial specifications of CORBA defined only the IDL, not the on-the-wire format. This meant that source-code compatibility was the best that was available for several years. With CORBA 2 and later this issue was resolved.

Location transparency

CORBA's notion of location transparency has been criticized; that is, that objects residing in the same address space and accessible with a simple function call are treated the same as objects residing elsewhere (different processes on the same machine, or different machines). This is a fundamental design flaw, as it makes all object access as complex as the most complex case (i.e., remote network call with a wide class of failures that are not possible in local calls). It also hides the inescapable differences between the two classes, making it impossible for applications to select an appropriate use strategy (that is, a call with 1µs latency and guaranteed return will be used very differently from a call with 1s latency with possible transport failure, in which the delivery status is potentially unknown and might take 30s to time out).

Design and process deficiencies

The creation of the CORBA standard is also often cited for its process of design by committee. There was no process to arbitrate between conflicting proposals or to decide on the hierarchy of problems to tackle. Thus the standard was created by taking a union of the features in all proposals with no regard to their coherence. This made the specification complex, expensive to implement entirely, and often ambiguous.

A design committee composed of a mixture of implementation vendors and customers created a diverse set of interests. This diversity made difficult a cohesive standard. Standards and interoperability increased competition and eased customers' movement between alternative implementations. This led to much political fighting within the committee and frequent releases of revisions of the CORBA standard that some ORB implementors ensured were difficult to use without proprietary extensions. Less ethical CORBA vendors encouraged customer lock-in and achieved strong short-term results. Over time the ORB vendors that encourage portability took over market share.

Problems with implementations

Through its history, CORBA has been plagued by shortcomings in poor ORB implementations. Unfortunately many of the papers criticizing CORBA as a standard are simply criticisms of a particularly bad CORBA ORB implementation.

CORBA is a comprehensive standard with many features. Few implementations attempt to implement all of the specifications, and initial implementations were incomplete or inadequate. As there were no requirements to provide a reference implementation, members were free to propose features which were never test-ed for usefulness or implementability. Implementations were further hindered by the general tendency of the standard to be verbose, and the common practice of compromising by adopting the sum of all submitted proposals, which often created APIs that were incoherent and difficult to use, even if the individual proposals were perfectly reasonable.

Robust implementations of CORBA have been very difficult to acquire in the past, but are now much easier to find. The SUN Java SDK comes with CORBA built-in. Some poorly designed implementations have been found to be com-plex, slow, incompatible and incomplete. Robust commercial versions began to appear but for significant cost. As good quality free implementations became available the bad commercial implementations died quickly.

Firewalls

CORBA (more precisely, GIOP) is not tied to any particular communications transport. A specialization of GIOP is the Internet Inter-ORB Protocol or IIOP. IIOP uses raw TCP/IP connections in order to transmit data.

If the client is behind a very restrictive firewall or transparent proxy server en-vironment that only allows HTTP connections to the outside through port 80, communication may be impossible, unless the proxy server in question allows the HTTP CONNECT method or SOCKS connections as well. At one time, it was difficult even to force implementations to use a single standard port — they tended to pick multiple random ports instead. As of today, current ORBs do have these deficiencies. Due to such difficulties, some users have made increas-ing use of web services instead of CORBA. These communicate using XML/SOAP via port 80, which is normally left open or filtered through a HTTP proxy inside the organization, for web browsing via HTTP. Recent CORBA implemen-tations, though, support SSL and can be easily configured to work on a single port. Some ORBS, such as TAO, omniORB and JacORB also support bidirec-tional GIOP, which gives CORBA the advantage of being able to use callback communication rather than the polling approach characteristic of web service implementations. Also, most modern firewalls support GIOP & IIOP and are thus CORBA-friendly firewalls.

Component Object Model

Component Object Model (COM) is a binary-interface standard for software compo-nents introduced by Microsoft in 1993. It is used to enable inter-process communica-tion and dynamic object creation in a large range of programming languages. COM is the basis for several other Microsoft technologies and frameworks, including OLE, OLE

Automation, Browser Helper Object, ActiveX, COM+, DCOM, the Windows shell, DirectX, UMDF and Windows Runtime. The essence of COM is a language-neutral way of implementing objects that can be used in environments different from the one in which they were created, even across machine boundaries. For well-authored components, COM allows reuse of objects with no knowledge of their internal implementation, as it forces component implementers to provide well-defined interfaces that are separated from the implementation. The different allocation semantics of languages are accommodated by making objects responsible for their own creation and destruction through reference-counting. Type conversion casting between different interfaces of an object is achieved through the QueryInterface method. The preferred method of "inheritance" within COM is the creation of sub-objects to which method "calls" are delegated.

COM is an interface technology defined and implemented as standard only on Microsoft Windows and Apple's Core Foundation 1.3 and later plug-in application programming interface (API). The latter only implements a subset of the whole COM interface. For some applications, COM has been replaced at least to some extent by the Microsoft .NET framework, and support for Web Services through the Windows Communication Foundation (WCF). However, COM objects can be used with all .NET languages through .NET COM Interop. Networked DCOM uses binary proprietary formats, while WCF encourages the use of XML-based SOAP messaging. COM is very similar to other component software interface technologies, such as CORBA and Java Beans, although each has its own strengths and weaknesses. Unlike C++, COM provides a stable application binary interface (ABI) that does not change between compiler releases. This makes COM interfaces attractive for object-oriented C++ libraries that are to be used by clients compiled using different compiler versions.

History

One of the first methods of interprocess communication in Windows was Dynamic Data Exchange (DDE), first introduced in 1987, that allowed sending and receiving messages in so-called "conversations" between applications. Antony Williams involved in the creation of the COM architecture, later distributed two internal papers in Microsoft that embraced the concept of software components: *Object Architecture: Dealing With the Unknown – or – Type Safety in a Dynamically Extensible Class Library* in 1988 and *On Inheritance: What It Means and How To Use It* in 1990. These provided the foundation of many of the ideas behind COM. Object Linking and Embedding (OLE), Microsoft's first object-based framework, was built on top of DDE and designed specifically for compound documents. It was introduced with Word for Windows and Excel in 1991, and was later included with Windows, starting with version 3.1 in 1992. An example of a compound document is a spreadsheet embedded in a Word for Windows document: as changes are made to the spreadsheet within Excel, they appear automatically inside the Word document.

In 1991, Microsoft introduced Visual Basic Extensions (VBX) with Visual Basic 1.0. A VBX is a packaged extension in the form of a dynamic-link library (DLL) that allows objects to be graphically placed in a form and manipulated by properties and methods. These were later adapted for use by other languages such as Visual C++. In 1992, when version 3.1 of Windows was released, Microsoft released OLE 2 with its underlying object model. The COM Application binary interface (ABI) was the same as the MAPI ABI, which was released in 1992. While OLE 1 was focused on compound documents, COM and OLE 2 were designed to address software components in general. Text conversations and Windows messages had proved not to be flexible enough to allow sharing application features in a robust and extensible way, so COM was created as a new foundation, and OLE changed to OLE2. In 1994 OLE custom controls (OCXs) were introduced as the successor to VBX controls. At the same time, Microsoft stated that OLE 2 would just be known as "OLE", and that OLE was no longer an acronym, but a name for all of the company's component technologies. In early 1996, Microsoft found a new use for OLE Custom Controls, expanding their Web browser's capability to present content, renamed some parts of OLE relating to the Internet "ActiveX", and gradually renamed all OLE technologies to ActiveX, except the compound document technology that was used in Microsoft Office. Later that year, DCOM was introduced as an answer to CORBA. In 2010, Wintempla incorporated the Com namespace; this namespace has a set of C++ classes to simplify the use of COM.

Related Technologies

COM was the major software development platform for Windows and, as such, influenced development of a number of supporting technologies.

COM+ and DCOM

In order for Microsoft to provide developers with support for distributed transactions, resource pooling, disconnected applications, event publication and subscription, better memory and processor (thread) management, as well as to position Windows as an alternative to other enterprise-level operating systems, Microsoft introduced a technology called Microsoft Transaction Server (MTS) on Windows NT 4. With Windows 2000, that significant extension to COM was incorporated into the operating system (as opposed to the series of external tools provided by MTS) and renamed COM+. At the same time, Microsoft de-emphasized DCOM as a separate entity. Components that made use of COM+ services were handled more directly by the added layer of COM+, in particular by operating system support for interception. In the first release of MTS, interception was tacked on - installing an MTS component would modify the Windows Registry to call the MTS software, and not the component directly. Windows 2000 also revised the Component Services control panel application used to configure COM+ components.

An advantage of COM+ was that it could be run in "component farms". Instances of a component, if coded properly, could be pooled and reused by new calls to its initializing routine without unloading it from memory. Components could also be distributed (called from another machine). COM+ and Microsoft Visual Studio provided tools to make it easy to generate client-side proxies, so although DCOM was used to make the remote call, it was easy to do for developers. COM+ also introduced a subscriber/publisher event mechanism called COM+ Events, and provided a new way of leveraging MSMQ (inter-application asynchronous messaging) with components called Queued Components. COM+ events extend the COM+ programming model to support late-bound events or method calls between the publisher or subscriber and the event system.

.NET

Microsoft .NET provides means both to provide component technology, and to interact with COM+ (via COM-interop-assemblies); .NET provides wrappers to most of the commonly used COM controls. Microsoft .NET hides most detail from component creation and therefore eases development. .NET can leverage COM+ via the System.EnterpriseServices namespace, and several of the services that COM+ provides have been duplicated in recent releases of .NET. For example, the System.Transactions namespace in .NET provides the TransactionScope class, which provides transaction management without resorting to COM+. Similarly, queued components can be replaced by Windows Communication Foundation with an MSMQ transport. (MSMQ is a native COM component, however.) There is limited support for backward compatibility. A COM object may be used in .NET by implementing a Runtime Callable Wrapper (RCW). NET objects that conform to certain interface restrictions may be used in COM objects by calling a *COM callable wrapper* (CCW). From both the COM and .NET sides, objects using the other technology appear as native objects. WCF (Windows Communication Foundation) eases a number of COM's remote execution challenges. For instance, it allows objects to be transparently marshalled by value across process or machine boundaries more easily.

Windows Runtime

Microsoft's new Windows Runtime programming and application model is essentially a COM-based API, although it relies on an enhanced COM. Because of its COM-like basis, Windows Runtime allows relatively easy interfacing from multiple languages, just as COM does, but it is essentially an unmanaged, native API. The API definitions are, however, stored in ".winmd" files, which are encoded in ECMA 335 metadata format, the same CLI metadata format that .NET uses with a few modifications. This common metadata format allows for significantly less overhead than P/Invoke when WinRT is invoked from .NET applications, and its syntax is much simpler.

Security

COM and ActiveX components are run as native code on the user's machine, with no sandboxing. There are therefore few restrictions on what the code can do. The prior practice of embedding ActiveX components on web pages with Internet Explorer did therefore lead to problems with malware infections. Microsoft recognized the problem with ActiveX as far back as 1996 when Charles Fitzgerald said, "We never made the claim up front that ActiveX is intrinsically secure". Recent versions of Internet Explorer prompt the user before installing ActiveX controls, enabling the user to disallow installation of controls from sites that the user does not trust. The ActiveX controls are signed with digital signatures to guarantee their authenticity. It is also possible to disable ActiveX controls altogether, or to allow only a selected few. The transparent support for out-of-process COM servers still promotes software safety in terms of process isolation. This can be useful for decoupling subsystems of large application into separate processes. Process isolation limits state corruption in one process from negatively affecting the integrity of the other processes, since they only communicate through strictly defined interfaces. Thus, only the affected subsystem needs to be restarted in order to regain valid state. This is not the case for subsystems within the same process, where a *rogue pointer* in one subsystem can randomly corrupt other subsystems.

Technical Details

COM programmers build their software using COM-aware components. Different component types are identified by class IDs (CLSIDs), which are Globally Unique Identifiers (GUIDs). Each COM component exposes its functionality through one or more interfaces. The different interfaces supported by a component are distinguished from each other using interface IDs (IIDs), which are GUIDs too. COM interfaces have bindings in several languages, such as C, C++, Visual Basic, Delphi, Python and several of the scripting languages implemented on the Windows platform. All access to components is done through the methods of the interfaces. This allows techniques such as inter-process, or even inter-computer programming (the latter using the support of DCOM).

Interfaces

All COM components implement the IUnknown (*custom*) interface, which exposes methods for reference counting and type conversion (casting). A *custom* IUnknown interface consists of a pointer to a virtual method table that contains a list of pointers to the functions that implement the functions declared in the interface, in the same order that they are declared in the interface. The in-process invocation overhead is therefore comparable to virtual method calls in C++. In addition to *custom* interfaces, COM also supports *dispatch* interfaces inheriting from IDispatch. Dispatch interfaces support late binding for OLE Automation. This allows *dispatch* interfaces to be natively accessed from a wider range of programming languages than *custom* interfaces.

Classes

A COM class ("coclass") is a concrete implementation of one or more interfaces, and closely resembles classes in object-oriented programming languages. Classes are created based on their class ID (CLSID) or based on their programmatic identifier string (progid). Like many object-oriented languages, COM provides a separation of interface from implementation. This distinction is especially strong in COM, where objects cannot be accessed directly, but only through their interfaces. COM also has support for multiple implementations of the same interface, so that clients at runtime can choose which implementation of an interface to instantiate.

Interface Definition Language and Type Libraries

Type libraries contain metadata to represent COM types. These types are described using Microsoft Interface Definition Language (MSIDL/IDL). IDL files define object-oriented classes, interfaces, structures, enumerations and other user-defined types in a language independent manner. IDL is similar in appearance to C++ declarations with some additional keywords such as "interface" and "library" for defining interfaces and collections of classes. IDL also supports the use of bracketed attributes before declarations to provide additional information, such as interface GUIDs and the relationships between pointer parameters and length fields. IDL files are compiled by the MIDL compiler. For C/C++, the MIDL compiler generates a compiler-independent header file containing struct definitions to match the vtbls of the declared interfaces and a C file containing declarations of the interface GUIDs. C++ source code for a proxy module can also be generated by the MIDL compiler. This proxy contains method stubs for converting COM calls into remote procedure calls to enable DCOM for out-of-process communication. IDL files can also be compiled by the MIDL compiler into a type library (TLB). TLB files contain binary metadata that can be processed by different language compilers and runtime environments (e.g. VB, Delphi, .NET etc.) to generate language-specific constructs to represent the COM types defined in the TLB. For C++, this will convert the TLB back to its IDL representation.

COM as an Object Framework

Because COM is a runtime framework, types have to be individually identifiable and specifiable at runtime. To achieve this, *globally unique identifiers* (GUIDs) are used. Each COM type is designated its own GUID for identification at runtime. In order for information on COM types to be accessible at both compile time and runtime, COM uses type libraries. It is through the effective use of *type libraries* that COM achieves its capabilities as a dynamic framework for the interaction of objects.

Consider the following example coclass definition in an IDL :

```
coclass SomeClass {

  [default] interface ISomeInterface;

};
```

The above code fragment declares a COM class named SomeClass which implements an interface named ISomeInterface.

This is conceptually equivalent to defining the following C++ class:

```
class SomeClass : public ISomeInterface {

    ...

    ...

};
```

where ISomeInterface is a C++ pure virtual class.

The IDL files containing COM interfaces and classes are compiled into type libraries (TLB) files, which can later be parsed by clients at runtime to determine which interfaces an object supports, and invoke an object's interface methods.

In C++, COM objects are instantiated with the CoCreateInstance function that takes the class ID (CLSID) and interface ID (IID) as arguments. Instantiation of SomeClass can be implemented as follows:

```
ISomeInterface* interface_ptr = NULL;

HRESULT hr = CoCreateInstance(CLSID_SomeClass, NULL, CLSCTX_ALL,
                              IID_ISomeInterface, (void**)&in-
terface_ptr);
```

In this example, the COM sub-system is used to obtain a pointer to an object that implements ISomeInterface interface, and coclass CLSID_SomeClass's particular implementation of this interface is required.

Reference Counting

All COM objects utilize reference counting to manage object lifetimes. The reference counts are controlled by the clients through the *AddRef* and *Release* methods in the mandatory IUnknown interface that all COM objects implement. COM objects are then responsible for freeing their own memory when the reference count drops to zero. Certain languages (e.g. Visual Basic) provide automatic reference counting so that COM object developers need not explicitly maintain any internal reference counter in their source codes. In C++, a coder may either perform explicit reference counting or use smart pointers to automatically manage the reference counts.

The following are guidelines for when to call *AddRef* and *Release* on COM objects:

- Functions and methods that return interface references (via return value or via "out" parameter) shall increment the reference count of the returned object before returning.

- *Release* must be called on an interface pointer before the pointer is overwritten or goes out of scope.

- If a copy is made on an interface reference pointer, *AddRef* should be called on that pointer.

- *AddRef* and *Release* must be called on the specific interface which is being referenced since an object may implement per-interface reference counts in order to allocate internal resources only for the interfaces which are being referenced.

All reference count calls are not sent out to remote objects over the wire; a proxy keeps only one reference on the remote object and maintains its own local reference count. To simplify COM development, Microsoft introduced ATL (Active Template Library) for C++ developers. ATL provides for a higher-level COM development paradigm. It also shields COM client application developers from the need to directly maintain reference counting, by providing smart pointer objects. Other libraries and languages that are COM-aware include the Microsoft Foundation Classes, the VC Compiler COM Support, VBScript, Visual Basic, ECMAScript (JavaScript) and Borland Delphi.

Programming

COM is a language agnostic binary standard that can be developed in any programming language capable of understanding and implementing its binary defined data types and interfaces. COM implementations are responsible for entering and leaving the COM environment, instantiating and reference-counting COM objects, querying objects for supported interfaces, as well as handling errors. The Microsoft Visual C++ compiler supports extensions to the C++ language referred to as *C++ Attributes*. These extensions are designed to simplify COM development and remove much of the plumbing code required to implement COM servers in C++.

Registry Usage

In Windows, COM classes, interfaces and type libraries are listed by GUIDs in the registry, under *HKEY_CLASSES_ROOT\CLSID* for classes and *HKEY_CLASSES_ROOT\Interface* for interfaces. COM libraries use the registry to locate either the correct local libraries for each COM object or the network location for a remote service.

Registration-free COM

Registration-Free COM (RegFree COM) is a technology introduced with Windows XP that allows Component Object Model (COM) components to store activation metadata and CLSID (Class ID) for the component without using the registry. Instead, the metadata and CLSIDs of the classes implemented in the component are declared in an assembly manifest (described using XML), stored either as a resource in the executable or as a separate file installed with the component. This allows multiple versions of the same component to be installed in different directories, described by their own manifests, as well as XCOPY deployment. This technique has limited support for EXE COM servers and cannot be used for system-wide components such as MDAC, MSXML, DirectX or Internet Explorer.

During application loading, the Windows loader searches for the manifest. If it is present, the loader adds information from it to the activation context. When the COM class factory tries to instantiate a class, the activation context is first checked to see if an implementation for the CLSID can be found. Only if the lookup fails is the registry scanned.

Manually Instantiating COM Objects

COM objects can also be created manually, given the path of the DLL file and GUID of the object. This does not require the DLL or GUID to be registered in the system registry, and does not make use of manifest files. A COM DLL exports a function named DllGetClassObject. Calling DllGetClassObject with the desired GUID and IID_IClassFactory provides an instance of a factory object. The Factory object has a CreateInstance method, which can create instances of an object given an interface GUID. This is the same process internally used when creating instances of registered COM components.

Process and Network Transparency

COM objects can be transparently instantiated and referenced from within the same process (in-process), across process boundaries (out-of-process), or remotely over the network (DCOM). Out-of-process and remote objects use marshalling to serialize method calls and return values over process or network boundaries. This marshalling is invisible for the client, who accesses the object as if it were a local in-process object.

Threading

In COM, threading is addressed through a concept known as *apartments*. All COM objects live in exactly one apartment, which might either be single-threaded or multi-threaded. There are three types of apartments in COM: *Single-Threaded Apartment (STA)*, *Multi-Threaded Apartment (MTA)*, and *Thread Neutral Apartment* (NA). Each apartment represents one mechanism whereby an object's internal state may be synchronized across multiple threads. A process can consist of multiple COM objects, some of which may use STA and others of which may use MTA. All threads accessing COM objects similarly live in one apartment. The choice of apartment for COM objects and threads are determined at run-time, and cannot be changed.

Apartment type	Description
Single-Threaded Apartment (STA), (ThreadingModel=Apartment)	A single thread is dedicated to execute the methods of the object. In such an arrangement, method calls from threads outside of the apartment are marshalled and automatically queued by the system (via a standard Windows message queue). Thus, the COM run-time provides automatic synchronization to ensure that each method call of an object is always executed to completion before another is invoked. The developer therefore does not need to worry about thread locking or race conditions.
Multi-Threaded Apartment (MTA), (ThreadingModel=Free)	The COM run-time provides no synchronization, and multiple threads are allowed to call COM objects simultaneously. COM objects therefore need to perform their own synchronization to prevent simultaneous access from multiple threads from causing a race condition. Calls to an MTA object from a thread in an STA are also marshalled.
Dynamically determined apartment (ThreadingModel=Both)	In the Both apartment mode, the server auto-selects STA or MTA at object creation to match the apartment type of the calling thread. This can be useful to avoid marshaling overhead when MTA servers are accessed by a STA thread.
Thread Neutral Apartment (NA), (ThreadingModel=Neutral)	A special apartment without any assigned threads. When a STA or MTA thread calls a NA object in the same process, then the calling thread temporarily leaves its apartment and executes code directly in the NA without any thread switching. Therefore, one can think of NA as an optimization for efficient interapartment method calls.

Threads and objects which belong to the same apartment follow the same thread access rules. Method calls which are made inside the same apartment are therefore performed directly without any assistance from COM. Method calls made across apartments are achieved via marshalling. This requires the use of proxies and stubs.

Criticisms

Since COM has a fairly complex implementation, programmers can be distracted by some of the "plumbing" issues.

Message Pumping

When an STA is initialized it creates a hidden window that is used for inter-apartment and inter-process message routing. This window must have its message queue regularly "pumped". This construct is known as a "message pump". On earlier versions of Windows, failure to do so could cause system-wide deadlocks. This problem is complicated by some Windows APIs that initialize COM as part of their implementation, which causes a "leak" of implementation details.

Reference Counting

Reference counting within COM may cause problems if two or more objects are circularly referenced. The design of an application must take this into account so that objects are not left orphaned. Objects may also be left with active reference counts if the COM "event sink" model is used. Since the object that fires the event needs a reference to the object reacting to the event, the latter's reference count will never reach zero. Reference cycles are typically broken using either out-of-band termination or split identities. In the out-of-band termination technique, an object exposes a method which, when called, forces it to drop its references to other objects, thereby breaking the cycle. In the split identity technique, a single implementation exposes two separate COM objects (also known as identities). This creates a weak reference between the COM objects, preventing a reference cycle.

DLL Hell

Because in-process COM components are implemented in DLL files and registration only allows for a single version per CLSID they might in some situations be subject to the "DLL Hell" effect. Registration-free COM capability eliminates this problem.

Distributed Component Object Model

Distributed Component Object Model (DCOM) is a proprietary Microsoft technology for communication between software components on networked computers. DCOM, which originally was called "Network OLE", extends Microsoft's COM, and provides the communication substrate under Microsoft's COM+ application server infrastructure.

The addition of the "D" to COM was due to extensive use of DCE/RPC (Distributed Computing Environment/Remote Procedure Calls) – more specifically Microsoft's enhanced version, known as MSRPC.

In terms of the extensions it added to COM, DCOM had to solve the problems of

- Marshalling – serializing and deserializing the arguments and return values of method calls "over the wire".

- Distributed garbage collection – ensuring that references held by clients of interfaces are released when, for example, the client process crashed, or the network connection was lost.

- It had to combine Hundreds/Tens of Thousands of objects held in the client's browser with a single transmission in order to minimize bandwidth utilization.

One of the key factors in solving these problems is the use of DCE/RPC as the underlying RPC mechanism behind DCOM. DCE/RPC has strictly defined rules regarding marshalling and who is responsible for freeing memory.

DCOM was a major competitor to CORBA. Proponents of both of these technologies saw them as one day becoming the model for code and service-reuse over the Internet. However, the difficulties involved in getting either of these technologies to work over Internet firewalls, and on unknown and insecure machines, meant that normal HTTP requests in combination with web browsers won out over both of them. Microsoft, at one point, attempted and failed to head this off by adding an extra http transport to DCE/RPC called *ncacn_http* (Network Computing Architecture connection-oriented protocol). This was later resurrected to support a Microsoft Exchange 2003 connection over HTTP.

DCOM is supported natively in Windows NT 4.0, Windows 2000, Windows XP, and Windows Server 2003, as well as Windows 7, Windows 8, Windows 10, Windows Server 2008, Windows Server 2008 R2, Windows Server 2012, Windows Server 2012 R2 and the Windows Server 2016 Technical Preview.

Hardening

As part of the initiative that began at Microsoft as part of Secure Development Lifecycle to re-architect insecure code, DCOM saw some significant security-focused changes in Windows XP Service Pack 2.

Alternative Versions and Implementations

COMsource: Its source code is available, along with full and complete documentation, sufficient to use and also implement an interoperable version of DCOM. According to that documentation, COMsource comes directly from the Windows NT 4.0 source code, and even includes the source code for a Windows NT Registry Service.

The Wine Team is also implementing DCOM for binary interoperability purposes; they are not currently interested in the networking side of DCOM, which is provided by MSRPC. They are restricted to implementing NDR (Network Data Representation) through Microsoft's API, but are committed to making it as compatible as possible with MSRPC.

TangramCOM is a separate project from Wine, focusing on implementing DCOM on Linux-based smartphones.

The Samba Team is also implementing DCOM for over-the-wire interoperability purposes: unlike the Wine Team, they are not currently interested in binary-interoperability, as the Samba MSRPC implementation is far from binary-interoperable with Microsoft's MSRPC.

References

- Arad, Cosmin (April 2013). Programming Model and Protocols for Reconfigurable Distributed Systems (PDF). Doctoral Dissertation. Stockholm, Sweden: KTH Royal Institute of Technology. ISBN 978-91-7501-694-8.

- Freeman, Eric; Freeman, Elisabeth; Sierra, Kathy; Bates, Bert (2004). Hendrickson, Mike; Loukides, Mike, eds. "Head First Design Patterns" (paperback). 1. O'REILLY: 23. ISBN 978-0-596-00712-6.

- Eric S. Raymond (2003). "The Art of Unix Programming: Unix and Object-Oriented Languages". Retrieved 2014-08-06.

- Tempero, Ewan; Yang, Hong Yul; Noble, James (2013). What programmers do with inheritance in Java (PDF). ECOOP 2013—Object-Oriented Programming. pp. 577–601.

- Waldo, Jim; Geoff Wyant; Ann Wollrath; Sam Kendall (November 1994). "A Note on Distributed Computing" (PDF). Sun Microsystem Laboratories. Retrieved 4 November 2013.

- Chappel, David (May 1998). "Trouble with CORBA". www.davidchappel.com. Archived from the original on 3 Dec 2012. Retrieved 15 March 2010.

- Knoernschild, Kirk (2002). Java Design - Objects, UML, and Process: 1.1.5 Composite Reuse Principle (CRP). Addison-Wesley Inc. Retrieved 2012-05-29.

- "Dijkstra, Wybe Edsger". Encyclopedia.com. Retrieved 2011-07-29. In his view, the key to a good computing science program was to consider it as a branch of mathematics.

## 8

Software Development Processes

Value stream mapping is a method that is used in analyzing the current state and also in analyzing and then designing a future state of the various stages that a product goes through from manufacture to distriburtion. The other software development practices used are kanban, queueing theory, test-driven development, node graph architecture and software architectural model. The aspects explained in this section are of vital importance and provide a better understanding of software development practices.

Value Stream Mapping

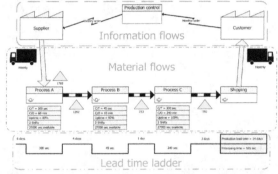

Value stream mapping usually employs standard symbols to represent items and processes, therefore knowledge of these symbols is essential to correctly interpret the production system problems.

Value stream mapping is a lean-management method for analyzing the current state and designing a future state for the series of events that take a product or service from its beginning through to the customer. At Toyota, it is known as "material and information flow mapping". It can be applied to nearly any value chain.

Using the Method

Applications

Value stream mapping has supporting methods that are often used in Lean environments to analyze and design flows at the system level (across multiple processes).

Although value stream mapping is often associated with manufacturing, it is also used in logistics, supply chain, service related industries, healthcare, software development, product development, and administrative and office processes.

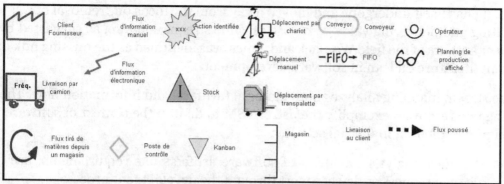

Value Stream Maps are usually drawn using a set of standard symbols, some of which can be seen here.

A paper value stream map.

In a build-to-the-standard form, Shigeo Shingo suggests that the value-adding steps be drawn across the centre of the map and the non-value-adding steps be represented in vertical lines at right angles to the value stream. Thus, the activities become easily separated into the value stream, which is the focus of one type of attention, and the 'waste' steps, another type. He calls the value stream the process and the non-value streams the operations. The thinking here is that the non-value-adding steps are often preparatory or tidying up to the value-adding step and are closely associated with the person or machine/workstation that executes that value-adding step. Therefore, each vertical line is the 'story' of a person or workstation whilst the horizontal line represents the 'story' of the product being created.

Value stream mapping is a recognised method used as part of Six Sigma methodologies.

Value Stream Mapping in Software Engineering

The success of Lean in manufacturing and production has led to an interest in its adoption in software development. However, it was noted that the current literature on adoption of Lean in software development had a disconnect between the high-level principles and the concrete practices related to lean and agile software development. The literature had also a limited focus on wastes that were literally mapped from the categories identified for manufacturing. This was ignoring the transformation that lean thinking has itself undergone and moved away from the focus on "removal of waste" to "creating and delivering value" The use of value stream mapping as suggested by the pioneer authors of the field Womack and Jones was identified as the missing link in the current literature on lean in software development.

Value stream mapping analyzes both material (artifact) and information flow. The following two resources exemplify the use of VSM to do it in the context of software process improvement in industrial settings:

- "Artifact analysis:" analysis of software artifacts like requirements, use case, change request or defect report through the development process

- "Information flow analysis:" analysis of information flows in the development process

Metrics

Two key metrics associated with value stream mapping are value adding times and non value adding times. Non value adding time is called waste or muda.

Associated Analysis Methods

Hines and Rich (1997) defined seven value stream mapping tools they are:

1. Process Activity Mapping
2. Supply chain responsiveness matrix
3. Product Variety Funnel
4. Quality filter mapping
5. Forrester effect mapping
6. Decision point analysis
7. Overall Structure Maps

Theory of Constraints

The theory of constraints (TOC) is a management paradigm that views any manageable system as being limited in achieving more of its goals by a very small number of constraints. There is always at least one constraint, and TOC uses a focusing process to identify the constraint and restructure the rest of the organization around it. TOC adopts the common idiom "a chain is no stronger than its weakest link." This means that processes, organizations, etc., are vulnerable because the weakest person or part can always damage or break them or at least adversely affect the outcome.

History

The theory of constraints (TOC) is an overall management philosophy introduced by Eliyahu M. Goldratt in his 1984 book titled *The Goal*, that is geared to help organizations continually achieve their goals. Goldratt adapted the concept to project management with his book *Critical Chain*, published in 1997.

An earlier propagator of a similar concept was Wolfgang Mewes in Germany with publications on *power-oriented management theory* (Machtorientierte Führungstheorie, 1963) and following with his *Energo-Kybernetic System (EKS, 1971)*, later renamed *Engpasskonzentrierte Strategie* as a more advanced *theory of bottlenecks*. The publications of Wolfgang Mewes are marketed through the FAZ Verlag, publishing house of the German newspaper *Frankfurter Allgemeine Zeitung*. However, the paradigm *Theory of constraints* was first used by Goldratt.

Key Assumption

The underlying premise of the theory of constraints is that organizations can be measured and controlled by variations on three measures: throughput, operational expense, and inventory. Inventory is all the money that the system has invested in purchasing things which it intends to sell. Operational expense is all the money the system spends in order to turn inventory into throughput. Throughput is the rate at which the system generates money through sales.

Before the goal itself can be reached, necessary conditions must first be met. These typically include safety, quality, legal obligations, etc. For most businesses, the goal itself is to make money. However, for many organizations and non-profit businesses, making money is a necessary condition for pursuing the goal. Whether it is the goal or a necessary condition, understanding how to make sound financial decisions based on throughput, inventory, and operating expense is a critical requirement.

The Five Focusing Steps

Theory of constraints is based on the premise that the rate of goal achievement by a goal-oriented system (i.e., the system's throughput) is limited by at least one constraint.

The argument by reductio ad absurdum is as follows: If there was nothing preventing a system from achieving higher throughput (i.e., more goal units in a unit of time), its throughput would be infinite — which is impossible in a real-life system.

Only by increasing flow through the constraint can overall throughput be increased.

Assuming the goal of a system has been articulated and its measurements defined, the steps are:

1. Identify the system's constraint(s).

2. Decide how to exploit the system's constraint(s).

3. Subordinate everything else to the above decision(s).

4. Elevate the system's constraint(s).

5. Warning! If in the previous steps a constraint has been broken, go back to step 1, but do not allow inertia to cause a system's constraint.

The goal of a commercial organization is: "Make more money now and in the future", and its measurements are given by throughput accounting as: throughput, inventory, and operating expenses.

The five focusing steps aim to ensure ongoing improvement efforts are centered on the organization's constraint(s). In the TOC literature, this is referred to as the *process of ongoing improvement* (POOGI).

These focusing steps are the key steps to developing the specific applications mentioned below.

Constraints

A constraint is anything that prevents the system from achieving its goal. There are many ways that constraints can show up, but a core principle within TOC is that there are not tens or hundreds of constraints. There is at least one but at most only a few in any given system. Constraints can be internal or external to the system. An internal constraint is in evidence when the market demands more from the system than it can deliver. If this is the case, then the focus of the organization should be on discovering that constraint and following the five focusing steps to open it up (and potentially remove it). An external constraint exists when the system can produce more than the market will bear. If this is the case, then the organization should focus on mechanisms to create more demand for its products or services.

Types of (internal) constraints

- Equipment: The way equipment is currently used limits the ability of the system to produce more salable goods/services.

- People: Lack of skilled people limits the system. Mental models held by people can cause behaviour that becomes a constraint.

- Policy: A written or unwritten policy prevents the system from making more.

The concept of the constraint in Theory of Constraints is analogous to but differs from the constraint that shows up in mathematical optimization. In TOC, the constraint is used as a focusing mechanism for management of the system. In optimization, the constraint is written into the mathematical expressions to limit the scope of the solution (X can be no greater than 5).

Please note: organizations have many problems with equipment, people, policies, etc. (A breakdown is just that – a breakdown – and is not a constraint in the true sense of the TOC concept) The constraint is the limiting factor that is preventing the organization from getting more throughput (typically, revenue through sales) even when nothing goes wrong.

Breaking a Constraint

If a constraint's throughput capacity is elevated to the point where it is no longer the system's limiting factor, this is said to "break" the constraint. The limiting factor is now some other part of the system, or may be external to the system (an external constraint).

Buffers

Buffers are used throughout the theory of constraints. They often result as part of the exploit and subordinate steps of the five focusing steps. Buffers are placed before the governing constraint, thus ensuring that the constraint is never starved. Buffers are also placed behind the constraint to prevent downstream failure from blocking the constraint's output. Buffers used in this way protect the constraint from variations in the rest of the system and should allow for normal variation of processing time and the occasional upset (Murphy) before and behind the constraint.

Buffers can be a bank of physical objects before a work center, waiting to be processed by that work center. Buffers ultimately buy you time, as in the time before work reaches the constraint and are often verbalized as time buffers. There should always be enough (but not excessive) work in the time queue before the constraint and adequate offloading space behind the constraint.

Buffers are *not* the small queue of work that sits before every work center in a Kanban system although it is similar if you regard the assembly line as the governing constraint. A prerequisite in the theory is that with one constraint in the system, all other parts of the system must have sufficient capacity to keep up with the work at the constraint and to catch up if time was lost. In a balanced line, as espoused by Kanban, when one work center goes down for a period longer than the buffer allows, then the entire system must wait until that work center is restored. In a TOC system, the only situation where work is in danger is if the constraint is unable to process (either due to malfunction, sickness or a "hole" in the buffer – if something goes wrong that the time buffer can not protect).

Buffer management, therefore, represents a crucial attribute of the theory of constraints. There are many ways to apply buffers, but the most often used is a visual system of designating the buffer in three colors: green (okay), yellow (caution) and red (action required). Creating this kind of visibility enables the system as a whole to align and thus subordinate to the need of the constraint in a holistic manner. This can also be done daily in a central operations room that is accessible to everybody.

Plant Types

There are four primary types of plants in the TOC lexicon. Draw the flow of material from the bottom of a page to the top, and you get the four types. They specify the general flow of materials through a system, and they provide some hints about where to look for typical problems. The four types can be combined in many ways in larger facilities.

- I-plant: Material flows in a sequence, such as in an assembly line. The primary work is done in a straight sequence of events (one-to-one). The constraint is the slowest operation.

- A-plant: The general flow of material is many-to-one, such as in a plant where many sub-assemblies converge for a final assembly. The primary problem in A-plants is in synchronizing the converging lines so that each supplies the final assembly point at the right time.

- V-plant: The general flow of material is one-to-many, such as a plant that takes one raw material and can make many final products. Classic examples are meat rendering plants or a steel manufacturer. The primary problem in V-plants is "robbing" where one operation (A) immediately after a diverging point "steals" materials meant for the other operation (B). Once the material has been processed by A, it cannot come back and be run through B without significant rework.

- T-plant: The general flow is that of an I-plant (or has multiple lines), which then splits into many assemblies (many-to-many). Most manufactured parts are used in multiple assemblies and nearly all assemblies use multiple parts. Customized devices, such as computers, are good examples. T-plants suffer from both synchronization problems of A-plants (parts aren't all available for an assembly) and the robbing problems of V-plants (one assembly steals parts that could have been used in another).

For non-material systems, one can draw the flow of work or the flow of processes and arrive at similar basic structures. A project, for example, is an A-shaped sequence of work, culminating in a delivered project.

Applications

The focusing steps, this process of ongoing improvement, have been applied to manufacturing, project management, supply chain/distribution generated specific solutions. Other tools (mainly the "thinking process") also led to TOC applications in the fields of marketing and sales, and finance. The solution as applied to each of these areas are listed below.

Operations

Within manufacturing operations and operations management, the solution seeks to pull materials through the system, rather than push them into the system. The primary methodology used is drum-buffer-rope (DBR) and a variation called simplified drum-buffer-rope (S-DBR).

Drum-buffer-rope is a manufacturing execution methodology based on the fact the output of a system can only be the same as the output at the constraint of the system. Any attempt to produce more than what the constraint can process just leads to excess inventory piling up. The method is named for its three components. The *drum* is the physical constraint of the plant: the work center or machine or operation that limits the ability of the entire system to produce more. The rest of the plant follows the beat of the drum. Schedule at the drum decides what the system should produce, in what sequence to produce and how much to produce. They make sure the drum has work and that anything the drum has processed does not get wasted.

The *buffer* protects the drum, so that it always has work flowing to it. Buffers in DBR provide the additional lead time beyond the required set up and process times, for materials in the product flow. Since these buffers have time as their unit of measure, rather than quantity of material, this makes the priority system operate strictly based on the time an order is expected to be at the drum. Each work order will have a remaining buffer status that can be calculated. Based on this buffer status work orders can be color coded into Red, Yellow and Green. The red orders have the highest priority and must worked on first since they have penetrated most into their buffers followed by yellow and green. As time evolves this buffer status might change and the color assigned to the particular work order change with it.

Traditional DBR usually calls for buffers at several points in the system: the constraint, synchronization points and at shipping. S-DBR has a buffer at shipping and manages the flow of work across the drum through a load planning mechanism.

The *rope* is the work release mechanism for the plant. Orders are released to the shop floor at one "buffer time" before they are due. In other words, if the buffer is 5 days, the order is released 5 days before it is due at the constraint. Putting work into the system earlier than this buffer time is likely to generate too-high work-in-process and slow down the entire system.

High-speed Automated Production Lines

Automated production lines that are used in the beverage industry to fill containers usually have several machines executing parts of the complete process, from filling primary containers to secondary packaging and palletisation. These machines operate at different speeds and capacities and have varying efficiency levels.

To be able to maximize the throughput, the production line usually has a designed constraint. This constraint is typically the slowest and usually the most expensive machine on the line. The overall throughput of the line is determined by this machine. All other machines can operate faster and are connected by conveyors.

The conveyors usually have the ability to buffer product. In the event of a stoppage at a machine other than the constraint, the conveyor can buffer the product enabling the constraint machine to keep on running.

A typical line setup is such that in normal operation the upstream conveyors from the constraint machine are always run full to prevent starvation at the constraint and the downstream conveyors are run empty to prevent a back up at the constraint. The overall aim is to prevent minor stoppages at the machines from impacting the constraint.

For this reason as the machines get further from the constraint, they have the ability to run faster than the previous machine and this creates a V curve.

Supply Chain and Logistics

In general, the solution for supply chains is to create flow of inventory so as to ensure greater availability and to eliminate surpluses.

The TOC distribution solution is effective when used to address a single link in the supply chain and more so across the entire system, even if that system comprises many different companies. The purpose of the TOC distribution solution is to establish a decisive competitive edge based on extraordinary availability by dramatically reducing the damages caused when the flow of goods is interrupted by shortages and surpluses.

This approach uses several new rules to protect availability with less inventory than is conventionally required. Before explaining these new rules, the term Replenishment Time must be defined. Replenishment Time (RT) is the sum of the delay, after the first consumption following a delivery, before an order is placed plus the delay after the order is placed until the ordered goods arrive at the ordering location.

1. Inventory is held at an aggregation point(s) as close as possible to the source. This approach ensures smoothed demand at the aggregation point, requiring proportionally less inventory. The distribution centers holding the aggregated stock are able to ship goods downstream to the next link in the supply chain much more quickly than a make-to-order manufacturer can.

2. Following this rule may result in a make-to-order manufacturer converting to

make-to-stock. The inventory added at the aggregation point is significantly less than the inventory reduction downstream.

3. In all stocking locations, initial inventory buffers are set which effectively create an upper limit of the inventory at that location. The buffer size is equal to the maximum expected consumption within the average RT, plus additional stock to protect in case a delivery is late. In other words, there is no advantage in holding more inventory in a location than the amount that might be consumed before more could be ordered and received. Typically, the sum of the on hand value of such buffers are 25–75% less than currently observed average inventory levels.

4. Once buffers have been established, no replenishment orders are placed as long as the quantity inbound (already ordered but not yet received) plus the quantity on hand are equal to or greater than the buffer size. Following this rule causes surplus inventory to be bled off as it is consumed.

5. For any reason, when on hand plus inbound inventory is less than the buffer, orders are placed as soon as practical to increase the inbound inventory so that the relationship On Hand + Inbound = Buffer is maintained.

6. To ensure buffers remain correctly sized even with changes in the rates of demand and replenishment, a simple recursive algorithm called Buffer Management is used. When the on hand inventory level is in the upper third of the buffer for a full RT, the buffer is reduced by one third (and don't forget rule 3). Alternatively, when the on hand inventory is in the bottom one third of the buffer for too long, the buffer is increased by one third (and don't forget rule 4). The definition of "too long" may be changed depending on required service levels, however, a rule of thumb is 20% of the RT. Moving buffers up more readily than down is supported by the usually greater damage caused by shortages as compared to the damage caused by surpluses.

Once inventory is managed as described above, continuous efforts should be undertaken to reduce RT, late deliveries, supplier minimum order quantities (both per SKU and per order) and customer order batching. Any improvements in these areas will automatically improve both availability and inventory turns, thanks to the adaptive nature of Buffer Management.

A stocking location that manages inventory according to the TOC should help a non-TOC customer (downstream link in a supply chain, whether internal or external) manage their inventory according to the TOC process. This type of help can take the form of a vendor managed inventory (VMI). The TOC distribution link simply extends its buffer sizing and management techniques to its customers' inventories. Doing so has the effect of smoothing the demand from the customer and reducing order sizes per SKU. VMI results in better availability and inventory turns for both supplier and customer.

More than that, the benefits to the non-TOC customers are sufficient to meet the purpose of capitalizing on the decisive competitive edge by giving the customer a powerful reason to be more loyal and give more business to the upstream link. When the end consumers buy more the whole supply chain sells more.

One caveat should be considered. Initially and only temporarily, the supply chain or a specific link may sell less as the surplus inventory in the system is sold. However, the immediate sales lift due to improved availability is a countervailing factor. The current levels of surpluses and shortages make each case different.

Finance and Accounting

The solution for finance and accounting is to apply holistic thinking to the finance application. This has been termed throughput accounting. Throughput accounting suggests that one examine the impact of investments and operational changes in terms of the impact on the throughput of the business. It is an alternative to cost accounting.

The primary measures for a TOC view of finance and accounting are: throughput, operating expense and investment. Throughput is calculated from sales minus "totally variable cost", where totally variable cost is usually calculated as the cost of raw materials that go into creating the item sold.

Project Management

Critical Chain Project Management (CCPM) are utilized in this area. CCPM is based on the idea that all projects look like A-plants: all activities converge to a final deliverable. As such, to protect the project, there must be internal buffers to protect synchronization points and a final project buffer to protect the overall project.

Marketing and Sales

While originally focused on manufacturing and logistics, TOC has expanded lately into sales management and marketing. Its role is explicitly acknowledged in the field of sales process engineering. For effective sales management one can apply Drum Buffer Rope to the sales process similar to the way it is applied to operations. This technique is appropriate when your constraint is in the sales process itself or you just want an effective sales management technique and includes the topics of funnel management and conversion rates.

Thinking Processes

The thinking processes are a set of tools to help managers walk through the steps of initiating and implementing a project. When used in a logical flow, the thinking processes help walk through a buy-in process:

1. Gain agreement on the problem

2. Gain agreement on the direction for a solution

3. Gain agreement that the solution solves the problem

4. Agree to overcome any potential negative ramifications

5. Agree to overcome any obstacles to implementation

TOC practitioners sometimes refer to these in the negative as working through *layers of resistance* to a change.

Recently, the *current reality tree* (CRT) and *future reality tree* (FRT) have been applied to an argumentative academic paper.

Despite its origins as a manufacturing approach (Goldratt & Cox, The Goal: A process of Ongoing Improvement, 1992), Goldratt's Theory of Constraints (TOC) methodology is now regarded as a systems methodology with strong foundations in the hard sciences (Mabin, 1999). Through its tools for convergent thinking and synthesis, the "Thinking processes", which underpin the entire TOC methodology, help identify and manage constraints and guide continuous improvement and change in organizations (Dettmer H., 1998).

The process of change requires the identification and acceptance of core issues; the goal and the means to the goal. This comprehensive set of logical tools can be used for exploration, solution development and solution implementation for individuals, groups or organizations. Each tool has a purpose and nearly all tools can be used independently (Cox & Spencer, 1998). Since these thinking tools are designed to address successive "layers of resistance" and enable communication, it expedites securing "buy in" of groups. While CRT (current reality tree) represents the undesirable effects of the current situation, the FRT (the future reality tree), NBR (negative branch) help people plan and understand the possible results of their actions. The PRT (Perquisite tree) and TRT (transition tree) are designed to build collective buy in and aid in the Implementation phase. The logical constructs of these tools or diagrams are the necessary condition logic, the sufficient cause logic and the strict logic rules that are used to validate cause-effect relationships which are modelled with these tools (Dettmer W., 2006).

A summary of these tools, the questions they help answer and the associated logical constructs used is presented in the table below.

	Sufficient thinking "If....... then"	Necessary Thinking "In order to...we must"
What to change?	Current Reality Tree	
What to change to?	Future Reality Tree Negative Branch Reservations	Evaporating cloud
How to change?	Transition Tree	Perquisite Tree

TOC Thinking Process Tools: Use of these tools are based on the fundamental beliefs of TOC that organizations a) are inherently simple (interdependencies exist in organizations) b) desire inherent harmony (win – win solutions are possible) c) are inherently good (people are good) and have inherent potential (people and organizations have potential to do better) (Goldratt E. , 2009). In the book "Through the clouds to solutions" Jelena Fedurko (Fedurko, 2013) states that the major areas for application of TP tools as:

- To create and enhance thinking and learning skills

- To make better decisions

- To develop responsibility for one's own actions through understanding their consequences

- To handle conflicts with more confidence and win-win outcomes

- To correct behavior with undesirable consequences

- Assist in evaluating conditions for achieving a desired outcome

- To assist in peer mediation

- To assist in relationship between subordinates and bosses

Development and Practice

TOC was initiated by Goldratt, who until his recent death was still the main driving force behind the development and practice of TOC. There is a network of individuals and small companies loosely coupled as practitioners around the world. TOC is sometimes referred to as "constraint management". TOC is a large body of knowledge with a strong guiding philosophy of growth.

Criticism

Criticisms that have been leveled against TOC include:

Claimed Suboptimality of Drum-Buffer-Rope

While TOC has been compared favorably to linear programming techniques, D. Trietsch from University of Auckland argues that DBR methodology is inferior to competing methodologies. Linhares, from the Getulio Vargas Foundation, has shown that the TOC approach to establishing an optimal product mix is unlikely to yield optimum results, as it would imply that P=NP.

Unacknowledged Debt

Duncan (as cited by Steyn) says that TOC borrows heavily from systems dynamics developed by Forrester in the 1950s and from statistical process control which dates back to World War II. And Noreen Smith and Mackey, in their independent report on TOC, point out that several key concepts in TOC "have been topics in management accounting textbooks for decades.

People claim Goldratt's books fail to acknowledge that TOC borrows from more than 40 years of previous management science research and practice, particularly from program evaluation and review technique/critical path method (PERT/CPM) and the just in time strategy. A rebuttal to these criticisms is offered in Goldratt's "What is the *Theory of Constraints* and How Should it be Implemented?", and in his audio program, "Beyond The Goal". In these, Goldratt discusses the history of disciplinary sciences, compares the strengths and weaknesses of the various disciplines, and acknowledges the sources of information and inspiration for the thinking processes and critical chain methodologies. Articles published in the now-defunct Journal of *Theory of Constraints* referenced foundational materials. Goldratt published an article and gave talks with the title "Standing on the Shoulders of Giants" in which he gives credit for many of the core ideas of Theory of Constraints. Goldratt has sought many times to show the correlation between various improvement methods. However, many Goldratt adherents often denigrate other methodologies as inferior to TOC.

Goldratt has been criticized on lack of openness in his theories, an example being him not releasing the algorithm he used for the Optimum Performance Training system. Some view him as unscientific with many of his theories, tools and techniques not being a part of the public domain, rather a part of his own framework of profiting on his ideas. According to Gupta and Snyder (2009), despite being recognized as a genuine management philosophy nowadays, TOC has yet failed to demonstrate its effectiveness in the academic literature and as such cannot be considered academically worthy enough to be called a widely recognized theory. TOC needs more case studies that prove a connection between implementation and improved financial performance. Nave (2002) argues that TOC does not take employees into account and fails to empower them in the production process. He also states that TOC fails to address unsuccessful policies as constraints. In contrast, Mukherjee and Chatterjee (2007) state that much of the criticism of Goldratt's work has been focused on the lack of rigour in his work, but not of the bottleneck approach, which are two different aspects of the issue.

Certification and Education

The Theory of Constraints International Certification Organization (TOCICO) is an independent not-for-profit incorporated society that sets exams to ensure a consistent standard of competence. It is overseen by a board of academic and industrial experts. It also hosts an annual international conference. The work presented at these conferences constitutes a core repository of the current knowledge.

Kanban

Kanban (literally signboard or billboard in Japanese) is a scheduling system for lean manufacturing and just-in-time manufacturing (JIT). Kanban is an inventory-control system to control the supply chain. Taiichi Ohno, an industrial engineer at Toyota, developed kanban to improve manufacturing efficiency. Kanban is one method to achieve JIT.

Kanban became an effective tool to support running a production system as a whole, and an excellent way to promote improvement. Problem areas are highlighted by reducing the number of kanban in circulation. One of the main benefits of kanban is to establish an upper limit to the work in process inventory, avoiding overloading of the manufacturing system. Other systems with similar effect are for example CONWIP. A systematic study of various configurations of kanban systems, of which CONWIP is an important special case, can be found in Tayur (1993), among other papers.

An English-language term that captures the meaning of the Japanese word, kanban, is *queue limiter*; and the beneficial result is *queue limitation*. Operationally, then, as process problems are dealt with, the queue limit (or maximum) should be reduced; for example, a former upper limit of five pieces is reduced to four, with queue time in the process reduced by 20 percent.

Origins

In the late 1940s, Toyota started studying supermarkets with the idea of applying shelf-stocking techniques to the factory floor. In a supermarket, customers generally retrieve what they need at the required time—no more, no less. Furthermore, the supermarket stocks only what it expects to sell in a given time, and customers take only what they need, because future supply is assured. This observation led Toyota to view a process as being a customer of one or more preceding processes, and to view the preceding processes as a kind of store. The "customer" process goes to the store to get required components, which in turn causes the store to restock. Originally, as in supermarkets, signboards guided "shopping" processes to specific shopping locations within the store.

Kanban aligns inventory levels with actual consumption. A signal tells a supplier to produce and deliver a new shipment when material is consumed. These signals are tracked through the replenishment cycle, bringing visibility to the supplier, consumer, and buyer.

Kanban uses the rate of demand to control the rate of production, passing demand from the end customer up through the chain of customer-store processes. In 1953, Toyota applied this logic in their main plant machine shop.

Operation

One key indicator of the success of production scheduling based on demand, *pushing,* is the ability of the demand-forecast to create such a *push.* Kanban, by contrast, is part of an approach where the "pull" comes from demand. Re-supply or production is determined according to the actual demand of the customer. In contexts where supply time is lengthy and demand is difficult to forecast, often, the best one can do is to respond quickly to observed demand. This situation is exactly what a kanban system accomplishes, in that it is used as a demand signal that immediately travels through the supply chain. This ensures that intermediate stock held in the supply chain are better managed, and are usually smaller. Where the supply response is not quick enough to meet actual demand fluctuations, thereby causing potential lost sales, stock building may be deemed more appropriate, and is achieved by placing more kanban in the system.

Taiichi Ohno stated that, to be effective, kanban must follow strict rules of use. Toyota, for example, has six simple rules, and close monitoring of these rules is a never-ending task, thereby ensuring that the kanban does what is required.

Toyota's Six Rules

Toyota has formulated six rules for the application of kanban:

- Later process picks up the number of items indicated by the kanban at the earlier process.

- Earlier process produces items in the quantity and sequence indicated by the kanban.

- No items are made or transported without a kanban.

- Always attach a kanban to the goods.

- Defective products are not sent on to the subsequent process. The result is 100% defect-free goods.

- Reducing the number of kanban increases the sensitivity.

Kanban Cards

Kanban cards are a key component of kanban and they signal the need to move materials within a production facility or to move materials from an outside supplier into the production facility. The kanban card is, in effect, a message that signals depletion of product, parts, or inventory. When received, the kanban triggers replenishment of that product, part, or inventory. Consumption, therefore, drives demand for more production, and the kanban card signals demand for more product—so kanban cards help create a demand-driven system.

It is widely held by proponents of lean production and manufacturing that demand-driven systems lead to faster turnarounds in production and lower inventory levels, helping companies implementing such systems be more competitive.

In the last few years, systems sending kanban signals electronically have become more widespread. While this trend is leading to a reduction in the use of kanban cards in aggregate, it is still common in modern lean production facilities to find use of kanban cards. In various software systems, kanban is used for signalling demand to suppliers through email notifications. When stock of a particular component is depleted by the quantity assigned on kanban card, a "kanban trigger" is created (which may be manual or automatic), a purchase order is released with predefined quantity for the supplier defined on the card, and the supplier is expected to dispatch material within a specified lead-time.

Kanban cards, in-keeping with the principles of kanban, simply convey the need for more materials. A red card lying in an empty parts cart conveys that more parts are needed.

Three-Bin System

An example of a simple kanban system implementation is a "three-bin system" for the supplied parts, where there is no in-house manufacturing. One bin is on the factory floor (the initial demand point), one bin is in the factory store (the inventory control point), and one bin is at the supplier. The bins usually have a removable card containing the product details and other relevant information—the classic kanban card.

When the bin on the factory floor is empty (because the parts in it were used up in a manufacturing process), the empty bin and its kanban card are returned to the factory store (the inventory control point). The factory store replaces the empty bin on the factory floor with the full bin from the factory store, which also contains a kanban card. The factory store sends the empty bin with its kanban card to the supplier. The supplier's full product bin, with its kanban card, is delivered to the factory store; the supplier keeps the empty bin. This is the final step in the process. Thus, the process never runs out of product—and could be described as a closed loop, in that it provides the exact amount required, with only one spare bin so there is never oversupply. This 'spare' bin allows for uncertainties in supply, use, and transport in the inventory system. A good kanban system calculates just enough kanban cards for each product. Most factories that use kanban use the coloured board system (heijunka box).

Electronic Kanban

Many manufacturers have implemented electronic kanban (sometimes referred to as E-kanban) systems. These help to eliminate common problems such as manual entry errors and lost cards. E-kanban systems can be integrated into enterprise resource planning (ERP) systems, enabling real-time demand signaling across the supply chain and improved visibility. Data pulled from E-kanban systems can be used to optimize inventory levels by better tracking supplier lead and replenishment times.

E-kanban is a signaling system that uses a mix of technology to trigger the movement of materials within a manufacturing or production facility. Electronic kanban differs from traditional kanban in that it uses technology to replace traditional elements such as kanban cards with barcodes and electronic messages such as email or Electronic data interchange.

A typical electronic kanban system marks inventory with barcodes, which workers scan at various stages of the manufacturing process to signal usage. The scans relay messages to internal/external stores to ensure restocking of products. Electronic kanban often uses the internet as a method of routing messages to external suppliers and as a means to allow a real time view of inventory, via a portal, throughout the supply chain.

Organizations such as the Ford Motor Company and Bombardier Aerospace have used electronic kanban systems to improve processes. Systems are now widespread from single solutions or bolt on modules to ERP systems.

Types of Kanban Systems

In a kanban system, adjacent upstream and downstream workstations communicate with each other through their cards, where each container has a kanban associated with it. Economic Order Quantity is important. The two most important types of kanbans are:

- Production (P) Kanban: A P-kanban, when received, authorizes the workstation to produce a fixed amount of products. The P-kanban is carried on the containers that are associated with it.

- Transportation (T) Kanban: A T-kanban authorizes the transportation of the full container to the downstream workstation. The T-kanban is also carried on the containers that are associated with the transportation to move through the loop again.

Queueing Theory

Queueing theory is the mathematical study of waiting lines, or queues. In queueing theory, a model is constructed so that queue lengths and waiting time can be predicted. Queueing theory is generally considered a branch of operations research because the results are often used when making business decisions about the resources needed to provide a service.

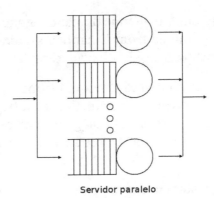

Servidor paralelo

Queue networks are systems in which single queues are connected by a routing network. In this image, servers are represented by circles, queues by a series of rectangles and the routing network by arrows. In the study of queue networks one typically tries to obtain the equilibrium distribution of the network, although in many applications the study of the transient state is fundamental.

Queueing theory has its origins in research by Agner Krarup Erlang when he created models to describe the Copenhagen telephone exchange. The ideas have since seen applications including telecommunication, traffic engineering, computing and the design of factories, shops, offices and hospitals.

Spelling

The spelling "queueing" over "queuing" is typically encountered in the academic research field. In fact, one of the flagship journals of the profession is named *Queueing Systems*.

Single Queueing Nodes

Single queueing nodes are usually described using Kendall's notation in the form $A/S/C$ where A describes the time between arrivals to the queue, S the size of jobs and C the number of servers at the node. Many theorems in queueing theory can be proved by reducing queues to mathematical systems known as Markov chains, first described by Andrey Markov in his 1906 paper.

Agner Krarup Erlang, a Danish engineer who worked for the Copenhagen Telephone Exchange, published the first paper on what would now be called queueing theory in 1909. He modeled the number of telephone calls arriving at an exchange by a Poisson process and solved the M/D/1 queue in 1917 and M/D/k queueing model in 1920. In Kendall's notation:

- M stands for Markov or memoryless and means arrivals occur according to a Poisson process

- D stands for deterministic and means jobs arriving at the queue require a fixed amount of service

- k describes the number of servers at the queueing node ($k = 1, 2,...$). If there are more jobs at the node than there are servers then jobs will queue and wait for service

The M/M/1 queue is a simple model where a single server serves jobs that arrive according to a Poisson process and have exponentially distributed service requirements. In an M/G/1 queue the G stands for general and indicates an arbitrary probability distribution. The M/G/1 model was solved by Felix Pollaczek in 1930, a solution later recast in probabilistic terms by Aleksandr Khinchin and now known as the Pollaczek–Khinchine formula.

After the 1940s queueing theory became an area of research interest to mathematicians. In 1953 David George Kendall solved the GI/M/k queue and introduced the modern notation for queues, now known as Kendall's notation. In 1957 Pollaczek studied the GI/G/1 using an integral equation. John Kingman gave a formula for the mean waiting time in a G/G/1 queue: Kingman's formula.

The matrix geometric method and matrix analytic methods have allowed queues with phase-type distributed inter-arrival and service time distributions to be considered.

Problems such as performance metrics for the M/G/k queue remain an open problem.

Service Disciplines

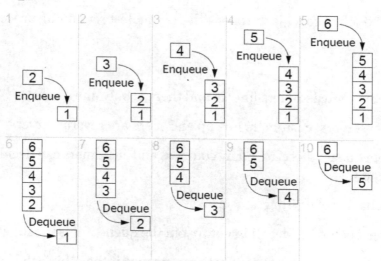

First in first out (FIFO) queue example.

Various scheduling policies can be used at queuing nodes:

First in first out

This principle states that customers are served one at a time and that the customer that has been waiting the longest is served first.

Last in first out

> This principle also serves customers one at a time, but the customer with the shortest waiting time will be served first. Also known as a stack.

Processor sharing

> Service capacity is shared equally between customers.

Priority

> Customers with high priority are served first. Priority queues can be of two types, non-preemptive (where a job in service cannot be interrupted) and pre-emptive (where a job in service can be interrupted by a higher-priority job). No work is lost in either model.

Shortest job first

> The next job to be served is the one with the smallest size

Preemptive shortest job first

> The next job to be served is the one with the original smallest size

Shortest remaining processing time

> The next job to serve is the one with the smallest remaining processing requirement.

Service facility

- Single server: customers line up and there is only one server

- Parallel servers: customers line up and there are several servers

- Tandem queue: there are many counters and customers can decide going where to queue

Customer's behavior of waiting

- Balking: customers deciding not to join the queue if it is too long

- Jockeying: customers switch between queues if they think they will get served faster by so doing

- Reneging: customers leave the queue if they have waited too long for service

Queueing Networks

Networks of queues are systems in which a number of queues are connected by customer routing. When a customer is serviced at one node it can join another node and queue for service, or leave the network. For a network of m the state of the system can be described by an m–dimensional vector $(x_1, x_2, ..., x_m)$ where x_i represents the number of customers at each node.

The first significant results in this area were Jackson networks, for which an efficient product-form stationary distribution exists and the mean value analysis which allows average metrics such as throughput and sojourn times to be computed. If the total number of customers in the network remains constant the network is called a closed network and has also been shown to have a product–form stationary distribution in the Gordon–Newell theorem. This result was extended to the BCMP network where a network with very general service time, regimes and customer routing is shown to also exhibit a product-form stationary distribution. The normalizing constant can be calculated with the Buzen's algorithm, proposed in 1973.

Networks of customers have also been investigated, Kelly networks where customers of different classes experience different priority levels at different service nodes. Another type of network are G-networks first proposed by Erol Gelenbe in 1993: these networks do not assume exponential time distributions like the classic Jackson Network.

Example of M/M/1

Birth and Death process

- A/B/C

Birth and death process.

A:distribution of arrival time

B:distribution of service time

C:the number of parallel servers

A system of inter-arrival time and service time showed exponential distribution, we denoted M.

λ : the average arrival rate

μ : the average service rate of a single service

P : the probability of n customers in system

n :the number of people in system

- Let E represent the number of times of entering state n, and L represent the number of times of leaving state n. We have $|E-L| \in \{0,1\}$. When the system arrives at steady state, which means t, we have, therefore arrival rate=removed rate.

- Balance equation

situation 0: $\mu_1 P_1 = \lambda_0 P_0$

situation 1: $\lambda_0 P_0 + \mu_2 P_2 = (\lambda_1 + \mu_1) P_1$

situation n: $\lambda_{n-1} P_{n-1} + \mu_{n+1} P_{n+1} = (\lambda_n + \mu_n) P_n$

By balance equation, $P_1 = \dfrac{\lambda_0}{\mu_1} P_0 \quad P_2 = \dfrac{\lambda_1}{\mu_2} P_1 + \dfrac{1}{\mu_2}(\mu_1 P_1 - \lambda_0 P_0) = \dfrac{\lambda_1}{\mu_2} P_1 = \dfrac{\lambda_1 \lambda_0}{\mu_2 \mu_1} P_0$

By mathematical induction, $P_n = \dfrac{\lambda_{n-1} \lambda_{n-2} \cdots \lambda_0}{\mu_n \mu_{n-1} \cdots \mu_1} P_0 = P_0 \displaystyle\prod_{i=0}^{n-1} \dfrac{\lambda_i}{\mu_{i+1}}$

Because $\displaystyle\sum_{n=0}^{\infty} P_n = P_0 + P_0 \sum_{n=1}^{\infty} \prod_{i=0}^{n-1} \dfrac{\lambda_i}{\mu_{i+1}} = 1$

we get $P_0 = \dfrac{1}{1 + \displaystyle\sum_{n=1}^{\infty} \prod_{i=0}^{n-1} \dfrac{\lambda_i}{\mu_{i+1}}}$

Routing Algorithms

In discrete time networks where there is a constraint on which service nodes can be active at any time, the max-weight scheduling algorithm chooses a service policy to give optimal throughput in the case that each job visits only a single service node. In the more general case where jobs can visit more than one node, backpressure routing gives optimal throughput.

A network scheduler must choose a queuing algorithm, which affects the characteristics of the larger network.

Mean Field Limits

Mean field models consider the limiting behaviour of the empirical measure (proportion of queues in different states) as the number of queues (m above) goes to infinity. The impact of other queues on any given queue in the network is approximated by a differential equation. The deterministic model converges to the same stationary distribution as the original model.

Fluid Limits

Fluid models are continuous deterministic analogs of queueing networks obtained by taking the limit when the process is scaled in time and space, allowing heterogeneous objects. This scaled trajectory converges to a deterministic equation which allows the stability of the system to be proven. It is known that a queueing network can be stable, but have an unstable fluid limit.

Heavy Traffic/Diffusion Approximations

In a system with high occupancy rates (utilisation near 1) a heavy traffic approximation can be used to approximate the queueing length process by a reflected Brownian motion, Ornstein–Uhlenbeck process or more general diffusion process. The number of dimensions of the RBM is equal to the number of queueing nodes and the diffusion is restricted to the non-negative orthant.

Software for Simulation/Analysis

- Java Modelling Tools, a GPL suite of queueing theory tools written in Java
- Queueing Package for GNU Octave
- Discrete Event Simulation for Python
- Queueing Process Models in the Wolfram Language
- PDQ software package for R statistical computing
- SimEvents for MATLAB

Test-Driven Development

Test-driven development (TDD) is a software development process that relies on the repetition of a very short development cycle: requirements are turned into very specific test cases, then the software is improved to pass the new tests, only. This is opposed to software development that allows software to be added that is not proven to meet requirements.

Kent Beck, who is credited with having developed or 'rediscovered' the technique, stated in 2003 that TDD encourages simple designs and inspires confidence.

Test-driven development is related to the test-first programming concepts of extreme programming, begun in 1999, but more recently has created more general interest in its own right.

Programmers also apply the concept to improving and debugging legacy code developed with older techniques.

Test-Driven Development Cycle

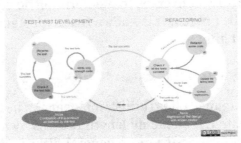

A graphical representation of the test-driven development lifecycle

The following sequence is based on the book *Test-Driven Development by Example*.

1. Add a Test

In test-driven development, each new feature begins with writing a test. Write a test that defines a function or improvements of a function, which should be very succinct. To write a test, the developer must clearly understand the feature's specification and requirements. The developer can accomplish this through use cases and user stories to cover the requirements and exception conditions, and can write the test in whatever testing framework is appropriate to the software environment. It could be a modified version of an existing test. This is a differentiating feature of test-driven development versus writing unit tests *after* the code is written: it makes the developer focus on the requirements *before* writing the code, a subtle but important difference.

2. Run all Tests and See if the New Test Fails

This validates that the test harness is working correctly, shows that the new test does not pass without requiring new code because the required behaviour already exists, and it rules out the possibility that the new test is flawed and will always pass. The new test should fail for the expected reason. This step increases the developer's confidence in the new test.

3. Write the Code

The next step is to write some code that causes the test to pass. The new code written at this stage is not perfect and may, for example, pass the test in an inelegant way. That is acceptable because it will be improved and honed in Step 5.

At this point, the only purpose of the written code is to pass the test. The programmer must not write code that is beyond the functionality that the test checks.

4. Run Tests

If all test cases now pass, the programmer can be confident that the new code meets the test requirements, and does not break or degrade any existing features. If they do not, the new code must be adjusted until they do.

5. Refactor Code

The growing code base must be cleaned up regularly during test-driven development. New code can be moved from where it was convenient for passing a test to where it more logically belongs. Duplication must be removed. Object, class, module, variable and method names should clearly represent their current purpose and use, as extra functionality is added. As features are added, method bodies can get longer and other objects larger. They benefit from being split and their parts carefully named to improve readability and maintainability, which will be increasingly valuable later in the software lifecycle. Inheritance hierarchies may be rearranged to be more logical and helpful, and perhaps to benefit from recognised design patterns. There are specific and general guidelines for refactoring and for creating clean code. By continually re-running the test cases throughout each refactoring phase, the developer can be confident that process is not altering any existing functionality.

The concept of removing duplication is an important aspect of any software design. In this case, however, it also applies to the removal of any duplication between the test code and the production code—for example magic numbers or strings repeated in both to make the test pass in Step 3.

Repeat

Starting with another new test, the cycle is then repeated to push forward the functionality. The size of the steps should always be small, with as few as 1 to 10 edits between each test run. If new code does not rapidly satisfy a new test, or other tests fail unexpectedly, the programmer should undo or revert in preference to excessive debugging. Continuous integration helps by providing revertible checkpoints. When using external libraries it is important not to make increments that are so small as to be effectively merely testing the library itself, unless there is some reason to believe that the library is buggy or is not sufficiently feature-complete to serve all the needs of the software under development.

Development Style

There are various aspects to using test-driven development, for example the principles of "keep it simple, stupid" (KISS) and "You aren't gonna need it" (YAGNI). By focusing on writing only the code necessary to pass tests, designs can often be cleaner and clearer than is achieved by other methods. In *Test-Driven Development by Example*, Kent Beck also suggests the principle "Fake it till you make it".

To achieve some advanced design concept such as a design pattern, tests are written that generate that design. The code may remain simpler than the target pattern, but still pass all required tests. This can be unsettling at first but it allows the developer to focus only on what is important.

Writing the tests first: The tests should be written before the functionality that is to be tested. This has been claimed to have many benefits. It helps ensure that the application is written for testability, as the developers must consider how to test the application from the outset rather than adding it later. It also ensures that tests for every feature get written. Additionally, writing the tests first leads to a deeper and earlier understanding of the product requirements, ensures the effectiveness of the test code, and maintains a continual focus on software quality. When writing feature-first code, there is a tendency by developers and organisations to push the developer on to the next feature, even neglecting testing entirely. The first TDD test might not even compile at first, because the classes and methods it requires may not yet exist. Nevertheless, that first test functions as the beginning of an executable specification.

Each test case fails initially: This ensures that the test really works and can catch an error. Once this is shown, the underlying functionality can be implemented. This has led to the "test-driven development mantra", which is "red/green/refactor", where red means *fail* and green means *pass*. Test-driven development constantly repeats the steps of adding test cases that fail, passing them, and refactoring. Receiving the expected test results at each stage reinforces the developer's mental model of the code, boosts confidence and increases productivity.

Keep the Unit Small

For TDD, a unit is most commonly defined as a class, or a group of related functions often called a module. Keeping units relatively small is claimed to provide critical benefits, including:

- Reduced debugging effort – When test failures are detected, having smaller units aids in tracking down errors.

- Self-documenting tests – Small test cases are easier to read and to understand.

Advanced practices of test-driven development can lead to acceptance test-driven development (ATDD) and Specification by example where the criteria specified by the customer are automated into acceptance tests, which then drive the traditional unit test-driven development (UTDD) process. This process ensures the customer has an automated mechanism to decide whether the software meets their requirements. With ATDD, the development team now has a specific target to satisfy – the acceptance tests – which keeps them continuously focused on what the customer really wants from each user story.

Best Practices

Test Structure

Effective layout of a test case ensures all required actions are completed, improves the readability of the test case, and smooths the flow of execution. Consistent structure helps in building a self-documenting test case. A commonly applied structure for test cases has (1) setup, (2) execution, (3) validation, and (4) cleanup.

- Setup: Put the Unit Under Test (UUT) or the overall test system in the state needed to run the test.

- Execution: Trigger/drive the UUT to perform the target behavior and capture all output, such as return values and output parameters. This step is usually very simple.

- Validation: Ensure the results of the test are correct. These results may include explicit outputs captured during execution or state changes in the UUT & UAT.

- Cleanup: Restore the UUT or the overall test system to the pre-test state. This restoration permits another test to execute immediately after this one.

Individual Best Practices

Individual best practices states that one should:

- Separate common set-up and teardown logic into test support services utilized by the appropriate test cases.

- Keep each test oracle focused on only the results necessary to validate its test.

- Design time-related tests to allow tolerance for execution in non-real time operating systems. The common practice of allowing a 5-10 percent margin for late execution reduces the potential number of false negatives in test execution.

- Treat your test code with the same respect as your production code. It also must work correctly for both positive and negative cases, last a long time, and be readable and maintainable.

- Get together with your team and review your tests and test practices to share effective techniques and catch bad habits. It may be helpful to review this section during your discussion.

Practices to Avoid, or "Anti-Patterns"

- Having test cases depend on system state manipulated from previously executed test cases (i.e., you should always start a unit test from a known and pre-configured state).

- Dependencies between test cases. A test suite where test cases are dependent upon each other is brittle and complex. Execution order should not be presumed. Basic refactoring of the initial test cases or structure of the UUT causes a spiral of increasingly pervasive impacts in associated tests.

- Interdependent tests. Interdependent tests can cause cascading false negatives. A failure in an early test case breaks a later test case even if no actual fault exists in the UUT, increasing defect analysis and debug efforts.

- Testing precise execution behavior timing or performance.

- Building "all-knowing oracles." An oracle that inspects more than necessary is more expensive and brittle over time. This very common error is dangerous because it causes a subtle but pervasive time sink across the complex project.

- Testing implementation details.

- Slow running tests.

Benefits

A 2005 study found that using TDD meant writing more tests and, in turn, programmers who wrote more tests tended to be more productive. Hypotheses relating to code quality and a more direct correlation between TDD and productivity were inconclusive.

Programmers using pure TDD on new ("greenfield") projects reported they only rarely felt the need to invoke a debugger. Used in conjunction with a version control system, when tests fail unexpectedly, reverting the code to the last version that passed all tests may often be more productive than debugging.

Test-driven development offers more than just simple validation of correctness, but can also drive the design of a program. By focusing on the test cases first, one must imagine how the functionality is used by clients (in the first case, the test cases). So, the programmer is concerned with the interface before the implementation. This benefit is complementary to design by contract as it approaches code through test cases rather than through mathematical assertions or preconceptions.

Test-driven development offers the ability to take small steps when required. It allows a programmer to focus on the task at hand as the first goal is to make the test pass. Exceptional cases and error handling are not considered initially, and tests to create these extraneous circumstances are implemented separately. Test-driven development ensures in this way that all written code is covered by at least one test. This gives the programming team, and subsequent users, a greater level of confidence in the code.

While it is true that more code is required with TDD than without TDD because of the unit test code, the total code implementation time could be shorter based on a model by Müller and Padberg. Large numbers of tests help to limit the number of defects in the code. The early and frequent nature of the testing helps to catch defects early in the development cycle, preventing them from becoming endemic and expensive problems. Eliminating defects early in the process usually avoids lengthy and tedious debugging later in the project.

TDD can lead to more modularized, flexible, and extensible code. This effect often comes about because the methodology requires that the developers think of the software in terms of small units that can be written and tested independently and integrated together later. This leads to smaller, more focused classes, looser coupling, and cleaner interfaces. The use of the mock object design pattern also contributes to the overall modularization of the code because this pattern requires that the code be written so that modules can be switched easily between mock versions for unit testing and "real" versions for deployment.

Because no more code is written than necessary to pass a failing test case, automated tests tend to cover every code path. For example, for a TDD developer to add an else branch to an existing if statement, the developer would first have to write a failing test case that motivates the branch. As a result, the automated tests resulting from TDD tend to be very thorough: they detect any unexpected changes in the code's behaviour. This detects problems that can arise where a change later in the development cycle unexpectedly alters other functionality.

Madeyski provided an empirical evidence (via a series of laboratory experiments with over 200 developers) regarding the superiority of the TDD practice over the classic Test-Last approach, with respect to the lower coupling between objects (CBO). The mean effect size represents a medium (but close to large) effect on the basis of meta-analysis of the performed experiments which is a substantial finding. It suggests a better modularization (i.e., a more modular design), easier reuse and testing of the developed software products due to the TDD programming practice. Madeyski also measured the effect of the TDD practice on unit tests using branch coverage (BC) and mutation score indicator (MSI), which are indicators of the thoroughness and the fault detection effectiveness of unit tests, respectively. The effect size of TDD on branch coverage was medium in size and therefore is considered substantive effect.

Limitations

Test-driven development does not perform sufficient testing in situations where full functional tests are required to determine success or failure, due to extensive use of unit tests. Examples of these are user interfaces, programs that work with databases, and some that depend on specific network configurations. TDD encourages developers to put the minimum amount of code into such modules and to maximize the logic that is in testable library code, using fakes and mocks to represent the outside world.

Management support is essential. Without the entire organization believing that test-driven development is going to improve the product, management may feel that time spent writing tests is wasted.

Unit tests created in a test-driven development environment are typically created by the developer who is writing the code being tested. Therefore, the tests may share blind spots with the code: if, for example, a developer does not realize that certain input parameters must be checked, most likely neither the test nor the code will verify those parameters. Another example: if the developer misinterprets the requirements for the module he is developing, the code and the unit tests he writes will both be wrong in the same way. Therefore, the tests will pass, giving a false sense of correctness.

A high number of passing unit tests may bring a false sense of security, resulting in fewer additional software testing activities, such as integration testing and compliance testing.

Tests become part of the maintenance overhead of a project. Badly written tests, for example ones that include hard-coded error strings or are themselves prone to failure, are expensive to maintain. This is especially the case with fragile tests. There is a risk that tests that regularly generate false failures will be ignored, so that when a real failure occurs, it may not be detected. It is possible to write tests for low and easy maintenance, for example by the reuse of error strings, and this should be a goal during the code refactoring phase described above.

Writing and maintaining an excessive number of tests costs time. Also, more-flexible modules (with limited tests) might accept new requirements without the need for changing the tests. For those reasons, testing for only extreme conditions, or a small sample of data, can be easier to adjust than a set of highly detailed tests. However, developers could be warned about overtesting to avoid the excessive work, but it might require advanced skills in sampling or factor analysis.

The level of coverage and testing detail achieved during repeated TDD cycles cannot easily be re-created at a later date. Therefore these original, or early, tests become increasingly precious as time goes by. The tactic is to fix it early. Also, if a poor architecture, a poor design, or a poor testing strategy leads to a late change that makes dozens of existing tests fail, then it is important that they are individually fixed. Merely deleting, disabling or rashly altering them can lead to undetectable holes in the test coverage.

Test-driven Work

Test-driven development has been adopted outside of software development, in both product and service teams, as test-driven work. Similar to TDD, non-software teams develop quality control checks (usually manual tests rather than automated tests) for each aspect of the work prior to commencing. These QC checks are then used to inform the design and validate the associated outcomes. The six steps of the TDD sequence are applied with minor semantic changes:

1. "Add a check" replaces "Add a test"

2. "Run all checks" replaces "Run all tests"

3. "Do the work" replaces "Write some code"

4. "Run all checks" replaces "Run tests"

5. "Clean up the work" replaces "Refactor code"

6. "Repeat"

TDD and ATDD

Test-driven development is related to, but different from acceptance test–driven development (ATDD). TDD is primarily a developer's tool to help create well-written unit of code (function, class, or module) that correctly performs a set of operations. ATDD is a communication tool between the customer, developer, and tester to ensure that the requirements are well-defined. TDD requires test automation. ATDD does not, although automation helps with regression testing. Tests used in TDD can often be derived from ATDD tests, since the code units implement some portion of a requirement. ATDD tests should be readable by the customer. TDD tests do not need to be.

TDD and BDD

BDD (behavior-driven development) combines practices from TDD and from ATDD. It includes the practice of writing tests first, but focuses on tests which describe behavior, rather than tests which test a unit of implementation. Tools such as Mspec and Specflow provide a syntax which allow non-programmers to define the behaviors which developers can then translate into automated tests.

Code Visibility

Test suite code clearly has to be able to access the code it is testing. On the other hand, normal design criteria such as information hiding, encapsulation and the separation of concerns should not be compromised. Therefore unit test code for TDD is usually written within the same project or module as the code being tested.

In object oriented design this still does not provide access to private data and methods. Therefore, extra work may be necessary for unit tests. In Java and other languages, a developer can use reflection to access private fields and methods. Alternatively, an inner class can be used to hold the unit tests so they have visibility of the enclosing class's members and attributes. In the .NET Framework and some other programming languages, partial classes may be used to expose private methods and data for the tests to access.

It is important that such testing hacks do not remain in the production code. In C and other languages, compiler directives such as #if DEBUG ... #endif can be placed around such additional classes and indeed all other test-related code to prevent them being compiled into the released code. This means the released code is not exactly the same as what was unit tested. The regular running of fewer but more comprehensive, end-to-end, integration tests on the final release build can ensure (among other things) that no production code exists that subtly relies on aspects of the test harness.

There is some debate among practitioners of TDD, documented in their blogs and other writings, as to whether it is wise to test private methods and data anyway. Some argue that private members are a mere implementation detail that may change, and should be allowed to do so without breaking numbers of tests. Thus it should be sufficient to test any class through its public interface or through its subclass interface, which some languages call the "protected" interface. Others say that crucial aspects of functionality may be implemented in private methods and testing them directly offers advantage of smaller and more direct unit tests.

Software for TDD

There are many testing frameworks and tools that are useful in TDD

xUnit Frameworks

Developers may use computer-assisted testing frameworks, such as xUnit created in 1998, to create and automatically run the test cases. Xunit frameworks provide assertion-style test validation capabilities and result reporting. These capabilities are critical for automation as they move the burden of execution validation from an independent post-processing activity to one that is included in the test execution. The execution framework provided by these test frameworks allows for the automatic execution of all system test cases or various subsets along with other features.

TAP Results

Testing frameworks may accept unit test output in the language agnostic Test Anything Protocol created in 1987.

Fakes, Mocks and Integration Tests

Unit tests are so named because they each test *one unit* of code. A complex module may have a thousand unit tests and a simple module may have only ten. The tests used for TDD should never cross process boundaries in a program, let alone network connections. Doing so introduces delays that make tests run slowly and discourage developers from running the whole suite. Introducing dependencies on external modules or data also turns *unit tests* into *integration tests*. If one module misbehaves in a chain of interrelated modules, it is not so immediately clear where to look for the cause of the failure.

When code under development relies on a database, a web service, or any other external process or service, enforcing a unit-testable separation is also an opportunity and a driving force to design more modular, more testable and more reusable code. Two steps are necessary:

1. Whenever external access is needed in the final design, an interface should be defined that describes the access available. See the dependency inversion principle for a discussion of the benefits of doing this regardless of TDD.

2. The interface should be implemented in two ways, one of which really accesses the external process, and the other of which is a fake or mock. Fake objects need do little more than add a message such as "Person object saved" to a trace log, against which a test assertion can be run to verify correct behaviour. Mock objects differ in that they themselves contain test assertions that can make the test fail, for example, if the person's name and other data are not as expected.

Fake and mock object methods that return data, ostensibly from a data store or user, can help the test process by always returning the same, realistic data that tests can rely upon. They can also be set into predefined fault modes so that error-handling routines can be developed and reliably tested. In a fault mode, a method may return an invalid, incomplete or null response, or may throw an exception. Fake services other than data stores may also be useful in TDD: A fake encryption service may not, in fact, encrypt the data passed; a fake random number service may always return 1. Fake or mock implementations are examples of dependency injection.

A Test Double is a test-specific capability that substitutes for a system capability, typically a class or function, that the UUT depends on. There are two times at which test doubles can be introduced into a system: link and execution. Link time substitution is when the test double is compiled into the load module, which is executed to validate testing. This approach is typically used when running in an environment other than the target environment that requires doubles for the hardware level code for compilation. The alternative to linker substitution is run-time substitution in which the real functionality is replaced during the execution of a test cases. This substitution is typically done through the reassignment of known function pointers or object replacement.

Test doubles are of a number of different types and varying complexities:

- Dummy – A dummy is the simplest form of a test double. It facilitates linker time substitution by providing a default return value where required.

- Stub – A stub adds simplistic logic to a dummy, providing different outputs.

- Spy – A spy captures and makes available parameter and state information, publishing accessors to test code for private information allowing for more advanced state validation.

- Mock – A mock is specified by an individual test case to validate test-specific behavior, checking parameter values and call sequencing.

- Simulator – A simulator is a comprehensive component providing a higher-fidelity approximation of the target capability (the thing being doubled). A simulator typically requires significant additional development effort.

A corollary of such dependency injection is that the actual database or other external-access code is never tested by the TDD process itself. To avoid errors that may arise from this, other tests are needed that instantiate the test-driven code with the "real" implementations of the interfaces discussed above. These are integration tests and are quite separate from the TDD unit tests. There are fewer of them, and they must be run less often than the unit tests. They can nonetheless be implemented using the same testing framework, such as xUnit.

Integration tests that alter any persistent store or database should always be designed carefully with consideration of the initial and final state of the files or database, even if any test fails. This is often achieved using some combination of the following techniques:

- The TearDown method, which is integral to many test frameworks.

- try...catch...finally exception handling structures where available.

- Database transactions where a transaction atomically includes perhaps a write, a read and a matching delete operation.

- Taking a "snapshot" of the database before running any tests and rolling back to the snapshot after each test run. This may be automated using a framework such as Ant or NAnt or a continuous integration system such as CruiseControl.

- Initialising the database to a clean state *before* tests, rather than cleaning up *after* them. This may be relevant where cleaning up may make it difficult to diagnose test failures by deleting the final state of the database before detailed diagnosis can be performed.

TDD for Complex Systems

Exercising TDD on large, challenging systems requires a modular architecture, well-defined components with published interfaces, and disciplined system layering with maximization of platform independence. These proven practices yield increased testability and facilitate the application of build and test automation.

Designing for Testability

Complex systems require an architecture that meets a range of requirements. A key subset of these requirements includes support for the complete and effective testing of the system. Effective modular design yields components that share traits essential for effective TDD.

- High Cohesion ensures each unit provides a set of related capabilities and makes the tests of those capabilities easier to maintain.

- Low Coupling allows each unit to be effectively tested in isolation.

- Published Interfaces restrict Component access and serve as contact points for tests, facilitating test creation and ensuring the highest fidelity between test and production unit configuration.

A key technique for building effective modular architecture is Scenario Modeling where a set of sequence charts is constructed, each one focusing on a single system-level execution scenario. The Scenario Model provides an excellent vehicle for creating the strategy of interactions between components in response to a specific stimulus. Each of these Scenario Models serves as a rich set of requirements for the services or functions that a component must provide, and it also dictates the order that these components and services interact together. Scenario modeling can greatly facilitate the construction of TDD tests for a complex system.

Managing Tests for Large Teams

In a larger system the impact of poor component quality is magnified by the complexity of interactions. This magnification makes the benefits of TDD accrue even faster in the context of larger projects. However, the complexity of the total population of tests can become a problem in itself, eroding potential gains. It sounds simple, but a key initial step is to recognize that test code is also important software and should be produced and maintained with the same rigor as the production code.

Creating and managing the architecture of test software within a complex system is just as important as the core product architecture. Test drivers interact with the UUT, test doubles and the unit test framework.

Node Graph Architecture

Node graph architecture is a type of software design which builds around modular node components which can be connected to form a graph. Often the software's underlying node graph architecture is also exposed to the end user as a two-dimensional visualization of the node graph. The node graph architecture is popular in the film and computer games industry.

There are often many different node types participating in the node graph. For example, in the Nuke Manual they list hundreds of nodes. Each node type performs one specific task. For example, Nuke's Merge node produces an output image in which a number of input images have been layered. By connecting many different node types together complex image effects can be produced.

The node graph architecture often allows grouping of nodes inside other group nodes. This hides complexity inside of the group nodes, and limits their coupling with other nodes outside the group. This leads to a hierarchy where smaller graphs are embedded in group nodes. In Nuke the group node is simply called the Group node.

In the paper Hierarchical Small Worlds in Software Architecture they argue that most large software systems are built in a modular and hierarchical fashion, and they use node graphs to analyze large software systems. In fact a large number of software analysis papers often use node graphs to analyze large software systems suggesting that node graphs are good models of the internal structure and operation of the software.

Many commercial and non-commercial software systems allow users to visualize and interact with internal components via the node graph. Below are a number of node graph based software applications from the film and games industry.

Commercial Applications

Grasshopper 3D is a procedural/parametric modeling add-on that runs within the Rhinoceros 3D computer-aided design (CAD) application. The nodes in its graph can be connected to create complex geometry for design and architecture.

Nuke is a compositing application for film made by The Foundry. The nodes in its graph can be connected to produce complex 2D image processing effects.

- Nuke Node Graph Basics
- Nuke Manual

Shake is a discontinued compositing application for film made by Nothing Real LLC and later purchased by Apple. The nodes in its graph can be connected to produce complex 2D image processing effects.

- Shake Screenshot
- Shake Manual

Maya is a modeling, animation, and rendering application made by Autodesk. The nodes in its graph are more general and produce 3D geometry and various other attributes.

- Maya Screenshot

- Maya Nodes

Houdini is a procedural modelling, animation, and rendering application made by Side Effects Software. The nodes in its graph produce procedural geometry. Side Effects Software refers to their node graphs as networks.

- Houdini Nodes and Networks

- Houdini Nodes

Valve Corporation's Source SDK allows players to create custom maps for all of their games. The nodes in its graphs are used in AI path planning and also in sending signals between game entities.

- Valve Nodes for Path Planning

- Entity Inputs and Outputs

Nodality is a free node based image editing and compositing application for iPad.

Open Source Applications

Blender is a modelling, animation, compositing, and rendering application. The nodes in its graph produce images, 3D geometry, and various other attriutes.

- Blender Node Graph Screen Shot

- Blender Node System

NodeBox is procedural image creation application. The nodes in its graph produce vector based images.

- NodeBox Screen Shot

- NodeBox Node Reference

Anahita is a knowledge networking platform and framework for building apps and services

- The Anahita Project

In-house Studio Applications

Many large movie studios are rumored to be using the node graph architecture to design many of their in-house software tools. Sony Pictures Imageworks uses an in-house compositing and lighting tool called Katana. In a recent press release (November 2009) it was announced that the Sony Pictures Imageworks' Katana software would be integrated into The Foundry's Nuke software.

- Katana and Nuke FAQ
- Katana and Nuke Press Release

Software Architectural Model

An architectural model (in software) is a rich and rigorous diagram, created using available standards, in which the primary concern is to illustrate a specific set of tradeoffs inherent in the structure and design of a system or ecosystem. Software architects use architectural models to communicate with others and seek peer feedback. An architectural model is an expression of a viewpoint in software architecture.

Some key elements in software architectural model are:

- rich: for the viewpoint in question, there should be sufficient information to describe the area in detail. The information should not be lacking or vague. The goal is to minimize misunderstandings, not perpetuate them.

- rigorous: the architect has applied a specific methodology to create this particular model, and the resulting model 'looks' a particular way. Here's the test of rigorousness: If two architects, in different cities, were describing the same thing, the resulting diagrams would be nearly identical (with the possible exception of visual layout, to a point).

- diagram: in general, a model may refer to *any* abstraction that simplifies something for the sake of addressing a particular viewpoint. This definition specifically subclasses 'architectural models' to the subset of model descriptions that are represented as diagrams.

- standards: standards work when everyone knows them and everyone uses them. This allows a level of communication that cannot be achieved when each diagram is substantially different from another. UML is the most often quoted standard.

- primary concern: it is easy to be too detailed by including many different needs in a single diagram. This should be avoided. It is better to draw multiple diagrams, one for each viewpoint, than to draw a 'mega diagram' that is so rich in content that it requires a two-year course of study to understand it. Remember this: when building houses, the architect delivers many different diagrams. Each is used differently. Frequently the final package of plans will include diagrams with the floor plan many times: framing plan, electrical plan, heating plan, plumbing, etc. They don't just say: it's a floor plan so 100% of the information that CAN go on a floor plan should be put there. The plumbing subcontractor doesn't need the details that the electrician cares about.

- illustrate: the idea behind creating a model is to communicate and seek valuable feedback. The goal of the diagram should be to answer a specific question and to share that answer with others to (a) see if they agree, and (b) guide their work. Rule of thumb: know what it is you want to say, and whose work you intend to influence with it.

- specific set of tradeoffs: the architecture tradeoff analysis method (ATAM) methodology describes a process whereby software architecture can be peer-reviewed for appropriateness. ATAM does this by starting with a basic notion: there is no such thing as a 'one-size-fits-all' design. We can create a generic design, but then we need to alter it to specific situations based on the business requirements. In effect, we make tradeoffs. The diagram should make those specific tradeoffs visible. Therefore, before an architect creates a diagram, he or she should be prepared to describe, in words, which tradeoffs they are attempting to illustrate in this model.

- tradeoffs inherent in the structure and design: a component is not a tradeoff. Tradeoffs rarely translate into an image on the diagram. Tradeoffs are the first principles that produced the design models. When an architect wishes to describe or defend a particular tradeoff, the diagram can be used to defend the position.

- system or ecosystem: modeling in general can be done at different levels of abstraction. It is useful to model the architecture of a specific application, complete with components and interactions. It is also reasonable to model the systems of applications needed to deliver a complete business process (like order-to-cash). It is not commonly useful, however, to view the model of a single component and its classes as software architecture. At that level, the model, while valuable in its own right, illustrates design much more so than architecture.

References

- Rother, Mike; Shook, John (1999). Learning to See: value-stream mapping to create value and eliminate muda. Brookline, MA: Lean Enterprise Institute. ISBN 0-9667843-0-8.

- Graban, Mark; Swartz, Joseph (2011). Healthcare Kaizen: Engaging Front-Line Staff in Sustainable Continuous Improvements. Boca Raton, FL: CRC Press. ISBN 9781439872963.

- Bell, Steven; Orzen, Michael. Lean IT: Enabling and Sustaining Your Lean Transformation. Boca Raton, FL: CRC Press. ISBN 9781439817568.

- Mascitelli, Ronald (2011). Mastering lean product development: a practical, event-driven process for maximizing speed, profits and quality. Northridge, CA: Technology Perspectives. ISBN 9780966269741.

- Shingo, Shigeo (1985). A Revolution in Manufacturing: The SMED System. Stamford, CT: Productivity Press. p. 5. ISBN 0915299097.

- Goldratt, Eliyahu M. Essays on the Theory of Constraints. [Great Barrington, MA]: North River Press. ISBN 0-88427-159-5.

- Goldratt, Eliyahu; Fox, Robert (1986). The Race. [Croton-on-Hudson, NY]: North River Press. p. 179. ISBN 978-0-88427-062-1.

- Waldner, Jean-Baptiste (September 1992). Principles of Computer-Integrated Manufacturing. London: John Wiley. pp. 128–132. ISBN 0-471-93450-X.

- Shingō, Shigeo (1989). A Study of the Toyota Production System from an Industrial Engineering Viewpoint. Productivity Press. p. 228. ISBN 0-915299-17-8.

- Shingō, Shigeo (1989). A Study of the Toyota Production System from an Industrial Engineering Viewpoint. Productivity Press. p. 30. ISBN 0-915299-17-8.

- Ohno, Taiichi (1988). Toyota Production System: Beyond Large-Scale Production. Productivity Press. p. 176. ISBN 9780915299140.

- Lindberg, Per; Voss, Christopher A.; Blackmon, Kathryn L. (eds.). International Manufacturing Strategies: Context, Content and Change. ISBN 0-7923-8061-4.

- Sundarapandian, V. (2009). "7. Queueing Theory". Probability, Statistics and Queueing Theory. PHI Learning. ISBN 8120338448.

- Harchol-Balter, M. (2012). "Scheduling: Non-Preemptive, Size-Based Policies". Performance Modeling and Design of Computer Systems. p. 499. doi:10.1017/CBO9781139226424.039. ISBN 9781139226424.

- Harchol-Balter, M. (2012). "Scheduling: Preemptive, Size-Based Policies". Performance Modeling and Design of Computer Systems. p. 508. doi:10.1017/CBO9781139226424.040. ISBN 9781139226424.

- Harchol-Balter, M. (2012). "Scheduling: SRPT and Fairness". Performance Modeling and Design of Computer Systems. p. 518. doi:10.1017/CBO9781139226424.041. ISBN 9781139226424.

- Madeyski, L. "Test-Driven Development - An Empirical Evaluation of Agile Practice", Springer, 2010, ISBN 978-3-642-04287-4, pp. 1-245. DOI: 978-3-642-04288-1

- Mayr, Herwig (2005). Projekt Engineering Ingenieurmässige Softwareentwicklung in Projektgruppen (2., neu bearb. Aufl. ed.). München: Fachbuchverl. Leipzig im Carl-Hanser-Verl. p. 239. ISBN 978-3446400702.

- Fowler, Martin (1999). Refactoring - Improving the design of existing code. Boston: Addison Wesley Longman, Inc. ISBN 0-201-48567-2.

Permissions

All chapters in this book are published with permission under the Creative Commons Attribution Share Alike License or equivalent. Every chapter published in this book has been scrutinized by our experts. Their significance has been extensively debated. The topics covered herein carry significant information for a comprehensive understanding. They may even be implemented as practical applications or may be referred to as a beginning point for further studies.

We would like to thank the editorial team for lending their expertise to make the book truly unique. They have played a crucial role in the development of this book. Without their invaluable contributions this book wouldn't have been possible. They have made vital efforts to compile up to date information on the varied aspects of this subject to make this book a valuable addition to the collection of many professionals and students.

This book was conceptualized with the vision of imparting up-to-date and integrated information in this field. To ensure the same, a matchless editorial board was set up. Every individual on the board went through rigorous rounds of assessment to prove their worth. After which they invested a large part of their time researching and compiling the most relevant data for our readers.

The editorial board has been involved in producing this book since its inception. They have spent rigorous hours researching and exploring the diverse topics which have resulted in the successful publishing of this book. They have passed on their knowledge of decades through this book. To expedite this challenging task, the publisher supported the team at every step. A small team of assistant editors was also appointed to further simplify the editing procedure and attain best results for the readers.

Apart from the editorial board, the designing team has also invested a significant amount of their time in understanding the subject and creating the most relevant covers. They scrutinized every image to scout for the most suitable representation of the subject and create an appropriate cover for the book.

The publishing team has been an ardent support to the editorial, designing and production team. Their endless efforts to recruit the best for this project, has resulted in the accomplishment of this book. They are a veteran in the field of academics and their pool of knowledge is as vast as their experience in printing. Their expertise and guidance has proved useful at every step. Their uncompromising quality standards have made this book an exceptional effort. Their encouragement from time to time has been an inspiration for everyone.

The publisher and the editorial board hope that this book will prove to be a valuable piece of knowledge for students, practitioners and scholars across the globe.

Index

CPSIA information can be obtained
at www.ICGtesting.com
Printed in the USA
BVHW011539270421
605871BV00039B/516